T·H·E
PROSPEROUS RETIREMENT
GUIDE TO THE NEW REALITY

MICHAEL K. STEIN, CFP

D1417878

EMSTCO PRESS
Boulder, Colorado

Project Editor: Jenifer Merchant
Book & Cover Design: Bob Schram, Bookends
Cover Art: Eunice M. Stein
Typeface: Goudy Old Style
Printer: Thomson-Shore, Inc.

Library of Congress Cataloging-in-Publication Data
Stein, Michael K.
   The Prosperous Retirement: Guide to the New Reality / by Michael K. Stein–1st ed.
   p. Cm.
   Includes illustrations, glossary and index
   ISBN 0-9663381-0-3
   1. Retirement Income—United States—Planning   2. Financial Planning, Personal—United States.   3. Investments. I. Title

   HG179.S819   1998
   332.024'01–dc20

                                                                98-92621
                                                                CIP

Printed in the United States of America
10 9 8 7 6 5 4

Discounts on quantity purchases of books by EMSTCO Press to be used for educational, or, charitable fund raising purposes can be arranged by contacting Pathway Book Service at 1-800-345-6665 or FAX (603) 357-2073

CONTENTS

*This book is dedicated to the people who have,
over the years, placed their trust in me—
particularly my wife, who has been kind about my mistakes
and generous about my successes.*

PREFACE

I HAVE ALWAYS BEEN INTERESTED IN FINANCES. My mother used to say that she knew I was destined to be a financial planner from the time that I was six. My Aunt Janet was the family financier; she had been a real estate broker before the Great Depression. In the wake of the Depression, she had purchased the assets of a defunct bank, which included hundreds of pieces of real estate. Over the years, Aunt Janet had cleaned up the titles of these properties and sold them, sometimes for substantial profits.

It was Aunt Janet's custom to give the children in the family silver dollars for their birthdays, one silver dollar for each year. On my sixth birthday, she laid six weighty silver dollars in my palm and asked, "What are you going to do with these?" I could tell by her penetrating stare that my thoughts of a baseball glove, or ice cream, were not what she had in mind. I looked her straight in the eye and told her what I thought was the "right answer." "I'm going to put them in the bank so that I can collect interest on them." She beamed, my mother beamed, and I knew I had passed the test.

My Aunt Janet had educated, tested, and certified me as a financial planner. Years later, when I told my mother that I had become a Certified Financial Planner®, she reminded me of this story and ended by saying, "It's taken a long time for you to find your calling, but I never doubted what it was."

One of my first financial planning clients was a man I will call Edward. Edward was in his 70s and had retired a few years earlier after a lifelong career as an engineer. He was a vigorous man, quick-witted, and in excellent health. He had accumulated a fair net worth over the years, and received Social Security and a nice pension annuity each month that allowed him and his wife, Sandy, to live a comfortable, but modest, life-style.

As we discussed his financial affairs, I discovered that virtually all of Edward's assets were in bank certificates of deposit and the bonds of utility companies. This was about 1980, and the current income he was receiving was adequate for their needs. We talked about investment objectives, and I suggested that Edward consider investing some portion of his assets in growth-oriented investments. It was clear to me that even in his 70s, a man in such good health had excellent prospects for living many more years and would need protection from inflation. He wasn't convinced. Instead, Edward taught me an important lesson that I will pass on in detail later in this book.

Edward told me that he tracked his budget carefully and that inflation, which in those days was in double digits, was not affecting his expenses. I pointed out that the cost of food, fuel, telephones—almost everything in his life—was growing more expensive by the day, but he was vehement that his budget was not increasing.

It took me a couple of years to understand what was happening, but when I finally figured it out, it turned out to be an important lesson. As I watched Edward and Sandy live out their retirement, I could see a subtle but continuous change in their life-style. Their trips to Europe became less frequent and finally stopped when Sandy was stricken with Alzheimer's Disease. They stopped buying new cars and then gave up their car entirely. They were making a transition from an active retirement to a passive life-style. Expenses in their budget were, in fact, increasing, but the increases in expenses were being offset by a shrinking life-style. Finally, in their late 80s, Edward and Sandy were reduced to a subsistence level of living, and Edward acknowledged that inflation was pinching their budget.

After I finally figured out the dynamics of this pattern, I searched the financial planning literature for a discussion of this phenomenon. I discovered that no one had discussed this interval in retirement when people seem to be immune from inflation. That led me to other important discoveries, and, ultimately, to the decision to write this book. When I asked myself the question, "How can it be that so many bright people have failed to observe and describe this important phenomenon?" I came to the important discovery that the ubiquitous discussions about retirement are not about today's retirement—they are about yesterday's retirement. These discussions were about my parents' and grandparents' retirement, not about my retirement and the retirements of my clients and friends. The more I thought about this discrepancy, the more discoveries I made about the differences between today's retirement and yesterday's retirement. I have been refining these ideas for more than 10 years. During that time, I have counseled many hundreds of people about retirement. Ironically, some of the people who have been the most conscientious in studying about and preparing for retirement—the people who have read the books and attended the seminars—are the very people who have loaded up with the most faulty concepts.

It is for these people that I am writing this book: the people who have prepared for The Prosperous Retirement, but who may not actually enjoy it unless they are taught the new rules of the game.

Modern retirement is not a simple matter. It is unlikely to be successful without planning, monitoring, professional assistance, and adjustments as circumstances and conditions change. Your life is not a dress rehearsal. It deserves the best thought you can give it, and you deserve the best professional assistance that you can find.

ACKNOWLEDGMENTS

A book like this cannot be written without the assistance of many people. Every author says that, but *only* an author really understands the depth of meaning. I have been blessed by the assistance of many bright and capable people who have worked long and hard to correct my errors and polish the text. If errors or unclear expressions remain, I apologize; they are entirely my responsibility. I am particularly grateful to Jenifer Merchant, my editor, whose expertise and good judgment went far beyond punctuation, grammar, and word use. Bob Schram designed both the cover and the interior of the book with style and skill. I am grateful to my wife, Eunice, for allowing me to use one of her paintings on the cover. Many of my professional friends and associates were kind enough to read the draft and offer their comments. Michael L. Wilson, MBA, CFP, a retirement specialist with the College for Financial Planning; Sandra Eve, CFP, a very talented financial planner; and Steven S. Shagrin, JD, CFP, CRPC, one of the leaders of the International Society for Retirement Planning, were kind enough to review the entire draft. Ronald P. Meier, MS, CMFC; Alan Weiss, CPA, CFP; and Dallas Powell, an expert on long-term care insurance, offered their comments on portions of the draft. A long-time friend, Seymour Jaye, gave me his good counsel on the overall management concept. Four of my trusted advisors, Mark Carson, CPA, JD; Amy Rappleye, CPA; Harley K. Look, Jr., JD; and Dr. Michael Perlman, M.D., were kind enough to offer their assistance with relevant sections of the book.

One values good friends—especially when there is a heavy load to lift.

INTRODUCTION

PICK UP A BOOK OR AN ARTICLE about retirement, or attend a retirement
seminar, and you are likely to get some misleading information. The
retirement advice that is being given to most Americans today frequently is
mistaken because it is based on the experiences of an earlier, radically different, generation of retirees. I call these people the "post-Depression retirement generation." They are those Americans who were born around the turn
of the century and who retired between 1960 and 1990. Even education for
financial professionals and the tools they use to plan retirements are based
on a series of ideas that have their roots in these earlier retirements. There
was recently an article in the *The Wall Street Journal*[1] that roundly criticized
the retirement planning software programs available to both individuals and
professionals. Beyond the problems with mathematics and the treatment of
ticklish issues like taxes and inflation, there are important deficiencies in the
actual model of how retirement works. Where did all these ideas come from?
They came from observing the retirements of these earlier retirees.

Many people in the post-Depression retirement generation were
denied the opportunity to acquire a higher education, and they never
had the chance to rise to highly compensated positions in business,
industry, or government. They began their working lives early and typically worked for many, many years. They were taught to live within their
means, avoid debt, and save what little they could. About the time they
managed to get a few dollars in the bank, the banks collapsed. They were

---

[1] "Personal Finance Software . . . ," *The Wall Street Journal*, December 27, 1996.

the principal victims of the Crash of 1929 and the following 10-year period of the Great Depression. Their hard-earned savings were destroyed. Their stocks, bonds, real estate, and even cash lost value. Millions of people found themselves unemployed and, without government intervention, they might have starved to death.

The government did intervene in a massive way that changed America forever. The Civilian Conservation Corps and the Works Project Administration provided jobs for millions. They built national parks, highways, dams, bridges, post offices, and other public projects that changed the physical face of the nation. Internally, and in less visible ways, the structure of American business and industry also was changed. The banking and securities industries were reorganized under new laws that insured investors against the worst excesses of the past. A Social Security safety net was placed under many workers. The nation was transformed, but the effects—both psychological and practical—lingered on for more than 10 years. The Great Depression truly created a psychological condition that profoundly affected the lives of the people who lived through it.

The Second World War finally lifted the nation out of the economic Depression, but the psychological scars lingered. The War gave us a national focus for our energy. It also gave us a reason to run our factories three shifts a day. At the same time, it created great scarcity, as we scrimped to send everything we could in support of the war effort. Wealth accumulation opportunities were limited because millions of Americans served in the armed forces with modest compensation, and the people on the home front were constrained by limited resources, rationing, and price controls. It was not a period in which most Americans were able to accumulate great wealth.

The final years of the 1940s brought rapid change, reorganization, and rapidly increasing inflation. Americans reorganized industry to direct their efforts at peacetime enterprises and the rebuilding of the war-torn world. The 1950s saw this reorganization begin to take effect when the Dow Jones Industrial Average finally rose above 200, never again to fall below that level. The Dow had been above 200 in the 1920s and recovered to that level again in 1936 and 1946. In other words, for 20 years, the stock market basically moved sideways, not creating a great opportunity for wealth building in the stock market.

The real estate market also had stagnated. There was little money to be made in real estate between 1930 and 1950. Many real estate projects that had been developed in the late 1920s never found buyers and eventually were lost in tax foreclosures. Those properties were not returned to productive use until the late 1940s or early 1950s.

By the time the opportunities of the 1950s were opening up, the generation of Americans who had been born around the turn of the century were approaching 50 to 60 years of age. They had spent 20 years maneuvering through the Great Depression, the Second World War, and the period of reorganization following the war. They approached middle age with few savings, limited career prospects, and a collective psyche that had been savagely scarred by the Great Depression. Savings and investment seemed to be futile. To many, it seemed most appropriate to direct their rising stream of earnings at current consumption. They bought new cars, new clothes, and new homes. They furnished those homes with appliances, furniture, and all the other fittings of the "Good Life." As far as retirement was concerned, they planned to do what their parents had done, but with two important differences. Their parents had worked as long as possible, then finally, when forced to retire, they lived with their family and did little in those few brief years between retiring and dying. I remember how my grandparents, who lived with us in the 1940s, took long walks and viewed their Saturday pint of ice cream as the high point of the week.

The two main differences that the post-Depression retirees were counting on to improve their situation were Social Security and corporate pensions. The new Social Security program ensured that they would never be totally impoverished if they had made the requisite contributions to the program. Secondly, increasing numbers of Americans could anticipate pension benefits from the rapidly rising number of corporate and union pension plans. The restructuring of the federal tax system gave corporations important incentives to contribute to pension plans that provided benefits based on the length of service and the level of wages earned.

As the first wave of the post-Depression retirees arrived at retirement in the 1950s and 1960s, the retirement advice they received was based on several assumptions:

- First, it was assumed that the duration of their retirement would be brief. Looking back at the previous generation who had worked as long as possible, it was assumed that the current generation would do the same. People were expected to work until age 65 or 70 and then live for only a few years.
- Secondly, looking again at the experience of the previous generation, it was assumed that inflation would not be a problem. In the 1930s, prices dropped, and in the 1940s, they were regulated by government price controls and rationing.

Accordingly, retirees were advised that, during their brief retirement, their need for income would remain fairly constant.

These post-Depression retirees were told to expect their retirement income to come from three sources: Social Security, their corporate retirement plan, and a small supplement from their personal savings. Based on the experiences of the 1920s, they were urged to invest their meager savings in only the safest investments, which in those days were yielding less than the rate of inflation. To make all of this come together in a way that suggested that retirement really was possible, they were told that retirees normally could expect to live on 50% to 65% of the income that they had been living on before retirement. To some extent, this advice was based on the actuality of retirees moving in with their family, but even more, it was based on the reality of what people were being forced to do. If retirees had income that was equal to only 50% of their pre-retirement income, they just had to make it work. It was a great demonstration of the first law of finance, "**Expenses tend to equal income.**"

That generation of post-Depression retirees is now approaching the end of their lives. They are being followed in the ranks of retirees by a new generation. Fortunately, the children of the post-Depression retirees, born in the 1930s and 1940s, have had a dramatically different life experience. Many of these post-Depression babies had the opportunity to go on to higher education, which positioned them for more productive lives and greater compensation than their parents ever earned. This new generation emerged from college in the 1950s during the early years of the post-war economic boom. Opportunities to earn a living, make money, and even inherit wealth seemed to be all around them.

The stock market between the early 1950s and 1998 has increased by more than 30 times. Houses that were built in the 1950s and sold for $10,000 are today worth $100,000 and more in many parts of the country. If you recall that the house could have been purchased for a $1,000 down payment, the price appreciation represents a 100 times return on investment. Even bank deposits and bonds were an easy place to make money. Do you remember that in the early 1980s, money market mutual funds were paying 21% and you could buy 30-year Treasury bonds to pay a guaranteed 15.25%?

The opportunities were abundant, and these babes of the post-Depression retirees had been well schooled in the virtues of thrift and saving. They were systematically saving toward a set of goals that seemed very real: home ownership, travel, education for their children, and a better retirement than their parents had experienced.

Not only were the opportunities abundant, but there was an increasing amount of consumer information about investments and a seductive stream of advertising urging people to invest. Some of those enticements proved to be siren calls, but many were true invitations to wealth building. There is talk of trillions of dollars passing from the generation of the post-Depression babies to their heirs over the next 20 years, which is a wealth transfer without precedent in the history of the world.

That is the legacy of a generation for whom the experiences of the post-Depression retirees is largely meaningless. Even worse, that experience is misleading. In spite of the obvious differences between the circumstances of these two generations, the common wisdom is very slow to change. The richly endowed post-Depression babies are being counseled by the financial press and many advisors using the same principles that their impoverished parents were given. Those who follow that advice will miss an important opportunity to enjoy the blessing that has been bestowed on them. They will miss the opportunity to enjoy "The Prosperous Retirement."

The model of The Prosperous Retirement differs from the post-Depression retirement model in six very important ways.

1. Retirees will live a long and active life in retirement.
2. The extended retirement will be divided into several phases.
3. The cost of the retirement life-style will be similar to the cost of the pre-retirement life-style.
4. Inflation will increase the need for income by two or three times during retirement.
5. The income sources for this new kind of retirement are different from the sources that were available to earlier retirees.
6. Taxes, estate planning, and insurance have become vital parts of the retirement planning process.

Unlike the retirees of earlier generations, today's retirees are likely to live for many years in retirement and lead an active retirement. This new, extended retirement is not one homogeneous phase; it is composed of several parts. Retirees are retiring earlier for a number of reasons:

- The pressures of the modern workplace often are extreme.
- Many people are able to accumulate enough wealth to retire at an early age.
- Many corporations are encouraging people to retire early.
- There are extremely attractive retirement life-styles available.
- Travel opportunities, retirement activities, and retirement groups exert their efforts to encourage people to retire as soon as they can.

Life expectancies are increasing. The retirement life-style often allows time for recreation and the maintenance of good health. Many of today's retirees can look forward to spending as many years in retirement as they spent working. However, all of those years will not be years of good health and high energy. Part of the retirement is likely to be quiet and part of it probably will be taken up with ill health.

In spite of all these changes, the first rule of finance, **"expenses tend to equal income,"** is alive and well as demonstrated by many retirees. There is no reason to think that the need for income decreases in retirement. If people have the means, it is not uncommon to see retirees spending more money in the first few years of their retirement than they had been used to spending before they retired. Given the higher level of income required and the greatly increased length of retirements, inflation has become an important consideration in retirement planning. Since 1925, inflation has averaged 3.1%, including the years of the Great Depression and the price controls of the Second World War period. Since the Second World War, inflation has averaged about 4.25%. Our research suggests that average inflation of 4% to 5% is a reasonable assumption for the next couple of decades. In that sort of an inflationary environment, prices double every 16 years. If today's typical retirees are living for 30 years in retirement, that means their budget will increase by a factor of four over the period of their retirement. However, as retirees reach their mid-70s, there is frequently a slowdown in their life-style and a slightly reduced need for income. Given this factor, retirees can expect their income needs to increase by about three times over the course of their retirement. In other words, if they begin their retirement with a budget of $2,500 per month, it is probable that during retirement their need for income will increase to $7,500 per month.

The income sources for The Prosperous Retirement generation are different than the sources for their parents' retirement, which has been characterized as a "three-legged stool." The legs of the stool were Social Security, corporate pension, and personal savings. Many observers believe that Social Security will survive, but the benefits will not keep pace with inflation. That shifts more burden to other income sources. Fewer and fewer retirees have the benefit of a corporate pension, and virtually no one, except a government retiree, has the luxury of a pension with cost-of-living adjustments. This also shifts more burden to other income sources. Fortunately, many retirees have accumulated very large pools of capital. With enlightened investment choices, that capital can provide an adequate and inflation-adjusted income stream. It is also prudent for today's retirees, who are relatively young and perhaps at the very height of their professional power, to think about some sort of activity to generate a stream of income during retirement. These retirement earnings should not be generated by long hours of work that is obnoxious. Many of today's retirees are able to generate income as part-time consultants or in activities related to their hobbies or other interests. There is no greater pleasure than being paid for doing something you love.

Given the length and expense of The Prosperous Retirement, the age-old wisdom advising retirees to use only the very safest investments just does not make much sense. Because of the impact of inflation on these long retirements, it is absolutely essential that retirees maintain a significant portion of their capital in assets that can keep pace with inflation. Current research about modern financial markets clearly indicates that only stocks and real estate have the ability to stay significantly ahead of inflation in the long term. Modern Portfolio Theory, the cornerstone of investment management, makes it clear that stocks must be the core of an investment portfolio designed to keep ahead of inflation. The volatility of stock market investments demands that the investor be prepared to hold them for long periods of time to persevere through market declines. Many retirees argue that, as they approach retirement, they must switch to less volatile investments because they no longer have the time to persevere through these periods of market volatility. That argument fails when retirees focus on the fact that they are likely to be investors for 20 to 30 years after they retire.

The professional financial advisor plays a central role in this new retirement. He or she must be prepared to hear these old arguments, explain where they come from, and then educate you in the realities of the new model and the ideas that flow out of these changed circumstances. It is the essence of professional advice that it prepares clients for the waves of change that constantly embroil their lives.

Millions of Americans have the opportunity to enjoy The Prosperous Retirement that was not available to earlier generations. To take advantage of that opportunity, they have to understand how The Prosperous Retirement differs from the earlier models of retirement with which they are familiar. They also need to understand the differences in the retirement environment and what those differences mean in terms of the way that they conduct their retirements.

Beyond the financial and demographic realities that help define The Prosperous Retirement, there is a new optimism and enthusiasm for retirement. The Prosperous Retirement is a frame of mind based on an understanding of the financial environment and the confidence that comes from understanding the factors that are shaping our lives. It is truly a time, to paraphrase the famous words of Napoleon Hill, "to think and live well."

1.

RETIREMENT IN
EARLIER GENERATIONS

"We rarely find a man who can say he has lived happy,
and content with his life,
can retire from the world like a satisfied guest."
—HORACE
65–8 B.C.

SYNOPSIS: The Prosperous Retirement is a relatively new concept. Americans traditionally have worked as long as possible and retired only when old age and infirmity made it necessary. They did not expect to live long in retirement. Pensions were not available to support them. Social Security did not exist before 1935. Retirees managed to live out a brief retirement by leading a modest life-style, depending on family, and earning a small income with whatever odd jobs might be available. In the years following the Second World War, dramatic changes resulted in the emergence of The Prosperous Retirement.

THE PROSPEROUS RETIREMENT is an invention of the last decades of the 20th Century. The word "retirement" means to withdraw from business, public service, or the affairs of state. The notion of an enjoyable and leisurely retirement goes against every fiber of our Puritan upbringing. Most of us were raised to believe that wealth and happiness flow out of hard work, that leisure, to the extent permissible, is won only through successful exertions. Generations of Americans believed that the withdrawal from work could lead to only one thing: ruin.

George Washington, on the occasion of his retirement from the presidency, expressed himself in the following words, "I anticipate with pleasing expectations that retreat in which I promise myself to realize, without alloy, the sweet enjoyment of partaking, in the midst of my fellow citizens, the benign influence of good laws under a free government, the ever favorite object of my heart, and the happy reward, as I trust, of our mutual cares, labors, and dangers." Here was the father of our nation, at the ripe old age of 64, just three years before his death, having to apologize for his retirement by noting his good works.

The example that Washington set, of working until declining health and advancing age forced him into retirement, served Americans for almost 200 years. For many generations of American workers, retirement was the precursor to death. It seemed clear that no healthy man retired.[1] It was natural that out of this mind-set came the belief that *"retirement = death."* The norm was to work as long as possible and to bear retirement as gracefully and as briefly as possible. Leisure was not something with which the average American was prepared to deal. The idea of older people playing golf and tennis, traveling the world, and generally enjoying life is a new development that would have seemed strange and unnatural to our grandparents, and possibly our parents.

Prior to the 20th Century, employer-provided pensions were not common. The concept of pensions for workers seems to have originated with Bismarck, the Chancellor of Germany, in the last decade of the 19th Century. Providing some sort of retirement income to older or disabled workers gradually caught on and became one of the battle cries of the labor

---

[1] I am sensitive to the use of gender-specific pronouns and have tried to avoid them or use them as appropriately as possible without slavish devotion to "political correctness."

movement. The goal of a pension was to replace some fraction of income—enough to keep the worker from being destitute in retirement. Few workers had any real opportunity to amass personal wealth, and so a comfortable retirement was the luxury of a few rather than the expectation of many.

The popular expectation in retirement was that a pensioner would live a straited life, enjoying simple home pleasures and perhaps living with other family members. A commonly used metaphor for retirement, "being put out to pasture," conveyed the image of a tired old horse, too lame to work, being put out to while away the remaining time in pastoral quiet. A similar picture of the pensioner, in shabby clothes, with bent back, tending a modest but meticulous flower garden also is part of our pictorial vocabulary. In truth, the pensioner probably was raising a few vegetables to supplement a meager diet.

At the same time that economic prospects for retirees were improving, life expectancy began a gradual but continuous and finally dramatic change for the better. Year after year, life expectancy has increased steadily as science found ways to prevent epidemics and childhood diseases. The widespread use of immunization against a whole series of diseases that threatened earlier generations of Americans added years to our life expectancy. Scientific laboratories mass produced new pharmaceuticals to treat diseases and the effects of aging. In 1945, the commercial introduction of penicillin proved to be a dramatic cure for bacterial infections of all sorts. By 1950, physicians in the United States reported that they were treating 60% of their patients with penicillin. Treatments for heart disease, ranging from anti-clotting drugs to heart transplants, have added years to the lives of millions. New diagnostic techniques have allowed doctors to detect the early stages of diseases and treat them more effectively. Science has pushed forward our understanding of body chemistry and genetics, which has allowed some dramatic improvements in the treatment of various ailments, including depression. Life expectancy of older Americans has increased by 53% since 1900 and the life expectancy of certain groups that were grossly disadvantaged at the turn of the century has increased even more.

We often hear the criticism that while medical science has been very successful in extending our life expectancy, those extra years are not always healthy, happy years. Increasingly, we see instances of people surviving some previously fatal disease or accident to live for a number of years in a state that does not always seem entirely desirable. In general, however, modern science has successfully added many years of high-quality life expectancy to the lives of Americans. We are living longer and, even more importantly, we are carrying energy, good health, and a high level of expectation further and further into old age.

Another important change in the pattern of retirement has come as a result of changing social attitudes. Before the 20th Century, leisure did not cross class boundaries. A small group of wealthy people—the leisure class—lived on the income generated by their investments. Working-class people had no real expectation of moving into the leisure class. There was more than an economic border between the rich and the poor in the early part of this century. The broad mass of the working class expected to work as long as possible. When they could no longer work, they didn't expect their employer or the government to provide for their old age. Gradually, the concept of society's responsibility for individuals began to assert itself through governments, businesses, and other social organizations. The labor unions played a role, but so did enlightened employers and politicians. On August 14, 1935, the Social Security Act was signed into law. It had been drafted by the treasurer of Eastman Kodak, a corporation well-known for its enlightened attitudes. Beginning in 1942, Social Security would provide up to $15[2] per month of federal aid to qualified retirees over the age of 65. It gradually became part of the American social consciousness that the responsibility for the welfare of older Americans rested on the shoulders of more than just their family. Corporations and labor unions, with the encouragement of the tax code, not only adopted pension plans but began programs to help employees prepare emotionally, psychologically, and practically for the eventuality of their retirement. They were joined in this beneficial work by churches and voluntary associations that were formed specifically to foster the interests of older Americans and retirees.

Out of these special-interest groups, a recognition began to form that something was happening among older Americans that had commercial

---

[2] This is the 1998 equivalent of about $156.64.

potential. New products were developed to accommodate the needs of older Americans, and special skills were developed to market those products to the newly identified consumers. Powerful organizations were formed to effectively represent the views of older Americans and to lobby governments to meet their needs. Retirement communities began to be developed. Thousands of golf courses were built. Recreational activities specifically designed for older people proliferated, and the stage was set for something interesting to happen. In the years following the Second World War, all of this began to come together in an interesting way that profoundly changed the shape of the American retirement. Suddenly, there were people who were old enough, wealthy enough, healthy enough, and who had the desire to live The Prosperous Retirement. A new era in retirement planning and retirement living was born.

2.

RETIREMENT FOR TODAY'S RETIREE

"If the only thing we have to offer is an improved version of the past, then today can only be inferior to yesterday. Hypnotized by images of the past, we risk losing all capacity for creative change."
—ROBERT HEWISON, *The Heritage Industry*, 1987

SYNOPSIS: Retirement at the end of the 20th Century is radically different from earlier retirements. It can be a lengthy, desirable, and greatly anticipated phase of life. The mechanics of retirement have changed because of increased longevity, wealth, and heightened expectations, but it is not just the statistics that have changed. The structure of retirement, as well as the intellectual and psychological contents, also has changed. Today's extended retirement is typically divided into three phases: the Active, Passive, and Final phases. Given the increased length of retirement and the greater vigor of retirees, intellectual stimulation, recreation, social involvement, and spiritual development have become important aspects of the new retirement. Attention to physical and mental health and their adjuncts, diet and exercise, also is essential to The Prosperous Retirement.

TODAY'S RETIREMENT DIFFERS from earlier retirements in three basic ways: it lasts longer, it is more affluent, and more is expected of life in retirement. People are retiring earlier because they want to and can afford to. They are living longer and carrying energy and vigor further into old age than previous generations. There have been enormous wealth-building opportunities in the last 50 years, and many people have taken advantage of those circumstances to build a strong capital base. Examples abound of people leading wonderful lives in retirement and, as a result, these younger, more affluent retirees are expecting to excel in retirement just as they did in earlier phases of their lives.

The retirement of earlier generations generally was so brief that no one made the observation that it was divided into phases. In fact, given the recognition that most Americans worked until deteriorating health forced them to retire, the entire retirement may have been characterized by failing health and medical problems. Today's retirement presents an entirely new, much more promising and complex, organization.

ACTIVE RETIREMENT PHASE

With people retiring earlier—often in the prime of life—full of health and vigor, it is no surprise that the first part of their retirement is a period of active living. Given the greater financial means of today's retirees and the amazing variety of retirement options, many retirees launch themselves into a frenzied pursuit of the "perfect retirement." Examples abound of enjoyable, sometimes exotic things to do in retirement. Whether the retirement dream is a round-the-world cruise in a sailing ship, or an apartment next to the Metropolitan Museum of Art, or a chicken farm in Montana, there are sources of information, encouragement, and help in pursuing the dreams. These resources may result in the first few years of retirement being the most active, and often most enjoyable, period of a person's life. Many people, freed of the necessity to go to work every day, find great joy in pursuing their athletic, philanthropic, intellectual, spiritual, and hobby interests—a sort of second childhood without parental supervision.

These activities also may result in expenditures that are well above the budget on which the retiree lived before retirement. If this seems surprising, reflect on how much you spend while traveling on vacation versus what you spend when you are at home in a more normal routine. After a while, reality generally takes over, things settle down to a less frenetic pace, and an active, satisfying, and thoroughly enjoyable phase of retirement begins. The budget during this active phase of retirement generally is equal to the pre-retirement budget; in fact, that is *Stein's First Rule of Retirement.*

STEIN'S FIRST RULE OF RETIREMENT

The active-phase retirement budget tends to equal the pre-retirement budget, if the retiree can afford it.

People generally want to continue the same life-style after retirement that they enjoyed before retirement. This life-style will cost about the same amount during retirement that it did before retirement. I know that this flies in the face of conventional wisdom, but it is true. There will be more discussion of why this is true in Chapter 3. During the years of the active phase, inflation will continue to act on the budget and drive it just as it did before retirement, but then a change begins to happen.

PASSIVE RETIREMENT PHASE

The "go-go" phase of retirement gives way to the "slow-go" phase. After some years of active retirement, people begin to grow weary of long vacations, feel less than enthusiastic about running through airports and train stations, grow tired of living out of suitcases on trips, and, in general, decide to let the pace of their lives slow down. This is the beginning of the passive phase of retirement.

The transition from active retirement to passive retirement generally begins when retirees reach the mid-70s and it lasts for about 10 years. There is no social science study to verify this observation, but watching hundreds of retirements has led me to this conclusion. Sometimes people feel like traveling and being active well into their 80s. Sometimes deteriorating health causes people to slow down before they reach their 70s. Typically, though, most people are able to be about as active as they want until their 70s, then, inexorably, old age creeps up on us and we slip quietly, without trauma, into the passive retirement phase. These older people take fewer and fewer trips and then, ultimately, no trips. They buy no new cars, no new houses. In fact, this may be the time that people downsize their homes, purchase fewer new clothes, and allow a quieter and less expensive life-style to take over. During the years of the passive phase, the budget typically declines by 20 to 30%, but the decline may be masked by the upward push of inflation. More about this later. It may have been this phase of life that prompted Somerset Maugham to write, "Old age has its pleasures which, though different, are not less than the pleasures of youth."

FINAL RETIREMENT PHASE

Finally, the quiet pleasures give way to the unpleasant realities of the third phase of retirement, the final phase. The "slow-go" phase gives way to the "no-go" phase. Failing health makes medical treatment and nursing care the defining characteristics. This phase may be prolonged or it may be blessedly brief. Managing this uncertainty is one of the principal challenges of The Prosperous Retirement and is discussed in more detail in Chapter 9.

THE RETIREMENT WHEEL

Given the length and complexity of the new retirement, it should come as no surprise that it is filled with all the challenges of the other phases of life, plus a few new ones. The concept of The Prosperous Retirement encompasses all of these complexities and helps to organize our understanding of the issues and their inter-relationships. I find it helpful to imagine retirement as an old wagon wheel. At the center of the retirement wagon wheel is the sturdy hub, from which the spokes radiate out to the wooden hoop of the wheel, and all is bound together by the iron rim. I picture retirement finances as the hub of the wheel. Nothing works very well without adequate finances, and accordingly, finances are the central issue. I think of money as the grease on which the hub turns around the axle of life. Radiating out from the financial hub, I imagine eight spokes:

1. Physical health
2. Mental health
3. Diet
4. Exercise
5. Social relations
6. Personal relations
7. Intellectual stimulation
8. Spiritual balance

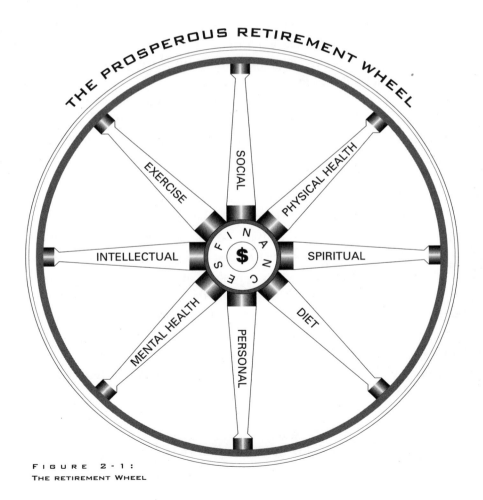

FIGURE 2-1:
THE RETIREMENT WHEEL

The concept of The Prosperous Retirement acts like the iron rim of the wagon wheel, holding all the other components of the wheel in place as it rolls across the years of retirement.

THE FINANCIAL HUB

This chapter is not primarily about finances, but before I dismiss finances as simply "the hub of the retirement wheel," I would like to make three points. First, a lot of money is not necessarily required to achieve The Prosperous Retirement. It is possible to have a satisfactory retirement on a slim budget, just as it is possible to have a happy life on a slim budget. While money is not the only factor in retirement, perhaps not even the main issue, it is hard to imagine a happy retirement in which one is constantly dogged by worries about finances. My father was fond of saying, "Money can't buy you happiness—but neither can poverty."

My second point is that most people approaching retirement have developed a life-style that is a reasonable compromise between extravagance and subsistence. Liberation from the obligations of the workplace does not mean that all the rules have lost their power. The first law of finance—expenses tend to equal income—continues to operate. The very essence of The Prosperous Retirement is maintaining the life-style that matches your tastes with your means.

My third point is that many people who have devoted their lives to the single-minded goal of becoming wealthy may not have developed the other skills that will be required to make retirement a success. Just as many people have to focus their pre-retirement planning on wealth accumulation, there are others whose pre-retirement planning has to focus on developing the other resources that will be required for The Prosperous Retirement, namely, physical and mental health, diet and exercise, social and personal relationships, intellectual stimulation, and spiritual balance. Just because a retiree has lots of money doesn't mean that retirement is going to be all cake and ale.

HEALTH

There is no possibility of having a wonderful retirement without reasonably good health. Modern medical science is making it increasingly clear that genes play a big role in the health of older people. Hopefully, you have inherited reasonably good genes, but whatever genetic hand you've been dealt, you can make the most of it by eating properly and getting enough exercise. The ideal diet and exercise regime varies not only from person to person but from time to time. I can remember when no one but a scientist knew what "cholesterol" was, and now it is party talk around every tray of canapés. I also can remember when it was generally accepted that the best exercise for older people was sitting in a rocking chair. As more and more Americans live to old age, the evidence is overwhelming that a low-fat diet and at least three, 30-minute periods of vigorous exercise a week are important steps toward maintaining good health in retirement.

DEPRESSION

One of the chief obstacles along the way to The Prosperous Retirement is depression. Depression is an ailment that does not get all the publicity of heart attacks and cancer, but I believe it is the true underlying cause of many deaths from heart attack, cancer, cirrhosis, suicide, and accidents. We all know that the loss of a long-time spouse is one of the greatest psychological strains that a person can experience. We also have heard the expression that people are "married to their work." Many people, when you ask them who they are, will answer with a description of their work. Is it any surprise, then, that when people become "divorced" from their work, they might experience a period of traumatic stress? A recent survey indicated that 18% of people over age 60 suffered from dysthymia, a chronic mild depression. Recent medical studies indicate that dysthymia is a treatable illness. Many retired people report that the transition to retirement is not as easy as they had expected. The changes that characterize retirement can thrust a person into a state of depression that can linger and deepen unless positive influences reverse the downward cycle.

Just as diet and exercise can have a positive effect on physical health, they also can help with mental health. There is no doubt that a good diet and an appropriate program of vigorous exercise can have a positive effect on mental health. A vicious cycle down into depression may develop from lack of exercise, poor diet, and the loss of intellectu-al and social stimulation that previously was drawn from the work-a-day world. This cycle may lead to a variety of self-destructive behaviors and the deterioration of personal, social, and spiritual relationships. If peo-ple find themselves in the grips of depression, if life has lost its savor, the only hope for a satisfactory retirement is to find help. Sometimes a change in diet and the pattern of exercise can be helpful. Some people find the stimulation of group involvement a powerful incentive to recapture the positive energy in their lives. For others, personal or fam-ily relations are the key, and for still others, spiritual involvement may provide the spark to get their fire burning. Whatever it takes, it is important not to allow a depressed state of mind to persist. If all else fails, medical science has a cartridge belt full of silver bullets that can help with depression.

Many older people find it distasteful or even abhorrent to seek medical assistance or to take drugs to correct a depressed state of mind. Among the miracles of modern science that help make The Prosperous Retirement a reality are the many products of the pharmacological industry. As we get older, we need all the help we can get. It is no more disgraceful today to take medicine for depression than it is to take aspirin for a headache. (See Appendix 1 for a questionnaire to assess your state of mind.)

SOCIAL RELATIONS

One of the keys to finding the positive energy in your retirement is to find the right social context. For some people, it is the country club, for others, it is a health club, a hobby group, or the great outdoors. There are groups for seniors everywhere you look. Senior centers, community centers, churches, and synagogues routinely sponsor social groups, dis-cussions, classes, exercise groups, and a variety of activities to keep your mind and body stimulated. Medical science seems to be coming to the conclusion that, given good health, seniors can engage in any physical activity that they want. There are even senior groups that engage in strenuous activities like hiking, bicycle riding, skiing, and running. I myself belong to a group called the "Over-the-Hill Gang." The club's motto is, "You pick up speed when you are over the hill."

MENTAL EXERCISE

Another important kind of "exercise" is mental exercise. The evidence is becoming abundant and clear that, as we age, it is important to keep mentally active. The evidence also seems clear that, as people age, they generally lose some of their mental agility, the "quickness" of their thought process. At the same time, a rich life experience and the time to reflect on things may have resulted in a kind of wisdom that younger people seldom command. To keep your mental faculties sharp, they need to be "exercised" on a regular basis. Inactivity and a lack of meaningful social and intellectual contact can lead to a dulling of intellect, depression, and a negative impact on both physical and mental health. An important component of The Prosperous Retirement is intellectual stimulation, and it is not enough to grumble over the daily newspaper during breakfast. It is important to be challenged by other people's ideas and to continue to seek opportunities to put your problem-solving skills to work in a rewarding way. Take classes, join discussion groups, learn new skills, visit museums, study nature, mentor a younger person, and look for positive energy and new ideas wherever you can find them.

SEEKING BALANCE

You can see where this discussion leads. It takes a combination of positive factors to make a truly prosperous retirement, to form a wagon wheel capable of rolling across the broad expanse of a modern retirement. At the center are finances. Money can be the tool that provides good nutrition, good medical care, good exercise facilities, and the ability to participate in enjoyable and uplifting activities. Just as a wagon wheel without spokes will not carry your wagon, money cannot, in itself, bring joy, satisfaction, fulfillment, and a sense of balance into your life. In fact, money sometimes can get in the way of achieving these non-financial goals. Money cannot buy health, either mental or physical. It cannot bring a sense of "getting your life straight," and it may make personal and social relations more complicated and less satisfying. Money is not the be-all and end-all of The Prosperous Retirement. Instead, the dominant theme of The Prosperous Retirement is to live your life in a way that truly makes you feel good about yourself and your life. It is about finding that golden mean, the balance of factors that keeps the wheel spinning smoothly and for a long time.

BUILDING RETIREMENT

Seen in the context of the wagon wheel and all its parts, retirement looks simple. However, the transition from a working life to retirement is not as easy as it may seem. Many retirees find that a gradual transition from working to retirement is easier to manage than an abrupt change. The transition to retirement may be easier if you keep a circle of friends and activities that were in place before retirement. In other words, it is important to begin building The Prosperous Retirement well before you begin living it. You would certainly understand that a person must begin planning their retirement finances before they retire, but many retirees think that they will deal with the other challenges of retirement "when the time comes." Building a circle of relationships, friends, activities, and interests that will play a positive role in retirement is not something that should wait until just before retirement. Retirement is something you should spend your life building.

LIFE-STYLE CHANGES

Many people imagine a retirement that is dramatically different from their working life. They dream of moving to the seashore, or a warm climate, or the mountains to pursue a different life-style. If your retirement plans call for a move to a new community, it is essential to plan this very carefully. Many retirees who move to a new location discover that the new place is not the paradise that they had imagined, and they find themselves moving again after just a few years. There are many books on selecting a retirement location that you can make use of. In addition, make a number of visits to the new place at various times of the year. Tucson may be wonderful in winter, but summer may not appeal to you. A few days of rain may not bother you, but a long rainy season in a coastal location may prove to be unendurable.

Make certain that the new location offers opportunities for the activities and hobbies that you enjoy. Many people move to a new location to enjoy an active outdoor life-style. This may be fine during the active phase of retirement, but as retirees move into the passive phase, other facilities that they might enjoy may be missing. If this leads to another relocation when you reach age 75, it may be difficult. As people slip into the final phase of retirement, good medical facilities and the support of family and friends may become very important. Having this support can add years of independent living to the retirement. Think about any relocation in the broadest and most detailed terms possible. It is an important decision, and a mistake may be costly and difficult to undo.

PERSONAL RELATIONS

Retirement can be a time when personal relations develop and flower in ways that can make the final phases of your life a very rewarding time. But retirement is no panacea. Retirement may provide the relief from pressure that allows some retirees to develop into the kind of people they have always wanted to be, but for others, the changes associated with retirement may make them unbearable. Many people find that the personal characteristics that described them in earlier phases of their life simply become more pronounced in retirement. For some retirees, this can pose a real problem. A sharp-edged personality that it was possible to cope with for a few hours a day may prove to be unbearable for 16 hours a day, 7 days a week. More than one spouse has said, "I married you for better or for worse, but not for lunch." It is important to maintain a good balance in retirement that involves a broad circle of relationships and activities, both at home and outside.

DEVELOPING RETIREMENT SKILLS

For many people, retirement seems like the time to do what they have always wanted to do. Freed of the everyday demands of the workplace, they imagine themselves fishing or gardening, playing tennis or golf, developing their intellectual skills, working on their hobbies, or just taking the time to smell the roses. Retirement is the time to take pleasure and find stimulation in these activities.

If you have not had the opportunity to develop these leisure activities during a busy lifetime, a part of your pre-retirement planning should be the development of some leisure interests. There are endless classes, groups, societies, and individuals who would be delighted to help you get involved in the activities that they find fascinating. Make an assessment of your interests and decide what seems stimulating.

Many people find retirement an ideal time to pursue some educational goal that they could not achieve in the earlier stages of their life. Many organizations actively solicit the involvement of retirees to help them pursue their organizational goals. These organizations may be political, social, healthcare-related, athletic, environmental, religious, or hobby-related. These involvements can be important in maintaining the all-around good balance that characterizes The Prosperous Retirement. These activities may provide the setting in which you can achieve personal, social, political, or intellectual goals for which you never had time.

RETIREMENT EMPLOYMENT

For many retirees, retirement employment may strengthen some of the spokes in their retirement wheel at the same time that it greases the hub. In today's world where retirements can last for 30 or 40 years, many people are finding it useful financially, intellectually, and personally to have some sort of post-retirement employment. It may seem like a contradiction to talk about retirement employment. After all, isn't retirement defined as the period when you don't have employment?

In The Prosperous Retirement, the active retirement phase frequently is characterized by retirement employment. This employment may be useful because it improves the financial picture, or because it eases the transition from work to leisure, or because it provides intellectual stimulation or personal contacts that are helpful in making all the spokes form a perfect circle. Retirement employment is not just a continuation of the same work that was done before retirement. It may involve the same kind of work but with reduced hours, less pressure, flexible deadlines, or some other features that make it compatible with retirement. For example, a marketing executive for a corporation may become a marketing consultant. As a consultant, she will have more flexibility in determining what work to take and what work to pass by. The consultant can set her own hours and take long vacations, but still supplement her retirement finances with earnings and continue to have the stimulation and contact of being active in the workplace.

In some cases, retirement employment may involve a completely different kind of work. Frequently, this new work is a reflection of some much-loved hobby. How many retirees might relish the idea of being a golf pro or a fly fishing coach? Still other retirees may choose to pursue an entirely new direction. I know of several people who have become mediators, employing the skills and experience they had acquired in their working careers to help other people resolve conflicts in their lives. While this is not a low-stress type of work, it can be very rewarding and may add the element of social purpose to the benefits to be derived. The old cliché of retirement as a time to go fishing without a line on your rod is part of the folklore from the old retirement, not part of The Prosperous Retirement.

KEEPING THE RETIREMENT WHEEL ROLLING

If you want your retirement to move smoothly through the many years that it is likely to encompass, you need to make certain that you have built a wheel that can cover the distance. The financial hub needs to be greased with adequate retirement capital and it will need an appropriate number of well-built spokes. Be certain to devote the necessary attention to health—both physical and mental, exercise, diet, recreation, intellectual stimulation, personal relations, social involvement, and spiritual development. There is a lot to consider in planning The Prosperous Retirement, but the rewards can be enormous. Remember, this is your life, not a dress rehearsal!

3.

WHAT WILL THE PROSPEROUS RETIREMENT COST?

"The man is the richest whose pleasures are the cheapest."
—HENRY DAVID THOREAU
Journal, March 11, 1856

SYNOPSIS: The cost of retirement is the first question that people ask and the last question to have an answer. This fundamental question is difficult to answer because it is based on so many different factors. Life-style and longevity are the key determinants. Contrary to what most retirement authorities tell you, your budget during the first phase of The Prosperous Retirement — the active retirement — is likely to be similar to the budget that you had before you retired, if you can afford it. Inflation will affect your active retirement budget. During the second phase of your retirement, the passive retirement, a slow-down in life-style will offset most of inflation's impact. The cost of the third and final phase is unpredictable because it is mainly a function of medical expenses, but it can be made predictable by the use of insurance.

WHEN CLIENTS ASK, "How much will it cost to retire?" I'm never certain that I understand exactly what they're asking. The classic way of planning retirement finances begins with the assumption that the retirement budget will be dramatically less than the budget was prior to retirement. Therefore, one meaning of the question might be, "What is my monthly budget likely to be in retirement?" The other meaning—and this is usually what clients have in mind—is, "How much capital do I need to accumulate to ensure a comfortable retirement?" Either way, I always know that I am at the beginning of a process of educating the client to the complexity of this fundamental and seemingly innocent question. Unfortunately, neither question really gets to the heart of the matter.

At the heart of The Prosperous Retirement is the question, "How am I going to be able to generate the cash flow[1] that I will need during retirement?" Cash flow—not capital—is the key to The Prosperous Retirement. My analysis indicates that there are at least 10 factors that influence the answer to this question:

1. Life-style
2. Age at retirement
3. Longevity
4. Health
5. Inflation
6. The nature of the retirement income
7. Retirement capital base
8. Investment policy
9. Risk tolerance
10. "Dispository inclinations"
   (i.e., your intention to leave wealth to others)

These topics will reappear frequently in the next chapters. As a result, I will discuss most of them only briefly here, but I must emphasize the complexity of this question. As anxious as I am to illustrate this com-

---

[1] There is a difference between "cash flow" and "income." Income comes from pensions, annuities, earnings, dividends, and interest. Cash flow includes all these plus the proceeds of liquidating assets. The difference is important to The Prosperous Retirement.

plexity for you, I also know you are anxious to get some sense of this vital number. So, before we get to the details, I'll give you a quick-and-dirty answer, if you promise to keep reading to get a more useful and accurate understanding of the factors that influenced the answer. I am going to spend the best part of five chapters explaining the main factors that influence this calculation and showing you how to come to a more precise number with which to guide your prosperous retirement.

THE QUICK-AND-DIRTY ANSWER

Here it is: $206,372! A 65-year-old retiree is likely to need about $206,372 in savings to provide each $1,000 per month of inflation-adjusted income during retirement. The assumptions on which this is based are as follows:

- The retiree will live for 30 years to age 95.
- Inflation will average 4.5%.
- Retirement capital will return 8.5% before-tax.
- The retiree will consume all retirement capital.

While this "answer" may seem helpful, it also is misleading, so keep reading. If it really were this easy, there would be little point in my writing this book, or in you reading this book or even seeking advice. The "real answer" is a lot more complicated, hedged with several imponderables, and it varies a great deal with changes in the underlying assumptions.

To illustrate just how much the "answer" varies, I have prepared Figure 3-1 that shows the capital required to produce $1,000 per month of inflation-adjusted income from various retirement ages to age 95 and at various rates of return on the capital. I have assumed inflation that averages 4.5%.

The overall pattern of the table is fairly obvious:

- ✔ The later you retire, the less money you need.
- ✔ The higher the return on capital is, the less money you need.
- ✔ Higher returns have more impact than later retirement.

The specifics are fairly noteworthy. At higher rates of return there is less change in the required capital for different ages. The difference between ages 50 and 65 at a 10.5% rate of return is only $20,097 ($184,664 versus $164,567), while at 6.5%, the difference is $82,511 ($349,147 versus $266,636). Looking across the table, you also can see that, at the younger ages, the various rates of return make a bigger difference. Note that at age 50, the difference between a 6.5% rate of return and a 10.5% rate of return means you need 89% more capital—an extra $164,483 ($349,147 versus $184,664). At age 65, the difference is only 62% more, or $102,069 ($266,636 versus $164,567). The implications of this observation will be discussed in greater detail, but it is a powerful argument for a more aggressive investment policy for younger retirees.

An example may make this chart a little clearer. A person retiring at age 60 would need $296,784 in capital to produce the inflation-adjusted equivalent of $1,000 per month until reaching age 95, if the retiree earned 6.5% before taxes on the capital. Those of you who are good with numbers will immediately see that 6.5% of $296,784 (296,784 x .065) is a lot more than $12,000—the first year's required income. It is $19,290.96. What may not be immediately obvious is that, over 35 years, the $1,000 per month, under the pressure of 4.5% inflation, grows to more than $4,877 per month. Thus, for the capital base to produce the required $56,008 of income in the 35th year, it needs to be earning more than is required in the

CAPITAL REQUIRED

to Produce $1,000 Per Month of Inflation-Adjusted Income to Age 95 at Various Ages and Rates of Return

FIGURE 3-1

Starting	Rates of Return				
Age	6.5%	7.5%	8.5%	9.5%	10.5%
50	$349,147	$291,202	$246,703	$212,042	$184,664
55	$324,206	$274,663	$235,691	$204,682	$179,726
60	$296,784	$255,608	$222,404	$193,384	$173,383
65	$266,636	$233,658	$206,372	$183,639	$164,567

earlier years. The capital base has to build up in the early years to carry the heavy burden of the inflation-swollen budget in later years. Well, so much for the simple version. Let's take a look at a more realistic version of the answer to our question about generating cash flow during retirement. We will consider each of the 10 factors listed earlier.

LIFE-STYLE

The first and primary determinant of the cost of retirement is life-style. Some people plan to change their life-style in retirement, but most people plan to live pretty much the same way that they were living before they retired. This is the essence of The Prosperous Retirement—a retirement life-style that is as similar to your pre-retirement life-style as you want it to be. So, for most people, the monthly cost of retirement is likely to be pretty much the same as it was before retirement. Over time, inflation will drive up the monthly budget just as it did before, and the impact of inflation will not change because of retirement.

The general rule reflects Stein's First Rule of Retirement, "The active-phase retirement budget tends to equal the pre-retirement budget, if the retiree can afford it." Round-the-world trips cost more, and so do 50-foot recreational vehicles, but selling a home and moving to a cabin in the woods might cost less. If you keep doing what you were doing, it is likely to cost the same as it was costing.

You are the only judge of what your retirement is going to cost, but don't fall for the old line that says you are going to be able to maintain your life-style in retirement on a lot fewer dollars than it cost you before you retired. This legend is deeply rooted in retirement lore, but it is based on observations of the post-Depression retirement, in which retirees simply did not have the resources to live a more prosperous retirement. People always tend to make do with what they have. If they have little, they live a modest life-style, look for ways to economize, and look to friends, family, and charity for help. No one wants to live that way today, and few are willing to settle for that kind of stunted retirement.

An interesting footnote for self-employed people is that, in retirement, you may not have your business to pay for some of your life-style expenses, so there could be a fairly dramatic *increase* in your personal budget.

MORTGAGE

Some people point at mortgage payments as a potential source for a budget reduction. They deduce, and quite correctly, "If I pay off my mortgage when I retire, I can eliminate the mortgage payment from my budget and lower my income needs significantly." What they fail to see, and this will be discussed in detail in Chapter 9, is that paying off the mortgage also deprives them of a potential source of income. Paying off the mortgage may or may not be a good idea, but it certainly does not change the bottom line on retirement income. It may reduce the need for income, but it also reduces the retiree's ability to generate income. When you transfer funds from savings to pay off the mortgage, you also are transferring them out of your retirement capital base and reducing your ability to generate growth and income in your retirement investment portfolio. Paying off the mortgage is a mixed blessing in which you trade financial benefits for peace of mind. For some people, this is a very desirable trade, but for financial planners, who focus on "financial efficiency," a frequent recommendation will be to allow the mortgage to stay in place.

AGE AT RETIREMENT

The age at which you retire will influence the cost of retirement in two ways. First, the younger you are at retirement, the longer your retirement is likely to be. The longer the retirement is, the more impact inflation will have and the more emphasis must be placed on retirement cash flow rather than retirement capital. A person retiring below the age of 65 needs to think about retirement earnings, not just living on Social Security, pension, and personal savings. Financial planners used to be fond of talking about "the three-legged stool of retirement income," which was constructed from Social Security, pension, and personal savings. That three-legged stool went out with hand milking. Retirees should now think in terms of a more stable four-legged stool that adds retirement earnings as the fourth leg.

The second point to consider is that the earlier a person retires, the longer the active phase of retirement is likely to be. If the retiree is vigorous and filled with dreams of expensive things to do with all his or her leisure time, the early years of retirement could be financially draining. This possibility needs to be factored into the calculation.

LONGEVITY

Longevity—the length of your lifetime—is the great imponderable. This complicated issue is examined in the next chapter, but let me make one fundamental point: You are likely to live longer than you think you will and longer than the longevity tables indicate. In addition, your expectation about longevity is based on your observation of family and friends. They lived in a different time; things look brighter for today's retiree. Generally, it is prudent to add at least 25% to your statistical longevity, or perhaps even as much as 50%. If the tables say that at age 65 you have a life expectancy of 17.30 years, you probably should plan on living at least to age 87 [65 + (17.30 x 1.25)].

HEALTH

The great variable in longevity is your health. If your health is excellent at age 65, that is above average. If your health is "only average," the statistical tables may be a reasonable indication of what to expect. If you are committed to maintaining your health with good diet and exercise, the tables probably understate your life expectancy. A researcher from the National Center for Health Statistics expressed the opinion that the recent dramatic increases in longevity of older Americans is largely due to improved diet and exercise regimes. If you have a serious health problem, your doctor may be helpful in assessing how long it is likely to be manageable. When health does begin to deteriorate in the passive and final phases of your retirement, the costs are assumed to be borne by insurance and Medicare. We will examine these issues more fully in Chapter 10.

INFLATION

Inflation is another imponderable. We have considerable data and a fairly clear historical trend to guide our thinking. We will examine that data in Chapter 5. The bottom line is that inflation will vary from year to year, but over the course of your retirement in the next few decades, I believe that inflation is likely to average a little more than it has since the Second World War—4% to 5% is a prudent range for assumptions. Right now, rates are low; but inflation is clearly a cyclical function.

INCOME SOURCES

The nature and sources of your retirement income are another factor. I am among those who believe that Social Security will survive; it will change, but it will survive. Increases in benefits are not likely to keep pace with inflation. The government may attempt to manipulate the Consumer Price Index (CPI) to understate inflation, and even then, increases are unlikely to keep up with the CPI, but benefits will be paid. The wealthy may find those benefits taxed and there could even be "means testing," but an effort will be made to keep up the appearance that you are getting the benefits that were promised.

If you have a pension, it is probably not cost-of-living adjusted and the burden of providing the inflation boost for the pension will fall on your personal savings. The issue of retirement earnings, making some current income in retirement, will be a make-or-break issue for many retirements. This issue will be examined in more detail in Chapter 9.

CAPITAL BASE

Your retirement capital base is the grease on which the wheel of your retirement will turn. The size and nature of this capital base will play a role in determining the risks and rewards of your retirement. If there is time before you retire, there may be some fairly dramatic increases that can be made through savings and wise investment policies.

The use of your retirement capital base—your investment policy—is another key issue. There are many misconceptions about the question of how to use your retirement savings, and we will devote Chapters 7 and 8 to this difficult and critical question. The difference between getting a 6.5% return on your assets and getting 10.5% involves your investment policy and, of course, the markets. You may be sufficiently astute to design a good portfolio of investments, but will you be able to maintain a steady hand on the tiller through the years of your retirement? This is an area where you should work with a trusted and skilled advisor. We will discuss some of the alternatives in Chapter 9. If you doubt that 10.5% before-tax returns actually are available over the long-term, look at the track records of the mutual funds that have been around for 40 to 50 years, or the return of the Standard and Poor's 500 since 1926. More about this in Chapters 7 and 8, *much* more.

One of the variables in your capital base that will affect your retirement income is whether your capital base is in taxable or tax-deferred accounts. Your tax-deferred accounts probably are concealing a substantial tax liability that will have to be paid as funds are withdrawn from these accounts. On the other hand, if your income is coming from taxable accounts, many fewer dollars probably will be going to taxes. This is a fairly complex issue and will be discussed in Chapter 9.

RISK TOLERANCE

Your risk tolerance reveals how much risk is likely to keep you awake at night. This is a key limitation on how productive your capital base is likely to be. This issue also will be considered in more detail in Chapter 9. Your ability to control your fears through education and confidence is a critical issue in determining and sticking with a wise investment policy. This, in turn, will determine the long-term productivity of your investments. No investment policy will work if your fears force you to change it because of changes in the marketplace. Working with a trusted and skilled financial professional can make the difference between insomnia and sleep and between sticking with a wise policy and being forced—by your fears—to abandon it.

DISPOSITORY INTENTIONS

The last factor that we will discuss is your vision of what you want to happen to your wealth when you have no further use for it—your dispository inclinations. Do you intend to leave a sizable inheritance to your heirs or charity or is it your aim to spend your last nickel with your last breath? The old model was to leave your wealth to your heirs. However, more and more people feel no obligation to leave large bequests. You probably have seen the bumper sticker, usually on a big recreational vehicle, that says, "I'm spending my kids' inheritance!"

The management of your resources to accomplish your purposes is not entirely under your control. Changes in government policies, programs, and taxation could affect your retirement. Health issues and changes in the insurance environment also may affect your retirement. The management of your retirement finances is an on-going challenge. You are likely to need a variety of dependable, professional resources to help you deal with these challenges.

By now, I'm certain you're convinced that predicting the cost of retirement is a complicated question that involves issues of life-style, risk tolerance, economic conditions, government policies, and a whole series of imponderables. The biggest imponderable is when the retiree will die, but there are many others. In spite of its complexity, the cost of retirement is a question that demands an answer not just because we want to plan the retirement, but because retirement has become the defining phase of people's lives and deserves careful attention.

LIFE-STYLE

This seems like the right place to recall that The Prosperous Retirement is defined as a retirement that has a life-style similar to the life-style before retirement. If a person was a careful spender during the working years, the retirement budget may be very modest. I have seen retirees who were living very happily on less than $2,000 a month of income. If this simple life-style satisfies their taste, and if there are enough resources to provide an inflation-adjusted cash flow over their life expectancy, this is The Prosperous Retirement.

On the other hand, I'm fond of telling the story of an actual client who had been a senior executive with a major corporation. Jason (name changed, of course) was earning $24,000 a month just before he retired. Over the years of his long and successful career, he and Agnes (also changed) had developed quite an expensive life-style. They were providing regular support for one of their children who was handicapped. They had a primary residence right by the club house of the local country club, a lovely condominium in the California Desert, and a third residence in the mountains. They were used to saving a few thousand dollars a month, and through successful investment management they had accumulated a net worth of about $2.5 million. When Jason retired, his pension was $14,000 a month, and at age 58, it would be some time until he received Social Security. This looked to me like another Prosperous Retirement, but surprise, surprise!

After his retirement, Jason and Agnes took a very nice cruise and then went up to their place in the mountains. I hadn't seen them in about 6 months when I got a Monday-morning call from Jason, "Have you got time to see me *today*?" I could tell that he was upset, so I agreed to meet him during the lunch hour. When he came in, his agitation was obvious. He explained that he had been studying his finances over the weekend and was in a panic. He concluded with an amazing question, "Is it really possible to be retired on $14,000 a month?" I managed to stifle my laughter and tried to understand what was going on. Jason had discovered that while $14,000 is a lot of monthly income, it is not $24,000. Stein's First Rule of Retirement was at work: **"*The active-phase retirement budget tends to equal the pre-retirement budget, if the retiree can afford it*."** While Jason was receiving income of $14,000, they were probably still spending about $20,000—the old $24,000 minus their savings. In the first six months of their retirement, I figured that they had probably spent about $35,000 more than they had received. Jason saw bankruptcy staring them in the eye. In fact, the situation was a little worse than I had surmised. On the advice of their estate planning attorney, they had made a round of $10,000 gifts to their five children, four spouses, and six grandchildren. Jason also had loaned $50,000 to one of their sons to finance a business venture. In addition, they had been spending even more in retirement than they had spent before retirement (first-class cruises are not cheap) and in six months they had managed to reduce their net worth by about $250,000—10%. They felt that bankruptcy was not just staring at them across the poker table of life, but breathing down their necks. It looked like they would be bankrupt in less than 5 years, at age 63. At this moment, Jason and Agnes were definitely not experiencing the joys of The Prosperous Retirement. After we went through their affairs and Jason saw that they actually *were* living within their means—as long as they used discretion on the gifts—they were once again enjoying The Prosperous Retirement.

The case of Agnes and Jason illustrates several interesting points, the first of which is the first corollary to Stein's First Rule of Retirement: "Your life-style tends to be based on the income that is available." Most Americans do not save a huge percentage of their income, so their pre-retirement life-style tends to absorb most of their income. It is probable that, if they can afford it, most Americans would prefer to live the same life-style after retirement that they were living before retirement. That life-style will continue to cost the same after retirement as it did before retirement. In fact, the first few years of retirement often are character-ized by even higher levels of expenses as people act on the dreams they have nurtured for all those years.

The next point is that the drop in income that comes with the tran-sition to retirement is offset in the minds of many retirees by the notion that it is now time to start taking income from their financial assets. They knew that their income was going to drop when they retired. They had planned for it, and they were not sufficiently disturbed by the change in income to really think it through. They expected to start drawing on their savings regardless of the impact that might have on their long-range financial stability.

The third point is that people tend to think of retirement finances in one of two modes. The first mode asks, "How much monthly income will I need?" They tend to think that this will be a fixed amount. They are not used to considering the impact of inflation on their income needs. There are two reasons why this doesn't seem important. First, most Americans are used to earning a market salary. As their skills improved and their seniority grew, they were used to receiving pay raises that exceeded the rate of inflation. They knew that inflation was out there, but it seemed like their finances automatically adjusted to compensate for it. The second reason that they think of their income needs as being fixed is that most Americans underestimate the number of years that they are likely to spend in retirement. It's almost as if they believe that if they say out loud, "I expect to live many, many years in a healthy and active retirement," it will jinx their life. That attitude may be a left-over from the days of the "bad old retirement." It is as though people really don't believe that they will be the beneficiary of the dramatic improve-ment in life expectancy that has extended the lives of Americans in the last century. I frequently hear clients say things like, "Sure, I know the statistics, but no one in my family has ever lived past 65." Remember, none of those relatives who died at an early age lived in the 21st Century. They probably never heard of organ transplants, genetic engineering, or the modern miracles of the pharmaceutical industry. The second mode in which Americans think about retirement finances is like this, "If I need

$5,000 a month to live, and if I get $2,000 from my pension and $1,000 from Social Security, I need to have a capital base of $400,000, because if I get 6% on $400,000, that makes up the other $2,000 per month of income that I need." It may seem like sound thinking, but it leaves out inflation and taxes, not to mention that there is no guarantee that 6% interest will always be available.

The final point to be drawn from Jason and Agnes is that, even given ample financial resources, The Prosperous Retirement is definitely a state of mind.

THE RETIREMENT BUDGET

Your retirement budget deserves a lot of study. Supplying your retirement budget with the cash flow it needs is the entire financial challenge of retirement. Therefore, it pays to study your budget, both as you are planning your retirement and as you are living your retirement. It is important to know not just how much you are spending, but to study the various expenses and see the budget in three ways that may be unfamiliar. The three unusual perspectives are:

1. Essential versus discretionary spending
2. Structural versus peripheral expenses
3. Fixed expenses versus inflation-driven expenses

One of the key "tricks" in The Prosperous Retirement is to structure your budget so that you can live a perfectly wonderful life-style when the funds are available and pull back to a merely great life-style when your investments are not quite so productive. Examining your budget with these three unusual perspectives will help to build in that flexibility.

Essential Versus Discretionary Spending

You need to know what portion of your budget is discretionary spending. What expenditures could be eliminated if push came to shove? The answer is not always obvious. Some expenditures that appear to be essential—food, shelter, clothing, taxes, transportation, and utilities—may prove to be at least partially non-essential. Other expenses that appear to be discretionary—gifts, charitable contributions, dining out, wine and liquor, and the cost of pets—may turn out to be essential. I have seen clients who spent $1,500 per month on groceries. There is probably room for savings. I have seen clients with mortgage payments in excess of $5,000 per month. Fur coats and cashmere sweaters are "clothing," but probably not essential. Everyone needs transportation, but not everyone needs a Mercedes. On the other side, I also know of people who believe that their 10% tithe to their church is a moral obligation. One client really believes his bumper sticker, which says, "Life is too short to drink cheap wine." Many people would rather cut their own food budget than skimp on their pet's food. Each retiree must examine his or her own budget and make judgments about what is essential and what is discretionary, but the discretionary part needs to be identified and quantified.

Structural Versus Peripheral Expenses

Another interesting perspective in which to view the budget is the separation of structural expenses from peripheral expenses. Some expenditures cannot be avoided because they are contractual obligations and default would result in legal consequences. These are structural expenses. Structural expenses are even more binding than essential expenses and generally are not subject to modification or negotiation. If you don't pay them, bad things happen. If you own property, you must pay the property taxes or lose the property. If you belong to a country club, you must pay the dues or lose your membership. If you have a mortgage, it must be paid. You have to service your automobile or risk losing it.

Other expenses are peripheral to the structure of your life. They generally are outside of the real structure of your life. They may be fun or desirable, but they are not required. You don't have to buy your spouse a solid gold watch for his 65th birthday. If you elect to take a vacation to Hawaii, you don't have to do it again next year. These are peripheral expenses, and you can eliminate them from your budget without changing the essential character of your life-style. When you are adding expenses to your retirement budget—a condominium, a country club, an expensive car—it is a good idea to recognize that these will add structural expenses that cannot be easily dropped if you have a bad year in the market. The peripheral expenses, such as vacations, trips, gifts, luxury purchases, can be made when the funds are available and eliminated when the funds are not available. They are not an essential part of the fabric of your retirement life-style. It is important to examine your budget in this perspective.

Inflated Versus Fixed Expenses

The third unusual perspective for examining the budget is to determine the portion of your budget that is exempt from inflation—expenses that are fixed. Most of your expenses are affected by inflation. Some items tend to go up more than others, but in general they are increased each year by the effect of inflation. Every budget has some expenses that are exempt from inflation. Some examples are mortgage payments, fixed insurance premiums, loan payments, and contracts that call for fixed payments. You should have an idea of what percent of your budget is composed of payments that are not affected by inflation. You probably will find that most of these are essential, structural expenses, although gifts and contributions which are not directly affected by inflation are discretionary and peripheral. You can control the impact of inflation on discretionary, peripheral expenses by selectively reducing them or eliminating them if inflation begins to stress your ability to generate income. It is important to know that you can reduce the impact of inflation by understanding your budget. There has been talk in the press recently about the ability of people to reduce the impact of inflation by substituting one product for another. If coffee goes up a lot, people can switch to tea. This is a real alternative. You do not have to plan your retirement in the belief that your budget is going to bear the full brunt of inflation.

Subsistence Budget

There is one more interesting perspective on the budget that is a key element to calculating the cost of The Prosperous Retirement. In Chapter 6, where we will develop a computer model for projecting the cost of retirement, one of the key factors will be the difference between your budget in the active phase of retirement versus the budget in the passive phase of retirement. The easiest way to develop this number, but not the most accurate, is to ask the question, "How many dollars a month do I need to exist?" This does not include peripheral or discretionary expenses. It includes only those expenses that are truly essential to staying alive physically and financially. An elaboration of this calculation goes on to apply the inflation factor and determine the degree to which this subsistence budget is driven by inflation. If your subsistence budget does not include mortgage payments, it is probably driven more by inflation than your active budget. The impact of inflation on the subsistence budget is a bit of an imponderable, so I recommend that you just focus on estimating an answer to the basic question, "How many dollars a month do I need to exist?"

Some people actually enjoy tracking their budget and studying it as suggested here. The odds are, you are not one of them, but you need to have a perspective on this important question to really understand the probable cost of your retirement. What do the Nike people say? "Just do it!"

CHAPTER 3

ACTION PLAN:

❏ Think about your retirement life-style—"bigger is better" or "small is beautiful."

❏ Study your current budget as a basis for estimating your retirement budget.

❏ Determine the "essential" portion of the budget versus the "discretionary" portion.

❏ Determine what portion of your budget is "structural" and what portion is "peripheral."

❏ Determine the portion of your budget that is not impacted by inflation.

❏ Study the "subsistence" budget to determine how much less it is than your current budget.

❏ Study your retirement income sources. Will there be retirement earnings?

4.

LONGEVITY AND
LIFE EXPECTANCY

*"Lord, make me to know mine end, and the measure
of my days, what it is; let me know how short-lived I am."*
—PSALMS 39:4

SYNOPSIS: Longevity is vitally important to the retirement equation, but totally unpredictable. Increased life expectancy affects every aspect of retirement: life-style choices, investment strategy, tax planning, estate planning, risk management, and all the non-financial aspects. An improved understanding of longevity helps to unlock the full potential of The Prosperous Retirement. Virtually everyone knows that life expectancy has increased dramatically in this century, but most people have no idea just how long they are likely to live. Since 1900, the life expectancy of older Americans has increased by 52% and the trend seems to be accelerating. We can expect further increases in longevity and life expectancy in the decades ahead. In addition to understanding the general statistics, it is important to take a realistic look at the specific longevity factors in your life.

WE ALL KNOW THAT DEATH is an integral part of life, but few of us deal with that knowledge in a very useful way. Most of us choose to let death walk toward us like a stranger in the crowd. A good deal of statistical information is available to give us a fair idea of how long we are likely to live. There are even implications in the history of that data about what is probably going to happen to life expectancies over the next few decades. We can choose to ignore that data, but we do so at the risk of running out of money before we run out of time. Making the available money last as long as necessary is the whole point of retirement planning.

There is a famous quip by a sports figure who said, "I understand that the point of retirement planning is to make your money last until you die. I'm in great shape—as long as I die after lunch next Tuesday." That humorous story really underscores the importance of longevity in retirement planning. If a retiree believes that he or she is likely to live a long and healthy life, it affects life-style choices, investment strategies, tax and estate planning, risk management, and virtually all of the non-financial aspects of retirement. If the retiree believes that he or she will not live long in retirement, that assumption ripples through all the retirement decisions and results in an entirely different kind of retirement.

All the other factors in the retirement equation can be controlled by conscious choices, or at least there is enough data to permit us a well-informed guess about the future. Only longevity is out of our control. A retiree with "terminal" cancer could have a remission and live longer than his or her statistical life expectancy, or a healthy person could have a fatal accident. It is difficult both emotionally and financially to deal with this uncertainty, but it is also one of the defining characteristics of our humanity. We just have to do the best that we can.

It seems to me that dealing with longevity in the most straightforward way possible involves two steps. First, you need to study and understand the abundant statistical data about life expectancy. Second, you need to modify the general statistical picture by considering the specifics of your personal longevity prospects.

LONGEVITY STATISTICS

Assuming that you plan to live beyond next Tuesday, we should examine the longevity data. The United States government collects and processes an impressive array of information about births, deaths, and life expectancy, and has been doing so for many years.[1] In addition, insurance companies have their own life expectancy tables and so does the Internal Revenue Service. In fact, organizations may have several different tables that they use for different purposes. There is no shortage of data. A relatively neutral source of life expectancy data is from the U.S. Department of Health and Human Services. That department's Center for Health Statistics publishes a table each year that gives us the latest available government information. The life expectancy table on the next page, Figure 4-1, is the most recently published table of information available.

The amazing improvements in childhood mortality have increased the life expectancy of newborns very dramatically. The improvement in life expectancy through the middle years has been less dramatic, but the life expectancy increase for older Americans 65 to 85 years of age has been as dramatic as the improvement for newborns. Good news for you and your retirement.

If you had been part of the post-Depression retirement generation, born in 1900, your life expectancy at birth would have been 49.2 years. Infant mortality was a huge hurdle in those days, so if you just survived your first year, your life expectancy jumped to 55.2 years. Let's reflect on that. That means that only 50% of the people who were one year old in 1901 would live to be 56 years and 73 days. Stated a slightly different way, you had only a 50% probability of living beyond 56 years and 73 days. There was more than a 50% probability that you would not live long enough to retire at age 65. If the person born in 1900 were lucky enough to live to age 20, his or her life expectancy would have been 42.8 years. In 1920, at age 20, the person had a 50% chance of living until just before his or her 63rd birthday. Chances were that the person still would

---

[1] Interestingly, it will be the second quarter of the 21st Century before the government will have a full century of uniform data.

UNITED STATES LIFE EXPECTANCY

At Various Ages–All Races (1900-1993)

FIGURE 4-1

AGE	1900-02	1909-11	1919-21	1929-31	1939-41	1949-51	1959-61	1969-71	1979-81	1993	CHANGE 1900-1993
0	49.24	51.49	56.40	59.20	63.62	68.07	69.89	70.75	73.88	75.50	53%
1	55.20	57.11	59.94	61.94	65.76	69.16	70.75	71.19	73.82	75.20	36%
5	54.98	56.21	57.99	59.29	62.49	65.54	67.04	67.43	70.00	71.30	30%
10	51.14	52.15	53.79	54.84	57.82	60.74	62.19	62.57	65.10	66.40	30%
15	46.81	47.73	49.37	50.25	53.10	55.91	57.33	57.69	60.19	61.50	31%
20	42.79	43.53	45.30	45.94	48.54	51.20	52.58	53.00	55.46	56.70	33%
25	39.12	39.60	41.47	41.85	44.09	46.56	47.89	48.37	50.81	52.00	33%
30	35.51	35.50	37.68	37.75	39.67	41.91	43.18	43.71	46.12	47.30	33%
35	31.92	31.90	33.89	33.68	35.30	37.31	38.51	39.07	41.43	42.70	34%
40	28.34	28.20	30.08	29.67	31.03	32.81	33.92	34.52	36.79	38.10	34%
45	24.77	24.54	26.25	25.79	26.90	28.49	29.50	30.12	32.27	33.60	36%
50	21.26	20.98	22.50	22.06	22.98	24.40	25.29	25.93	27.94	29.20	37%
55	17.88	17.55	18.90	18.53	19.31	20.57	21.37	21.99	23.85	24.90	39%
60	14.76	14.42	15.54	15.24	15.91	17.04	17.71	18.34	20.02	20.90	42%
65	11.86	11.60	12.47	12.23	12.80	13.83	14.39	15.00	16.51	17.30	46%
70	9.30	9.11	9.74	9.58	10.00	10.92	11.38	12.00	13.32	14.00	51%
75	7.08	6.99	7.49	7.32	7.62	8.40	8.71	9.32	10.48	10.90	54%
80	5.30	5.25	5.63	5.50	5.73	6.34	6.39	7.10	7.98	8.30	57%
85	3.96	4.00	4.21	4.19	4.31	4.69	4.58	5.28	5.96	6.00	52%

Source: *Vital Statistics of the United States, 1993* (Latest data available in March 1998).

LONGEVITY AND LIFE EXPECTANCY

not live long enough to retire at age 65. If that person were lucky enough to be in the minority who lived to reach age 65, his or her life expectancy, at age 65, was 11.9 years, but he or she probably did not have the means to retire, so continued to work if the person were in good health. If the average person did not live long enough to retire, and if retirement was very likely to be relatively brief, it is easy enough to understand why many workers of that generation—who were 65 years of age in 1965—believed that retirement was inextricably linked to death. What they had seen around them during their entire lives were people working as long as health would allow them. When they were finally forced to retire, they generally did not live very long because failing health was the reason they had retired. For many people of the generation born around 1900, retirement did equal death. The people of that generation now are almost all gone, but their observations and attitudes still are part of the current retirement culture.

IMPROVEMENTS IN LONGEVITY

In the last century, modern medicine and enhanced living conditions have made an incredible improvement in the life expectancy of the average American. A baby born in 1993 had a life expectancy of 75.5 years, an increase of 53% over the 93-year period since 1900. This has been a solid, even accelerating, trend. Figure 4-2 shows the pattern of how the increase in the longevity of older Americans actually has occurred.

INCREASE IN LONGEVITY		
of Older Americans–By 30-Year Periods (1900-1993) FIGURE 4-2		
	1900-1930	1930-1960	1960-1993
65	3%	18%	20%
70	3%	19%	23%
75	3%	19%	25%
80	4%	16%	30%
85	6%	9%	31%

(Source: Derived from Figure 4-1)

It is just short of amazing to note that more than half of the longevi-ty increases for older Americans has occurred in the last 30 years. The trend of increased longevity for the oldest Americans seems to be accel-erating. Over the last 90 years, longevity has increased an average of about .5% per year. In the last 33 years, the increase has averaged close to 1%. If the trend continues over the next couple of decades, the remaining life expectancy of a 65-year-old could increase by about 25% to 30%. In other words, instead of the life expectancy of a 65-year-old woman being about 20 years, it may actually be 25 years.

The chances are very good—much better than 50%—that an American born in 1993 will live long enough to be retired at age 65. If that person retires at age 65, he or she will, according to current statis-tics, have a life expectancy of 17.3 years. That person, born in 1993, is now about 5 years old. Over his or her remaining life expectancy of about 70 years, we can expect a dramatic improvement in life expectan-cy just from this very positive trend. The trend could easily increase life expectancy at age 65 from its current 17.3 years to something like 35 to 40 years without any major scientific breakthroughs.[2] My daughter just had a baby girl. It is probable that my granddaughter, born in 1997, will live in three different centuries, the 20th, 21st, and 22nd. What a won-derful time to be alive!

This very positive trend of increased longevity hides an increasingly important aspect of the statistics. If you are retiring at age 65 with a sta-tistical life expectancy of 17.3 years, there is a 50% probability that you will live longer than 17.3 years. The definition of the statistic tells us that 50% of the 65-year-old people will live longer than the average. In fact, more than 20% of the 65-year-olds will live beyond age 90, and a white female has almost a 50% probability of living beyond 85. A couple, man and woman, both aged 65 currently have a 10% probability that one of them—probably the woman—will live to age 100.

---

[2] This assumes that the longevity of older people will continue not just to improve, but to improve at an accelerating pace. From 1960 to 1993, the longevity of older people increased about 60%. If that pace of improvement continues until 2050, the longevity of a 65-year-old will be 40 years.

LONGEVITY PLUS 50%

In planning your retirement, you may elect to assume that you will live only until your statistical life expectancy, but there is a 50% chance that you will live longer and the chance is growing every day. If you are content to have a plan that has a 50% margin for error, you are more tolerant than the average person, who wants no more than a 10% or 20% margin for error in a plan that represents the rest of their life.

Figure 4-3 represents a group of 10,000 65-year-olds. Current government statistics give us some details of their mortality until age 85, but after that they become "85+" and are assumed to die. In fact, we know that many will live beyond 85, but we can assume that almost everyone will be gone by age 105. This graph extrapolates the government statistics and fills in the detail from age 85 to age 105. The graph gives you a concrete basis for adjusting your statistical life expectancy to meet some criteria other than a 50% probability.

Assume that you are 65 years old and in "average" health. You would like to know the age beyond which you have only a 20% chance of surviving. Put another way, this would be the age beyond which you are 80% certain that you do not have to plan. This allows you to find an age which increases the probability that your plan will be fully adequate. An example will be helpful in seeing how this works. Look on the left scale for the 20% mark. This shows the level at which only 20% of the 10,000 people were still alive. Trace that level over to the right, until it hits the

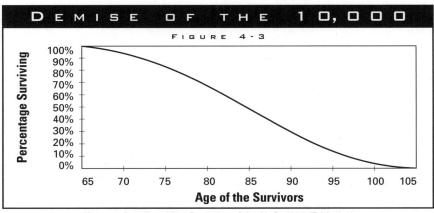

(Source: Based on Vital Statistics of the U. S. 1993, Table 6-2)

curve. Then come straight down and find that it hits the age scale just before age 90. This means that if you make plans to age 90, you have only about a 20% probability of outliving your planning assumption.

Your statistical life expectancy (50%) at age 65 is about 17.3 years, or the expectation that you will live to age 82.3. The 20% expectation (80% probability of not living longer) is about 7.4 years longer than the median expectation of 17.3 years. This increases the longevity assumption by about 43%. If you increase the statistical longevity by 50%, it gives you something like an 80% to 90% probability that you will not outlive your planning, and this does not consider the accelerating trend of increasing longevity for older Americans.

THE IMPACT OF RACE AND GENDER

It also is interesting to look at the life expectancy data for 65-year-olds in various decades broken down by race and gender, as in Figure 4-4. The pattern probably comes as no surprise. Life expectancies for all groups have increased over the years. In every decade, women have tended to live longer than men regardless of race, and white men and women tend to live longer than black men and women. The statistics are not available to support this thesis, but I would guess that educated people of all races tend to have similar life expectancies, and that expectancy probably is

U. S. LIFE EXPECTANCY

At Age 65–By Race and Sex (1900-1993)
FIGURE 4-4

YEAR	TOTAL Female	TOTAL Male	WHITE Female	WHITE Male	BLACK Female	BLACK Male
1993	17.8	14.3	19.0	15.4	17.1	13.4
1990	17.8	14.0	19.1	15.2	17.2	13.2
1980	17.6	13.8	18.6	14.3	17.1	13.3
1970	16.0	12.9	16.9	13.0	15.7	12.5
1960	15.1	12.8	15.9	13.0	–	–
1900	–	–	12.2	11.5	11.4	10.4

(Source: Vital Statistics of the United States 1991 and 1993)

longer than the average. I also will speculate that as we move into the 21st Century, the difference between the life expectancies of men and women probably will decrease, but not completely disappear.

If your retirement involves two of you, it makes sense to use the general statistic that, at age 65, life expectancy was 17.3 years in 1993. You then should assume that the life expectancy for which you need to plan is 50% greater—26 years. One of you is likely to live beyond age 91 and there is that 10% chance that one of you will live beyond age 100.

FUTURE DEVELOPMENTS

According to recent articles about genetic research, we may be on the verge of still another dramatic increase in the life expectancy of older Americans. The prediction is that in the 21st Century, genetic "fixes" will largely replace surgery and pills. Even more recent news announces that researchers may have discovered the secret of the human aging process. The implications not only for longevity, but for the vigor and enjoyment of retirement, are incredible. Think of what a greatly extended active retirement might do for your enjoyment of life and to your financial planning.

THE IMPACT ON PLANNING

There are enormous practical implications to these seemingly arcane statistics and improvements in medical science. They affect every aspect of the retirement plan. One of the most profound effects of increased longevity and extended retirements is the discovery that retirement is not one homogeneous period in our lives. Now that the length of retirements is increasing, it is easy to observe that retirement is divided into at least three phases. It is not inconceivable that, as longevity continues to increase, we may see that retirement can be divided into more than three phases.

Right now the largest implication in increased longevity is the increased variability of longevity. Some people will die early and some will live very long lives. Rather than a difference of 20 or 25 years between the first and last deaths in a retirement generation, the difference may be moving toward 50 years. This increased variability raises some enormous problems in planning retirement.

I want to summarize some of the major retirement planning problems that arise from increased longevity so that you can see clearly how the blessing of increased longevity has complicated retirement planning.

- Retirement must be funded for a greatly increased period of time.
- Longevity is less predictable.
- Retirement is now divided into three phases: Active, Passive, Final.
- Inflation impacts the retirement budget over a longer period.
- Estate planning has become more complicated.
- Insurance has become much more important.
- Cash flow, not capital, has become the main focus of retirement planning.
- Investment management has become more challenging.
- Income tax planning has become more complicated.

PERSONAL LONGEVITY PLANNING

All these important changes flow directly out of increased longevity. There is nothing that we can do or would even want to do with the increased longevity that older Americans are enjoying. It would be helpful, however, if we could improve our insights into the unpredictability factor by looking at the specifics of family and personal health and life-style.

FAMILY HISTORY

Consider the longevity of your family: grandparents, parents, siblings, and close blood relations. Does your family tend to live a long life or not so long? Are there patterns of disease or illness that have affected earlier generations? Are there changes in the treatment of those health problems that might change the pattern in your generation? If there is some risk factor that you can see in your family history, it might make sense to discuss it with your physician, who can make suggestions that may ward off the danger or at least detect a problem in an early stage. Your physician also can help in understanding the risk factor and explaining its likely impact on your life expectancy.

It is clear that earlier generations did not have the benefit of recent health studies that show smoking, drinking, high-fat diets, and lack of exercise take years off life expectancy. Habits are changing. In a recent conversation with a scientist at the National Center for Health Statistics, he expressed the opinion that the greatest factor in the increased longevity of older people in the last few decades is improvement in their diet and exercise regimes. Fewer people smoke. People are much more conscious of fat in their diets. Many more older people are getting regular exercise. Many people are moderating their drinking. We have already noted the potential impact of genetic research and the ability of the pharmaceutical industry to create new drugs specifically targeted to narrowly defined body functions. All of this research and technical wizardry is likely to help the affluent, educated, and well-informed members of society before the benefits spread more broadly through society. If you are responding in a sensible way to the new findings, you are probably adding years to your statistical life expectancy.

ASSESS YOUR HEALTH REGIME

You should assess your personal health regime periodically. A good time to do that is in conjunction with your annual physical checkup.

LONGEVITY IS THE KEY

Longevity is the key to The Prosperous Retirement. Many people are reluctant to count their good fortune in living in a time and a place when they can hope to live for so many years with health and vigor. You must deal realistically with your longevity if you want to realize the full potential of your retirement. Enjoy the active years, smile through the passive years, and plan for the reality of the last years.

CHAPTER 4

ACTION PLAN:

❏ Have you had a complete physical recently?

❏ Were you frank in telling your doctor about your concerns and symptoms?

❏ Did you respond in a constructive way to your physician's recommendations?

❏ Have you taken steps to limit your intake of fat and increase the fiber in your diet?

❏ Are you taking any recommended medications or diet supplements on a regular basis?

❏ Are you getting the recommended amount and type of exercise?

❏ Have you cut the amount of red meat that you are eating and increased the amount of fish?

❏ Have you quit smoking?

❏ Are you limiting your alcohol intake?

❏ Do you have a regular source of information about recent medical findings that might guide your personal health regime?

5.

INFLATION

"Inflation is not all bad, it has allowed every American family
to live in a more expensive neighborhood without moving."
—ATTRIBUTED TO SENATOR ALAN CRANSTON

SYNOPSIS: Inflation was not an important factor in planning for retirement until after the Second World War. The post-Depression retirement generation
largely ignored its effects because they didn't expect to live for very many years in
retirement, they had not experienced the ravages of inflation in their adult lives, and
they couldn't afford to worry about it. With longer retirements, higher rates of inflation, and a more affluent retirement life-style, inflation has become a central issue in
retirement planning. To deal successfully with inflation, a retiree needs to know the
history of American inflation, prospects for inflation, and how to figure a personal
inflation index.

PEOPLE TALK ALMOST AS MUCH about inflation as they do about the weather. In fact, the two have a few traits in common. Like the weather, most people feel there isn't much they can do about inflation except put up with it, and most people can't tell you where either one comes from. We all know from practical experience that inflation is an increase in the overall cost of goods and services. We pay more for a candy bar, more for the health club where we work off the candy, and more for the doctor who tells us to stop eating the candy. There is a general understanding that inflation comes from too much money chasing too few goods, but there is a good deal of uncertainty, even among experts, about the exact mechanics of inflation. In today's world, even the concept of "money" is a little bit tricky, but it generally is understood to include both currency and all forms of credit, including borrowing by the U.S. government. The precise relationship between money supply and inflation is controversial; if you ask three economists, you are likely to get six answers. You may recall the quip from Harry Truman, in which he wished he could find a one-armed economist who couldn't say, ". . . and on the other hand. . . ."

I have a book in my library, published in 1917, that says, "Some of our foremost economists contend that gold in recent years has been mined in such large quantities as to cause the higher cost of living and correspondingly to reduce investors' income."[1] In other words, inflation was caused by excess gold mining. Before you laugh too loudly, remember that in 1917 gold was monetized; in other words, mining gold was equivalent to creating money. That same book also expresses the opinion that, "The federal reserve system under the wise administration and intelligent co-operation on the part of bankers makes an old-time financial panic less likely—one might say, almost impossible." This, just 12 years before the Great Crash of 1929. The Talmud tells us that, "The beginning of wisdom is the recognition of ignorance." When talking about inflation, it is best to be humble.

The exact mechanics of inflation are largely irrelevant to our discussion, but it is important to understand a few key issues: the history of

---

[1] Guenther, Louis. *Investment and Speculation*. Chicago: LaSalle Extension University, 1917, p.12.

inflation in the United States, the current state of inflationary pressures, and what inflation is likely to do in the next few decades.

INFLATION IN THE UNITED STATES

The United States is no stranger to inflation. Have you ever heard the expression, "Not worth a Continental"? Well, the first American currency was called the "Continental" and it was used to finance the Revolutionary War. During the war, they say that it took a cartload of money to buy a cartload of goods. Too much money chasing too few goods resulted in "hyper-inflation," a period of rapidly rising prices and, finally, the collapse of the currency. The financial demands of the war were such that the new government had issued more IOUs denominated in Continentals than it could ever repay, so the currency became worthless. In 1785, Congress adopted the "dollar" as the new currency unit and repudiated the debts of the Revolutionary War. We have data which shows that since 1790, inflation has averaged about 1.17% per annum. That doesn't seem very high, but over the course of 200 years, that inflation rate has resulted in a dollar having about 10% of the buying power it had in 1790. In other words, it takes $10 today to buy what $1 would have bought in Colonial America.

WARS AS A SOURCE OF INFLATION

In general, up until the last couple of decades, wars were the principal source of inflation. The War of 1812, the Civil War, the First World War, the Second World War, the Korean War, and the Vietnam War all were potent sources of inflation. Inflation during the Civil War totaled more than 25%, and World War I and the Korean War each saw price increases of about 15%. Until the Second World War, prices generally declined after each war. With strict rationing and price controls during World War II, some of the inflationary increases were pushed into the post-war period. By the time that deflation started in 1949, we found ourselves in the Korean War. The Korean War never really ended, but it was followed by a period of moderate inflation that was boosted by our involvement in Vietnam. In 1973, the entire focus of inflation concerns shifted from the cost of military operations to the cost of importing energy. The Arab Oil

Embargo heightened fears of inflation to the point that people began to worry about hyper-inflation—which might lead to economic and possibly political chaos.

INFLATION AS A POLICY

While modest levels of inflation—mainly associated with the cost of financing wars—have been part of the American economic scene from the beginning of the Republic, it is fair to say that in modern times, inflation has been an intentional economic policy consciously pursued by politicians. Sir John Maynard Keynes, whose economic philosophy has dominated the 20th Century, convinced politicians that a modest level of inflation is an important antidote to the inefficient use of capital by individuals. As a result, modern monetary policy has had the task of maintaining a tightly controlled, moderate level of inflation.

PROSPECTS FOR CONTROLLED INFLATION

The modern American goal has been to keep the economy moving down what I call "the 80% Track." This represents the track of controlled, moderate inflation. I believe that we have an 80% probability of continuing to achieve that goal in the foreseeable future. The alternatives are a depression, in which prices plunge, or a hyper-inflation, in which prices soar. We have a recent and influential example of an American depression in the Crash of 1929 and the ensuing period of economic malaise. The memory of that experience seems to remain in the minds of most Americans. The period of the Revolutionary War as an example of American hyper-inflation apparently is too distant in time to be very instructive.

More recent periods of hyper-inflation mainly have affected the economies of rapidly growing and immature nations, such as Brazil, Israel, Chile, and others. An example of a disastrous hyper-inflation in a more mature economy was Weimer Germany. During the period of 1919 to 1924, the cost of sending a postcard across the city of Berlin rose from 3 pfennigs in 1919 (.03 Mark) to 10 billion Marks in December of 1924. Money became worthless. The economy collapsed, the government followed, and the Nazis took over. This phenomenon is indeed worrisome, but such a well-understood and greatly feared consequence seems unlikely to engulf the U.S. economy. If it ever did, there would be a lot more to worry about than finances.

POLITICS AND INFLATION

There are many examples of the relationship between inflation and politics. In the last half of the 19th Century, silver was discovered in large quantities in the western states. Politicians thought that it might be useful to use that wealth to help develop the nation by putting purchasing power in the hands of millions of Americans. The Bland-Allison Act of 1878 obligated the U. S. Treasury to purchase $2 million to $4 million worth of silver bullion every month to be minted into silver dollars. In 1890, the Sherman Silver Purchase Act forced the Treasury to buy $4 million to $8 million of silver bullion every month to be minted into silver dollars. In 1893, in the face of dwindling gold reserves, Congress repealed the Sherman Silver Purchase Act and returned the country to the Gold Standard. Silver prices collapsed, bankrupting the "silver barons," including Colorado's Horace Tabor, and this plunged the nation into a three-year depression. The collapse of silver prices led to the creation of the Populist Party, which advocated unlimited silver coinage to expand the money supply and make it easier for farmers and laborers to repay their debts. This chapter out of American history is still instructive because it demonstrates how politicians can intentionally use inflation to pursue political goals.

LESSONS ABOUT INFLATION

Several important lessons flow out of this thumbnail sketch. First, politics and inflation are intertwined. Populist parties that depend on the support of the underprivileged will always advocate inflationary policies. (As George Bernard Shaw observed, "Any government that robs Peter to pay Paul can always count on Paul's vote.") Wars lead to an over-expansion of the money supply and then inflation. Inflation can be inflicted by external economic events. The expansion of the money supply beyond increases in productivity—either through direct expansion of the money supply or the provision of easy credit (low interest rates)—leads to inflation. The oil embargo demonstrated that a critical shortage also can lead to inflation.

THE PROGRESSION OF INFLATION

Figure 5-1 shows the year-by-year progression of inflation during the 72-year period from 1926 to 1997. The current measure of inflation, as reported by the Department of Labor, is the Consumer Price Index for All Urban Consumers (CPI-U), which is just one of several similar

I N F L A T I O N

As Measured by the Consumer Price Index (CPI)
F I G U R E   5 - 1

1926	-1.5%	1950	5.8%	1974	12.2%
1927	-2.1%	1951	5.9%	1975	7.0%
1928	-1.0%	1952	0.9%	1976	4.8%
1929	0.2%	1953	0.6%	1977	6.8%
1930	-6.0%	1954	-0.5%	1978	9.0%
1931	-9.5%	1955	0.4%	1979	13.3%
1932	-10.3%	1956	2.9%	1980	12.4%
1933	0.5%	1957	3.0%	1981	8.9%
1934	2.0%	1958	1.8%	1982	3.9%
1935	3.0%	1959	1.5%	1983	3.8%
1936	1.2%	1960	1.5%	1984	4.0%
1937	3.1%	1961	0.7%	1985	3.8%
1938	-2.8%	1962	1.2%	1986	1.1%
1939	-0.5%	1963	1.7%	1987	4.4%
1940	1.0%	1964	1.2%	1988	4.4%
1941	9.7%	1965	1.9%	1989	4.7%
1942	9.3%	1966	3.4%	1990	6.1%
1943	3.2%	1967	3.0%	1991	3.1%
1944	2.1%	1968	4.7%	1992	2.9%
1945	2.3%	1969	6.1%	1993	2.8%
1946	18.2%	1970	5.5%	1994	2.7%
1947	9.0%	1971	3.4%	1995	2.5%
1948	2.7%	1972	3.4%	1996	3.3%
1949	-1.8%	1973	8.8%	1997	1.7%

Source: U. S. Department of Labor, Bureau of Labor Statistics, Washington, D. C. 1926-1978, as measured by the Consumer Price Index (CPI), more recently measured by the Consumer Price Index for All Urban Consumers (CPI-U).

indices. Until 1978, only one Consumer Price Index existed, but even that was changed from time to time to reflect what the Department of Labor deemed to be a more representative basket of goods and services. Recent proposals to make further changes in the CPI are not an entirely new phenomenon.

The seemingly random progression of inflation is difficult to understand without a fairly comprehensive knowledge of both the economic and political history of the period and the events leading up to the Crash of 1929.

UNDERLYING FACTORS

The period from 1914 to 1920 had seen a dramatic increase in prices based on the demands of the First World War. The wholesale price index had risen from 33 in 1914 to 80 in 1920, a 16% annual rate of increase, as the world struggled to recover from the devastating economic effects of World War I. The years immediately following 1920 saw a period of declining prices in this country, while Europe struggled with hyper-inflation.

The Crash of 1929 was not just a stock market collapse; it brought down the entire banking structure of the United States. It caused millions of Americans to lose their jobs, and millions of others to find it impossible to sell the goods and services that they were producing. Over three years, from 1930 to 1933, prices fell by more than 25%. This was followed by a period of moderate inflation (Yes! Prices were increasing even during part of the Great Depression), until the onset of World War II created a shortage of goods and services that drove prices up by more than 25% during the four years of that war. This wartime inflation occurred in spite of strict rationing and price controls imposed by the federal government. This period of inflation was largely driven by a shortage of labor, as industry attempted to "draft" the men and women who were not recruited by the Armed Forces.

After the war, Americans used their wartime savings to make up for the time lost in the war. They married, had children, and bought cars and homes in record numbers. As a result, the period from 1946 to 1951 was a classic period of inflation, with excess dollars chasing goods that were still in short supply. Prices rose more than 45% in 6 years.

The next 17 years, from 1952 to 1968, was a period of modest inflation with average annual increases of only 1.75%. Even so, an item that cost $100 in 1952 cost $134 in 1968.

Beginning in 1969, it looked like the United States was headed for real trouble on the inflation front. For 13 unlucky years, from 1969 to 1981, inflation averaged 7.8%, well above the 5% limit that many authorities thought marked the upper limit of "controlled inflation." For three years, it crossed "the double digit" barrier that everyone acknowledged was difficult and frightening. Prices during the period increased by 2.5 times.

For the next 8 years, from 1982 to 1989, inflation seemed like it was back under control, averaging only 3.75%. Then, in 1990, inflation spurted up to 6.1%. Many people were concerned that the cycle was headed upward because of spiraling federal deficits.

Surprise, surprise! The last seven years have had the lowest rates of inflation since the 1960s. The 1997 rate of 1.7% was the lowest in 11 years. Even in hindsight, some of these periods are not easy to explain, although some were quite predictable. The overall lesson seems to be that longer-term trends probably are easier to predict than the year-to-year level of inflation.

THE INFLATION CYCLE

The seemingly random progression of inflation is only partly explained—at least in retrospect—by the economic and political events of the time. To a greater extent, inflation seems to run in cycles. Figure

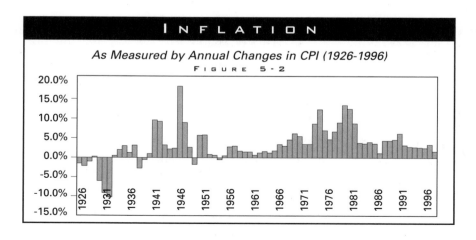

INFLATION

As Measured by Annual Changes in CPI (1926-1996)

FIGURE 5-2

5-2, a graph of the annual inflation rates from 1926 to 1997, seems to show an interesting trend. The period of the Second World War and the Arab Oil Embargo stand out clearly, but the current trend, if indeed there is one, appears to be headed downward. There is, of course, controversy around this opinion, but some authorities (there are no real experts) believe that the next few decades will see lower rates of inflation, perhaps even modest disinflation.

MODIFYING FACTORS

A number of factors could easily confound the rosy predictions of those authorities. High rates of inflation in the economies of many emerging nations could add to our inflation. Their demand for raw materials and consumer goods builds some inflationary pressures into the world economy.

The U.S. economy seems healthy, but the level of indebtedness—particularly federal indebtedness—concerns many observers. I do not view the federal debt as a great problem. The federal government does not carry as an asset any of the things that are built with federal expenditures. (The roads, schools, government buildings, airports, harbors, and other facilities that the government has built obviously are worth a great deal of money, and they are not carried on the federal books.)

Another source of inflation worries is the very low level of unemployment. Many observers are concerned that high levels of employment will eventually lead to higher wages and the beginning of an inflationary spiral.

The continuing imbalance in the value of American imports and exports is another part of the concern about debt. The impending crises in Social Security and Medicare make prospects for taxes, the economy, and our ability to repay debts and protect the international value of the dollar look very interesting. (You know the Chinese curse, "May you live in interesting times.")

Another factor that could lead to inflationary pressures is our continuing dependence on fossil fuels and the fact that there are finite quantities of these fuels. In the 1970s, there were acute concerns about the world supply of petroleum, and many observers were predicting that the world would run out of petroleum early in the 21st Century. Since then,

consumption has increased, and while there have been some major discoveries, it now looks like petroleum supplies will dwindle by the year
2025. Rising prices for energy were a potent source of inflationary pressure in the 1970s and could be again.

ONE MAN'S OPINION

It is my opinion that inflation over the next couple of decades—the
period relevant to your retirement—may average 4% to 5%. I believe
that 4.5% is a reasonable basis for planning.

I would rather err on the side of expecting too much inflation than
too little inflation, but this may be an irrelevant argument. The reason
that it may not make much difference is because the return on investments tends to be related to the rate of inflation. If inflation rates trend
upward, the return on investments tends to move upward, as well.

Given the choice of having too much money or too little money, I'll
go for too much every time, so let's proceed on the basis that inflation
will average 4.5% per year over the next couple of decades. This is more
than the 3.1% average of the period from 1925 to 1997, slightly more
than the 4.4% average of the period from 1946 to 1997, but slightly less
than the 4.9% average of the period from 1978 to 1997. The "right"
answer will probably prove to be something other than 4.5%, but to
make any kind of a plan, it is necessary to make some kind of an assumption, and 4.5% is my inflation assumption.

A BRIEF ASIDE

Critics of financial planning complain that financial planners often
use excessive inflation assumptions to drive their clients into aggressive
investment strategies. There is no reason why this should be true. The
financial planner is better served by recommending a conservative
investment strategy to the client, if the conservative strategy will get the
client where he or she wants to go. The conservative strategy is less likely to provide the kind of disappointment that might motivate the client
to find another financial planner. The problem is that the financial planner is competing with the entire brass band of American advertising for
the client's financial resources. It is probable that Reeboks, vacations,

and even gambling parlors will claim a portion of the client's wealth. The wealth remaining is likely to be only marginally adequate for the client's retirement needs, so the planner frequently must conspire with the client to stretch $1 to cover a $2 gap. It is not the financial planner's desire to use aggressive investments, but the client's financial need which forces the planner to recommend these aggressive strategies. A wise investor and a professional financial planner will never (almost never) embark on an investment strategy which has risks that truly exceed the investor's risk tolerance, but this is a complicated issue that will be dealt with more fully in Chapters 7, 8, and 9.

WHAT DOES 4.5% MEAN?

If 4.5% proves to be the "right" inflation answer, it means that over the period of your retirement, the general costs of goods and services are likely to increase by two or three times, even more if you retire at a young age. Fortunately, in practice, your budget is not likely to increase quite that much for two principal reasons. The first reason is that not everything in your budget is subject to inflation. If you have a mortgage payment, a life insurance premium, a long-term health care policy premium, they probably are fixed and will not increase over time. Your charitable contributions and gifts are not necessarily tied to inflation, nor are other discretionary expenditures, such as vacations and luxury items. These luxury expenditures are affected by the second reason, the active-to-passive retirement offset. This factor is discussed in more detail in Chapters 3 and 6, but for our purpose here, it is enough to simply recognize that you will reach a point when your life-style will slow down and your cost of living will level out, or even decrease, in spite of inflation.

A PERSONAL CPI

It is fairly easy to look at your current budget and pick out the costs that are not subject to inflation. Let's say your budget is $5,000 per month after taxes. Of that $5,000, assume that your mortgage is $875, you have a life insurance premium of $70, and your long-term health care insurance premium is $55. That means that $1,000 of your $5,000 budget is not subject to inflation. Only 80% of your budget is subject to inflation, so your Personal Inflation Index is 80% of the CPI. If the five o'clock news reports that inflation is 3%, your personal rate of inflation is only 80% of that, or 2.4%. Instead of doubling your cost of living in 24 years, which is what 3% inflation will do, with a Personal Inflation Index of only 2.4%, it will take 30 years to double your budget. It is important to have an idea of what portion of your budget is not subject to inflation so that you can plan your retirement on a realistic basis.

An interesting implication of this discussion is that retirees with mortgage payments to make are relatively less susceptible to inflation than retirees who have paid off their mortgage.

PLANNING FOR INFLATION

Inflation is a key issue in planning your retirement. It will have a considerable effect on your budget over the many years of your Prosperous Retirement. It will affect your life-style, your investment planning, and the comfort of your retirement. To the extent that your retirement budget is funded by the returns on your retirement capital base, inflation also may affect the returns that you can expect on your assets.

You need to stay alert for signs that the pattern of inflation may be changing, so you can make the necessary changes in your plans. But don't overreact because year-to-year inflation is more volatile than the overall trend. Much of what you hear about inflation makes it sound like a tidal wave that engulfs everything in its path. Some of your expenditures are immune from inflation and others are under your control. Inflation needs to be considered, but don't let it become an excuse for not enjoying The Prosperous Retirement.

By understanding the history of inflation, and the specifics of how it affects your budget now and in the future, you can make plans that will allow you to use your capital in a wise way to provide the kind of prosperous retirement that you want.

6.

RETIREMENT MODELING

"To have his path made clear for him is the aspiration of every human being in our beclouded and tempestuous existence."
—JOSEPH CONRAD, 1906

SYNOPSIS: It is possible to create a mathematical model of a retirement that allows you to explore a range of retirement strategies and the impact of alternative assumptions. The model is based on some facts, some assumptions, and some guesses. It is a powerful and indispensable tool for achieving The Prosperous Retirement. This chapter is crucial because it weaves together the threads of information that have been developed in other chapters. You may find this chapter difficult if you have not read the other chapters because the concepts that appear here, and which are explained elsewhere in the book, may not be entirely clear.

RETIREMENT MODELING HAS NOTHING TO DO with cameras or fashion shows. It has a little more to do with the model airplanes that I liked to build when I was a kid. What it really concerns is the use of computers to create a model of your retirement. The magic of having a mathematical computer model is that it allows you to test the impact of various assumptions on the outcome of your retirement. It allows you to see, for example, the impact that different inflation rates might have on your ability to enjoy The Prosperous Retirement. Using computer models is partly science and partly art. The art aspect involves asking all the relevant questions about your retirement, accurately gathering the facts, and making reasonable assumptions concerning those questions that have no "correct" answers. The science part involves figuring out the relationship between all this information.

We will go through the model-building process one step at a time in this chapter, so that you can fully appreciate each step and better understand the interplay of the factors. Some of the steps will be surprising, and some of the results may not be what you hoped. Remember, however, that this is just a model, so you do get to change things if you want. In fact, that is the very reason that we build the model—to see what changes can be made to put you on a smoother path to The Prosperous Retirement. We are going to build a model of your retirement so you can see if you like the way it flies. Get out the balsa wood, tissue paper, and airplane cement, but don't inhale the fumes!

THE RETIREMENT CONCEPT

The process of modeling begins with the creation of a model. The model of a retirement is not difficult to conceptualize. It asks the basic question, "Can I make my money last as long as I do?" This question obviously involves longevity determinations, the costs of retirement, available retirement income, and the management of retirement capital. If you weave together these four strands, you will have a basic retirement model. In addition, a series of other issues make subtle differences that can have a profound impact on the outcome. Questions like taxes, estate planning, and risk management can make an important difference in the success or failure of a retirement. It is important to consider a broad range of questions and to bring everything relevant into the modeling process. Beyond that—and I will say this over and over—it is important to monitor the plan, see how the assumptions are working when compared with reality, and make changes if the plan seems to be heading off track. Things do change. No one can predict the future, but a plan gives you a basis for making decisions in the context of unfolding reality. General Dwight D. Eisenhower was fond of saying, ". . . plans are useless, but planning is indispensable." You have to know where you are going. You have to know what can affect your journey. If you know where you are going and how you intend to get there, you can tell when you are off course and make decisions about what is to be done to get you back on track. Retirement planning is the key to The Prosperous Retirement. The Prosperous Retirement is based on confidence that things are going well and that resources are available to deal with contingencies. That confidence can come only from a comprehensive, well grounded, and carefully designed plan.

THE ELEMENTS OF THE MODEL

The retirement model weaves together 10 threads of information. The rope that results from this combination is your retirement. The 10 information threads are:

1. **Boundary Issues**–Who is to be included in your plan?
2. **Age and Longevity Factors**–When will your retirement start and how long is it likely to last?
3. **Income Issues**–What income can you expect in retirement?
4. **Savings Issues**–Will there be savings between now and your retirement or during the retirement?
5. **Budget and Expense Issues**–What is your budget likely to be in retirement?
6. **Capital Base**–How much capital will you have to support your retirement?
7. **Risk Management Issues**–Are the risks in your retirement properly covered or could one of them torpedo the whole plan?
8. **Tax Planning Issues**–Are income taxes under control?
9. **Estate Planning Issues**–Has consideration been given to estate planning issues?
10. **Investment Planning**–Is there a system in place for maximizing the productivity of your financial assets?

TWINING THE THREADS

Once the 10 threads are completely twined, the completion of the model is a rather straightforward technological task. From there, it is also a simple matter to change various assumptions one at a time, or in combinations, to see what effect they will have on your retirement. The typical way of seeing whether the retirement "works" is to watch the capital base. If the capital base becomes exhausted before the expected longevity is attained, the model needs some adjustments.

The sensitivity of the model to minor changes is remarkable. The change of $100 a month in the budget or 1/10th of a percent in rate of return can extend the life of the capital base for a couple of years. Knowing that these factors can have that kind of impact gives you the opportunity to make minor changes throughout the course of your retirement that will add greatly to your comfort and security. There is a saying in financial planning circles, "If you have no goal, any road will get you there." A journey without a destination is not a very happy or fulfilling experience. The quotation with which this chapter begins says it all. Everyone wants their path to be made clear, and, I will add, to have frequent reassurances that they continue to be on track. The trick to obtaining this clarity in the retirement planning process is in the twining of the threads, so we will examine that process in some detail.

BOUNDARY ISSUES

The first thread to be twined involves the so-called boundary issues: "Who is to be included in the retirement plan?" In the "Beaver Cleever" model, the plan obviously includes the client and spouse, and assumes that everyone else is standing on their own two feet. Today's world often is more complicated. Sometimes you are not dealing with a client and spouse. There are times when the retirement plan encompasses a couple who is not married. In that case, questions about the extent to which the "significant other" is to be included in the plan are important. In some cases, children will receive support. Sometimes there is an expected limit to that support and, in other cases, say a handicapped child, the support may go on without limit. In other cases, financial support for aged parents, other relatives, or, in rare cases, non-related persons will be required. Sometimes this scenario can be finessed with long-term care insurance, but in other cases only cash will do the trick. The amount of support and the length of that support needs to be defined using carefully thought-out assumptions. Remember, if the assumptions are troubling, we can easily try alternatives once we have filled in the other factors.

AGE AND LONGEVITY

The next set of factors revolve around age and longevity questions. We need to know the current age of everyone to be included in the planning. We need to know when you plan to retire and when your spouse plans to retire, if these times are different. It is reassuring to note that some of the factors in this modeling are either facts—like your age—or are under your control—like when you will retire. Unfortunately, not all of the model input falls into place as easily as these factors.

The next part is the great imponderable: How long will everyone in the plan live? Chapter 4 deals with this issue at some length, so you can just review the results of those thoughts. We will start with the statistical life expectancy of each person in the plan and increase that by 50% to reflect the fact that they are likely to be "luckier than average" and that longevities are increasing as we talk. We then will take that 150% longevity and adjust it to reflect current health, family history, the person's "health regime," and other factors we can identify that might affect their longevity. If there are serious problems in the family history or in the genes, we may need a physician's opinion about the impact on longevity. The longevity numbers are the most difficult issue in the entire plan, but they affect everything else, so they deserve more attention than they generally get in retirement planning.

INCOME AND SAVINGS

The next set of issues concerns income and savings. Most of this data is fairly easy to find. How much are you and your spouse currently making? What is likely to happen to your earnings between now and retirement? How much are you currently saving? Is there a match from your employer? What is your anticipated savings trend between now and retirement? How many dollars will this savings trend allow you to add to your retirement capital in the time remaining before you retire?

The good news on this topic is that, generally in the last few years before retirement, people find that their earnings are at a lifetime peak, while expenses have flattened out or are even falling. In many families, this reflects the time when tuitions are finally covered, the mortgage was fixed a long time ago, and currently two salaries are being earned. The gap between earnings and expenses is increasing rapidly, and if people can capture that difference and save it, they can greatly improve their retirement prospects. Figure 6-1 is a pictorial representation of this important concept.

Note how the savings line rises much more rapidly than either income or expenses. Income during this period increased about 50%, from $72,000 to $108,000. Expenses grew, but less rapidly, from $64,800 to $86,400. Savings exploded 200% from only $7,200 in the first year to more than $21,600 in the tenth year. In many cases, the growth of savings is even more dramatic.

Social Security

The next income factor is Social Security. Will both you and your spouse collect Social Security or some similar government benefit? When will you start collecting it, and what do you expect benefits to be? If you haven't filed a Form SSA-7004-SM (Request for Earnings and Benefit Estimate Statement), you should do so right away. You can request the form by calling the Social Security Administration at 1-800-772-1213. The response from the Social Security Administration will tell

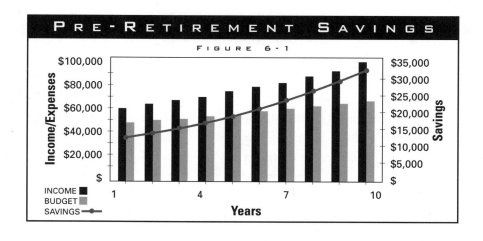

you the year-by-year credits that have been posted to your Social Security account and the benefit that you will get at retirement. Checking your Social Security account from time to time to ensure that your credits have been properly posted is important because there are time limits for correcting your account if it is not properly posted. I have seen a case where an employer recorded an employee's Social Security number incorrectly and the payments that were intended for the employee's account went to another account. Fortunately, the error was detected within the time limit and it was corrected.

After you find out your projected benefits, you need to make an assumption about the cost-of-living adjustments that will be made to the benefits. The government's stated policy is to increase Social Security benefits at the rate of inflation. In the past 20 years, these benefits have increased by more than the rate of inflation, but it is likely that they will increase less than the rate of inflation in the future. My best guess is that benefits will increase at half the rate of inflation, the taxability of benefits will be increased, and "means testing" is likely. If you "don't need" Social Security—by the government's definition—you may not get it. I think that an optimistic assumption is that Social Security benefits will increase at half the rate of inflation, they will be fully taxable, and they will not be means tested. A pessimistic assumption is that, for people who are enjoying The Prosperous Retirement, means testing will eliminate Social Security benefits.

Pension

The next issue concerns pension benefits. Do you and your spouse expect to receive pension benefits? What are the benefits expected to be? Is the benefit a single-life benefit or a joint-life benefit? In other words, if the person receiving the benefit dies, does the survivor continue to receive a benefit? If it is a single-life benefit, is there life insurance in place to replace the stream of income (see Chapter 10–Pension Maximization Strategy)? Will there be cost-of-living adjustments to the pension?

A potential danger pertaining to cost-of-living adjustments is looming. The government is talking about the fact that the Consumer Price Index "overstates" the actual rate of inflation. This is a definitional problem; it can be proven to be either understated over overstated, depending on your frame of analysis. The result, however, is that we are likely to see the government fiddling with the CPI to make it appear that inflation is less than it might appear to be under the current system. That may result in cost-of-living adjustments being less than the inflation factor that you are experiencing in your retirement budget. You can model this by assuming that the cost-of-living increases will be slightly less than the inflation rate.

Retirement Earnings

Do you and your spouse plan to generate retirement earnings? I think that this is a great idea, particularly for people retiring at ages younger than 60 or 65. If there will be retirement earnings, how much do you expect to earn and how long will the earnings last? Will the earnings go up or down over the years? The best method of modeling these earnings is to make a little table showing the estimated earnings on a year-by-year basis. It is not important to get these numbers "exactly right." Reasonable estimates are a lot more helpful than a blank.

Other Income Sources

Are there other potential sources of income? Is there a trust in place that will provide income? Is there the possibility of gifts or perhaps a potential inheritance? Do you own any assets that might generate regular income? This could be an investment of some sort, a business interest that pays royalties or licensing fees, or other income from intellectual property like patents, trademarks, or copyrights. Income generators of this sort can be a very important support for The Prosperous Retirement because they tend to respond to inflation.

BUDGET AND EXPENSES

The next thread to twine together concerns the budget and expenses. You need to study your current budget because it is probably the key to estimating your retirement budget. I suggest that you consider using Quicken[1] software to track your budget. This is a very popular package that makes it easy to track expenses. It will give you reports that make your budget clear

---

[1] Trademark of Intuit Inc. 1-800-446-8848.

and easy to understand. If you are "technologically challenged," I suggest that you track your expenses for three months manually by using checks and credit cards, and as little cash as possible. Take the cash in small amounts and account for the last batch of cash before you take the next. The result will not be as glitzy as the computer version, but it will give you a good handle on your expenditures. Remember not to drastically curtail your spending[2] during the period in which the budget is being examined. Try to keep your expenditures pretty much as they are when you are not tracking them. Be certain to add in the expenses that didn't show up during this particular period. Auto insurance premiums, life insurance premiums, and other payments that are not made monthly typically can be found in last year's checkbook, and they need to be added into your budget estimate.

Chapter 3 explains that there are various cross sections that you can do on your budget to determine some interesting aspects. For example, not all of your budget is subject to inflation. You need to know what part of the budget is fixed and not subject to inflation so that you can determine your own Personal Inflation Index. If only 75% of your budget is subject to inflation, and inflation is running at 4%, your Personal Inflation Index is only 3% [.75 x .04 =.03]. Figure 6-2 shows schematically how a monthly budget of $3,500 at age 55 is likely to grow, because of inflation, over the years of your retirement.

---

[2] My editor wouldn't let me say "Suck it in."

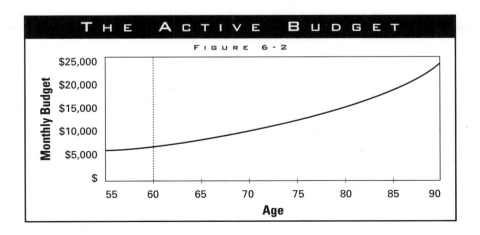

Active Versus Passive Budget

Chapter 3 also discussed the Active Budget and the Passive Budget, suggesting that the offset from active to passive is a function of how much of the active budget is discretionary. The passive budget (or subsistence budget) typically equals the active budget minus all or most of the discretionary expenditures. This is the basis on which you will calculate your passive budget. Take your current budget minus discretionary expenses and inflate it at your Personal Inflation Index. Figure 6-3 shows that, over time, the gap between the active budget and the passive budget will increase. Another factor that causes the two curves to diverge is that a larger percentage of the passive budget tends to be composed of fixed expenses, which causes the active budget to rise more rapidly than the passive budget. This increasing gap makes the concept of the active-to-passive offset a powerful force in helping to keep the projected cost of The Prosperous Retirement within your reach.

The Active to Passive Transition

At age 75, we assume that you will start moving from the active budget to the passive budget, arriving at the passive budget at age 85. Figure 6-4 shows what this transition looks like. After 85, the budget traces the inflated curve of the passive budget. The three-phase curve is the composite retirement budget. The composite budget is the basic pattern of the budget on which you will live over the years of your retirement.

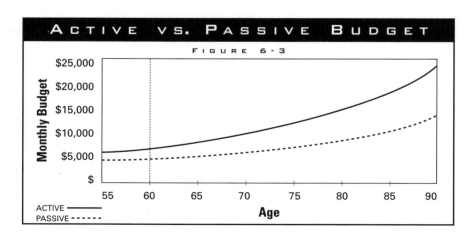

ACTIVE VS. PASSIVE BUDGET

FIGURE 6-3

Life-Style

I have assumed that Stein's First Rule of Retirement is in operation and that your active retirement budget will be very similar to
your pre-retirement budget. This is not always true, though, so you
need to think about your expectations for your retirement life-style.
Do you expect your life-style to change one way or the other in retirement? What is the estimated impact of any change on your retirement
budget? Do you plan to live the life-style of the rich and famous or are
you moving to a hermitage in Utah? Do you have special plans for
your retirement? Is there a grand trip, a recreational vehicle, a hobby
facility, or an exercise room that needs to be included in your retirement budget? What will be the cost of these special plans and when
will the funds be required?

Terminated Expenses

A budget issue that needs to be examined in detail is whether
there are expense factors that will completely drop out of your budget at some point. Are there child support or alimony payments that
will end at some point? When will the mortgage or other loans be
paid off? Are there home maintenance costs that you currently pay
that will end when you have the time to do these things for yourself?
Remember that your contributions to retirement plans will end when
you retire.

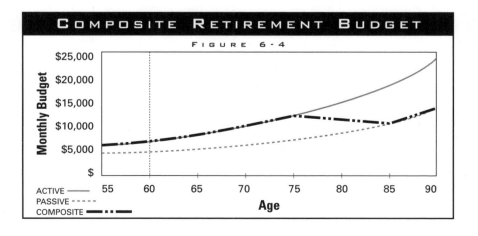

COMPOSITE RETIREMENT BUDGET

FIGURE 6-4

Increased Expenses

A tricky issue for self-employed people is the question of the tax-free benefits that they derive from their business: medical insurance, life insurance, disability insurance, possibly an auto, and other benefits that come to them without being regarded as taxable personal income. When these people sell or terminate their business and these expenses have to be paid with after-tax dollars, not only are there new costs in their budget, but the size of the costs will increase because the income with which to pay them will be subject to income taxes. If you are in this situation, you will have to examine this issue carefully and add the appropriate amount to your retirement budget.

When all of these budget and expense issues are twined together—including the special plans—it should give a reasonably accurate picture of your cash flow requirements during the years of your retirement. The pattern of these expenses is likely to look like the graph in Figure 6-5. Note that, in the early years of your retirement, the actual budget is higher than a continuation of your pre-retirement budget as you do all those things that you have always wanted to do. Then, in your 70s, the budget flattens out as you slide from the active retirement to the passive retirement. From then on, the actual budget is less than the inflated continuation of the active budget. This does not include medical and nursing home expenses, because those are covered by the insurance that you have so wisely obtained.

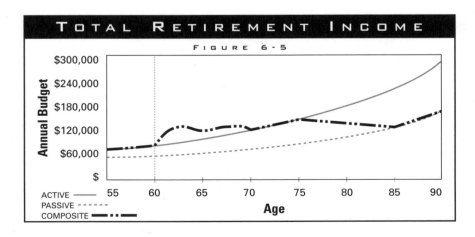

CAPITAL BASE

The next thread to be formed concerns the capital base that will provide the rest of the cash flow required for The Prosperous Retirement, and
which will provide the bulk of your inflation protection. We begin this
process by looking at your net worth statement. What do you own and
what do you owe? You need to compile a detailed list of assets owned and
the form of ownership in which they are held. There may even be assets
that are beneficially owned, which do not show up on your balance sheet
and are not even under your control. For example, you may be the income
beneficiary of a trust, the corpus of which does not belong to you. Perhaps
your Uncle Elmer set up a generation-skipping-trust from which you get
the income while you are alive, but when you die, your children get the
corpus. The trust may be managed by Uncle Elmer's attorney and you just
get monthly checks. It also makes a difference if your assets are held in
individual names, joint names, trusts, retirement plans, or possibly other
forms. All of these may belong to you and your spouse, but they must be
treated differently in terms of when they are to be used and what kind of
results we can expect from them. For example, let's go back to Uncle
Elmer's trust. What can you expect to happen to the monthly checks over
time? You need to know what the trust tells the attorney to do and then
make a judgment about whether the income will stay the same, increase,
or decrease over time.

You need to segregate your assets by their ability to grow on a tax-
deferred or tax-free basis, because the tax-protected assets will have higher
effective rates of return than the fully taxable assets. You need to take into
consideration any taxes that may be due on appreciated assets. You may
have $100,000 of stock in some company that cost you $1,000 many year
ago. The balance sheet value of the stock is $100,000 but the net value is
only $80,000 because there are $20,000 of taxes due on the capital gains if
the stock is sold.

Additions to the Capital Base

You now need to bring forward the results of your study in the savings section about additions that will be made to your capital base from
now until your retirement. There also may be situations in which the

capital base is earning so much that there will continue to be savings even after retirement. This is called "being between a mattress and a down pillow." You may have to consider your alternatives, either enhancing your life-style or increasing your gifting program to keep estate taxes under control. A tough choice, but I know you can do it!

There may be other income-generating assets that do not show up on the balance sheet. Such things as patents, copyrights, trademarks, etc., may not show up as valuable assets, but they may have the ability to generate income. Assets that do not have current value but may have future value should be carried on your personal balance sheet with a $1 value, just so they will not be forgotten. Interests in a business need to show in this listing, as well as notes and loans outstanding and any personal property that is going to be sold to help finance the retirement. One of my clients had a valuable collection of antique cars that he expected to sell to finance his retirement.

Still other assets, like escrow accounts with utility, mortgage, and insurance companies, should show up on the balance sheet if they are significant. Real estate assets, other than the home, need to be analyzed for their income-generating capacity versus their value in the marketplace. It may be necessary to do an analysis to see if it makes sense to hold such assets or to convert them into better income generators. This is discussed in more detail in Chapter 10.

The Residence as an Asset

The residence can be a dilemma. Typically, it is the biggest asset that people own and yet it is needed to provide shelter. I usually recommend that the home not be included in the retirement capital base unless there is a specific plan to sell the residence and buy another home or to rent. If you have such a plan, you need to know the market value of the home and when you plan to sell it. Then you can estimate the rate of appreciation on the home from now until it is sold. That will give you the expected sales proceeds. Then subtract the mortgage balance that will be due and the capital gains taxes that will be owed, if any. Then you need to figure what the replacement residence will cost. What is the current value of a likely replacement and what rate of appreciation shall you assume on that property? Alternatively, you need to know what rent might cost today and how much it is likely to increase between now and when the transition is to be made.

Liquid Assets

A final issue pertaining to the capital base is the question of liquid assets. How many dollars of liquid assets are required to keep the wheel of retirement turning smoothly? How many dollars do you need in an emergency reserve to give you the quiet assurance you need to sleep well? These assets are not terribly productive financially, but you must always assure that there are adequate liquid reserves to provide income even when the markets are in turmoil for a period. In retirement, I think that it is prudent to have 6 months of your subsistence budget in a money market mutual fund at all times. That is a minimum, and sometimes it makes sense to let that build up.

RISK MANAGEMENT

The risk management thread mainly represents an effort to ensure that there are no catastrophic perils lurking in the shadows just waiting to scuttle your retirement. If you are counting on income between now and retirement, is it insured with life and disability insurance? Do you have plans to provide medical insurance throughout this whole process? If you are eligible for Medicare, do you have the appropriate supplemental coverage? Is there a long-term care policy in place and is it "tax qualified" (Chapter 10) so that any benefits received will be free of income taxes? Have all the estate planning uses of insurance been considered and are you making appropriate use of tax-deferred annuities? Lastly, are your home, vehicles, and personal liabilities properly covered with insurance?

TAX PLANNING

You will want to look at tax planning issues in two different lights. First, you need to make certain that taxes have been filed properly and that there are no tax liabilities from previous periods. Then you want to know if the tax burden that is currently in place is really the smallest amount of taxes that you can legally pay. You will find a lot of comfort on both of these scores if the tax returns are prepared by a competent tax professional. (See Chapter 12.) If you have been doing your own taxes, it makes sense to have a tax professional check your last three years of returns for any "time bombs." Have all the possible tax minimization strategies been considered? In the discussion of the budget, we noted that self-employed persons might be losing some benefits when they end their business. Conversely, it may make sense to have a retirement business in conjunction with your retirement earnings strategy to provide the ability to pay some of these expenses as business expenses rather than subjecting your business expenses to the 2-1/2% threshold that applies to miscellaneous business expenses on a personal tax return.

ESTATE PLANNING

The next thread of issues concerns estate planning. The biggest question under this category is whether you intend to leave assets to your heirs or spend everything during your lifetime. There are a lot of folks who believe that perfect retirement planning involves running out of money simultaneously with running out of time. Are there specific assets that need to be left to specific family members?

This kind of planning can get tricky in a second marriage where there is a "mixed family"—his, hers, and theirs. Frequently, planners suggest that the assets brought into the marriage by one party should go to that person's children. Typically, more of a motivation exists to make certain that assets are left for the heirs in these cases, and planning provisions need to be made to ensure that the objective is met. This may entail the creation of life insurance trusts, or income trusts which leave the principal to a designated heir. This situation needs to be discussed with your estate planning attorney and financial advisor, because it may mean that certain assets simply are not available for the retirement. The bottom-line question, after the final estate planning is in place, is this: "Are all assets available for retirement or are some to be reserved?"

INVESTMENT PLANNING

The final thread, which is perhaps a bit thicker and more important than many of the others, is investment planning. The bottom-line question in this section is: "How much cash flow can the investments generate?" The following three chapters cover this topic in detail, but there are some fundamental points to be made here. First, I am convinced that you will have much better investment results if you find a trusted advisor with whom you can work over time. The magic is not necessarily in their superior knowledge of investment questions, but in the discipline and continuing process that they will bring to your investment decisions. In my view, the issue is not a point or two of better performance, but success or failure when the going gets tough and you need all the help you can get to stay on course.

The disciplined process of investment management should be manifested in a written investment policy that includes all the relevant issues: risk tolerance, target asset allocation, investment objective, expected rate of return, and a procedure for making decisions about purging investments. In addition, the discipline also should be apparent in a regular program of investment review. The reviews should include a written report that tells you the current rate of return of your assets and compares these with your target returns and the returns that are available in the market. The review should answer the questions, "How are we doing?" and "What can we do to improve our performance in the future?" There also must be a plan to actually generate the cash flow that you need to keep your retirement wheel turning.

It is wonderful to have your portfolio generating a high rate of return, but there must be a procedure in place for turning assets into cash to meet your budget requirements. This procedure needs to be clear to all parties so that generating the cash does not lead to excess taxes, or a panic over the liquidation of assets because it is perceived as a dreaded "invasion of principal." We need to come away from this process with two clear numbers. First, what is the total rate of return expected on the financial assets? This is a percentage that includes interest, dividends, and growth of capital. Second, we need to know how much income the portfolio is going to generate. Generally, we back into this by saying the portfolio will generate the income required to make up the difference between what you need and the income available from all other sources. The process of supplementing dividends and income to meet this need is called "the equity-income strategy." This strategy involves the periodic liquidation of assets to generate cash. The capital base and the budget are the shock absorbers that take up the slack when it is necessary to curtail the equity-income strategy. They will help you to deal with all the bumps that we expect as your retirement wheel rolls across the many years of your retirement.

WEAVING THE THREADS

We now have 10 important threads. What comes next? You can take these numbers, and put them into a spreadsheet program and work out the results. Figure 6-6 is a sample retirement planning spreadsheet. The first column tracks the years. Next are two columns that trace out your age in one column and your spouse's age in the other. The next column is the active retirement budget, followed by the passive budget and a column for special plans. The next column shows the composite budget. It actually comes from a separate spreadsheet where you have blended together the active budget, increased by inflation, until age 75. From 75 to 85, the budget is moving in equal steps from the active budget at age 75 to the passive budget at age 85. Beyond 85, out to an age that represents 150% of your life expectancy, you are tracing the passive budget increased by inflation. To this budget, you need to add the cost of your special plans and any support that you expect to give others. Remember to decrease the budget for any expenditures that will stop at some time in the future.

In the next columns, you trace out your income from various sources. The columns for client and spouse earnings reflect both earnings until retirement and any retirement earnings that are expected. It may take some work to get these estimates to be realistic, but it is vital. Social Security starts at age 62 or 65 and increases at your assumed rate of increase. Your pension comes next, with any expected cost-of-living adjustments. Then there is a column or perhaps multiple columns to show the income that may be coming from any other sources: real estate, intellectual property, licenses, trusts, gifts and inheritances.

The next two columns trace the ebb and flow of your retirement capital. The first column shows tax-deferred assets and the second column shows your taxable assets. Each of these increases at some assumed rate of return on the capital base. This number, you will recall, is dependent on your choice of

SAMPLE RETIREMENT PLANNING SPREADSHEET

FIGURE 6-6

	INIT. VAL.	60	59	$60,000	$48,000			$48,000	$32,000	$1,200	$650	$16,000	$3,500	$600,000	$400,000
	MODIFIER	1	1	4.5%	3.4%			5.0%	5.5%	2.25%	2.25%	4.5%	5.5%	8.75%	8.25%
YEAR		CLIENT AGE	SPOUSE AGE	ACTIVE BUDGET	PASSIVE BUDGET	SPECIAL PLANS	COMPOS. BUDGET	CLIENT EARNINGS	SPOUSE EARNINGS	CLIENT SOC. SEC.	SPOUSE SOC. SEC.	SPOUSE PENSION[1]	RENTAL INCOME	TAX DEFERRED CAPITAL	TAXABLE CAPITAL
1998		60	59	$60,000	$48,000		$60,000	$48,000	$32,000				$3,500	$623,500	$400,000
1999		61	60	$62,700	$49,632		$62,700	$50,400	$33,760				$3,693	$684,368	$454,348
2000		62	61	$65,522	$51,319		$65,522	$52,920	$35,617				$3,896	$750,891	$514,721
2001		63	62	$68,470	$53,064		$68,470	$55,566	$8,500			$16,000	$4,110	$821,399	$554,820
2002		64	63	$71,551	$54,869		$71,551	$58,344	$8,500		$650	$16,720	$4,336	$898,284	$614,714
2003		65	64	$74,771	$56,734	$15,000	$89,771	$61,262	$8,500		$665	$17,472	$4,574	$982,116	$680,127
2004		66	65	$78,136	$58,663	$20,000	$98,136	$10,000	$8,500	$1,200	$680	$18,259	$4,826	$1,069,439	$686,305
2005		67	66	$81,652	$60,658	$15,000	$96,652	$10,000	$8,500	$1,227	$695	$19,080	$5,091	$1,164,402	$686,881
2006		68	67	$85,326	$62,720	$10,000	$95,326	$10,000	$8,500	$1,255	$711	$19,939	$5,371	$1,267,675	$690,119
2007		69	68	$89,166	$64,852	$10,000	$99,166	$10,000		$1,283	$726	$20,836	$5,667	$1,379,347	$888,269
2008		70	69	$93,178	$67,057	$10,000	$103,178	$10,000		$1,312	$743	$21,774	$5,979	$1,500,790	$683,665
2009		71	70	$97,371	$69,337	$7,500	$104,871			$1,341	$760	$22,754	$6,307	$1,632,109	$666,712
2010		72	71	$101,753	$71,695		$101,753			$1,371	$777	$23,778	$6,654	$1,774,918	$648,024
2011		73	72	$106,332	$74,132		$106,332			$1,402	$794	$24,848	$7,020	$1,930,223	$632,330
2012		74	73	$111,117	$76,653		$111,117			$1,434	$812	$25,966	$7,406	$2,099,118	$612,247
2013		75	74	$116,117	$79,259		$116,117			$1,466	$830	$27,134	$7,814	$2,282,791	$587,277
2014		76	75	$121,342	$81,954		$116,077			$1,499	$849	$28,355	$8,243	$2,482,535	$556,873

The spreadsheet headings and the formulas in the columns reflect the specific circumstances of the retirement being planned.
[1] In this scenario, the client's pension amount is zero, so this column has been omitted to save space.

asset allocation and is projected on the basis of the past performance of a portfolio of the composition that you have selected (Chapter 8). The return on the taxable assets is reduced by your income tax rate. This reduction is based on the somewhat unrealistic assumption that all capital gains are realized in the year that they occur. A way of making this a bit more realistic is to reduce the rate of return on taxable asset not by your marginally tax rate, but by your overall tax rate. The rate of return on the tax-deferred assets can be assumed to be reduced by 50% of your tax bracket to reflect the fact that someday you will have to pay taxes on the gains achieved. In other words, if you are getting a 10% return on your assets and you are in a 36% marginal tax bracket, your taxable assets are increasing at a net 6.4% and your tax-deferred assets are increasing at 8.2%. (This is an approximation based on the assumption that the taxes on the tax-deferred assets will not be paid for 10 to 15 years and that the future value of those taxes are discounted at the rate of return on the portfolio. This is more fully discussed in Chapter 9.)

If the annual budget is less than the income from all sources, the excess is added to the capital base. You can put it into taxable or tax-deferred assets, depending on your preference, your practical alternatives, and the number of years until the balance shifts and the funds will have to come back out. If the balance will shift within 8 years, the funds should be added to the taxable assets.

If the income from all sources is less than the current budget, then the difference should be subtracted from the taxable assets. This continues until the taxable assets are equal to the next year's budget. When that occurs, no further funds are withdrawn from the taxable assets and the withdrawals to meet the budget are made from the tax-deferred assets.

If the capital base in both categories hits zero before you reach your expected longevity, adjustments need to be made. You can try reducing the budget a little. Try taking out some of the special plans. Try a slightly more optimistic projection on retirement earnings. Examine the asset allocation that you have selected and see if you might be comfortable with a slightly more aggressive portfolio that might give a slightly higher projected rate of return. You will be amazed to see the difference that small adjustments make when they are projected out over all the years of your retirement.

If the actual manipulation of these calculations is more than you want to deal with, you should have your financial advisor use his retirement software to make the projection. If you do this, make certain that the advisor is using a model that incorporates the ideas we have discussed. Many of the older software programs do not allow the planner to reflect the important ideas that we have discussed. They typically offer no help with longevity modeling. They do not include the active-to-passive transition. This alone can add as much as 35% to the total cost of your retirement. In addition, older software does not easily accommodate retirement earnings or the idea of savings continuing after retirement. Another important deficiency in many of these older programs is that they do not reflect the difference in return on your taxable and tax-deferred assets. As a result, they tend to understate the productivity of your capital base.

Whichever way you choose to go, this step is of vital importance. You need to see what it is going to take to allow you to enjoy The Prosperous Retirement. In addition, you need to see the track on which you are to run so that you can be confident that your retirement really is under control. This is the payoff—the ability to have your path made clear.

7.

INVESTMENT ALTERNATIVES

"'Tis money that begets money."
—ENGLISH PROVERB

SYNOPSIS: Investments are the vehicles by which capital is put to work. There is a mind-boggling confusion of investment alternatives, with more added daily. Effective selections must be made from this jungle of alternatives. Choices always seem easier when the full range of possibilities is clear.

The world of investments is divided between debt-based assets and equity-based assets. Within each sphere, there are wise alternatives and foolish alternatives. Investments are like corks bobbing on the tides of economic, political, and social change. It is hard to predict where the tides will take them, but it is clear that we want investments that will survive. We must watch constantly for signs that our investments are not carrying us in the desired direction.

A S SURELY AS WATER FLOWS DOWNHILL, talk of money and finances inevitably turns to investments. Investments are said to be the vehicles by which capital is put to work. The real point to saving and investing is to put accumulated capital to work. "You worked hard for your money. Now, make it work hard for you." Imagine a farmer whose sweat and skill brings in a bountiful harvest. A part of that harvest is set aside as seed for a future crop. Like the farmer, the wise investor uses part of the harvest to sow dollars with the hope that they will grow into more dollars. If dollars are the seeds, investments are the furrows in which those dollars are sown.

TWO KINDS OF INVESTMENTS

Literally hundreds of thousands of investment alternatives exist today. We count thousands of types of investments. However, there are only two fundamentally different ways of investing money: The first way is to loan money; the second way is to buy an ownership share. In other words, when you are investing, you are either loaning money or you are buying an ownership interest. Either way, you expect the investment to return more money than you invested, and, either way, you know that there are risks involved. The trick is to balance the risk with the reward and—this is important—never to take more risk than you need to achieve your goals.

There is an old and wise saying in the stock market: "Bulls make money, and Bears make money, but Pigs get slaughtered." Translated into Main Street-speak, this means that investors who take risks can make money and investors who avoid risks can make money, but greedy people come to grief.

LOAN-TYPE INVESTMENTS

When you loan your money, you expect not only to get it back, but to be paid whatever return has been promised. When you place your money in a bank account, buy a bond, loan money to a friend,[1] or put

---

[1] My grandmother had it right when she said, "Loan money to a friend—lose the money and lose the friend."

cash into a cash-value insurance policy, you are loaning your capital and you hope to have two guarantees:

- A guarantee to return your capital at some time in the future
- A guarantee to pay you some amount of money for the use of your capital

These can be important guarantees or they can be useless, depending on the reliability of the issuer of the guarantees. Rating services can help determine reliability of debt-based investments by issuing opinions about the creditworthiness of banks, corporations, municipalities, insurance companies, and other entities that borrow money. It is wise to note that the very useful opinions of these prestigious rating services are based on the facts known to them, and, like the rest of us, they cannot predict the future. It is possible that today's AAA-rated credit risk can be tomorrow's default, but the odds are higher that today's C-rated bond is going to be tomorrow's default. Furthermore, a number of other risks can affect loan-type investments, and many investments that pose as loan-type investments lack both of the usual guarantees.

OWNERSHIP-TYPE INVESTMENTS

The other half of the investment universe is composed of ownership investments that generally are called "equity investments." When you make an equity investment, you are investing in a business. There are no guarantees with equity investments. If the business succeeds, you expect to make a profit, but this profit is not guaranteed even if the business does succeed. Generally, equity investments are involved with the stock market or real estate, but they also may be direct investments into a business or property, real or personal. Investors buy equity investments only for the opportunities they represent because, unlike debt-based investments, there are absolutely no guarantees.[2]

---

[2] Anyone who offers a guarantee with an equity investment should be regarded with great suspicion.

INVESTMENTS FOR RETIREES

In the past, investment advice for retirees has emphasized investments in bonds[3]. Popular thinking on bonds was that the guarantees that came with them were significant because retired people were not in a position financially to be able to replace capital if it were lost. Furthermore, the then-popular belief was that retirement would not last long, so the loss of buying power through inflation was not a major risk. The traditional strategy in the early part of this century was to take your "safe and sane" money to the bank and your "mad" money to the stock market. People banked their "capital" and took their greed to the stock market, where they engaged in "speculation." This mind-set—and the reality that engendered it—was part of the reason that our parents and grandparents were unable to enjoy The Prosperous Retirement.

During the 1930s, the reality changed as the financial marketplace became more highly regulated and the financial industry made efforts to give everyone a much more equitable—if not entirely level—playing field. In the last 50 years, the popular perception also has undergone a massive change. Millions of American families have become exposed to the stock market through a hurricane of new investment products and services. Mutual funds have proliferated, as evidenced by the fact that more than 62 million Americans have investments in mutual funds. These investors represent more than 37% of all American families. In addition, many employees in the 1990s—unlike employees of earlier generations—are responsible for investing their own retirement accounts. Gone are the days when the boss and his advisors sat in a smoke-filled room and decided which insurance company or bank to entrust with the funds in the corporate pension plan.

Today's Individual Retirement Accounts (IRAs), 401(k) plans, 403(b) plans, and other retirement accounts generally are under the

---

[3] Throughout the book, I will refer to all "loan-like investments" as "bonds." All loans are not bonds, but rather than make a "laundry list" of the various "loan-like investments," —notes, bills, bonds, municipal bonds, money market accounts, savings accounts, credit union shares, certificates of deposit, deferred annuities, commercial paper, cash-value life insurance, mortgages, debentures, collateralized mortgage obligations, zero coupon bonds, and a host of other "loan-like investments"—I will just refer to "bonds."

management of the very employee whose retirement will depend on the success of these investments. Increasingly, these employees are wisely electing to invest their retirement savings in vehicles that derive their value from the stock market, generally in the form of mutual funds.

The choice of investments for a retiree is a complex process and will be discussed at length in the next chapter.

BOND INVESTMENTS FOR RETIREES

It has long been thought that the value of bonds was fundamentally more stable than the value of stocks. The perception was that if you held a high-quality bond to its maturity, you had a very great probability of recapturing your principal and enjoying the interest paid by the bond on a regular basis. The history of the economy over the last 50 years has blasted enormous holes in this theory.

Investors have discovered that bonds are subject to a broad range of risks[4]:

- Buying power risk
- Interest rate risk
- Business and credit risk
- Conversion rate risk

BUYING POWER RISK

Buying power risk means that the dollars you get back from your bond investment may have less buying power than the dollars you invested. In an inflationary environment—and I believe we are in one for the foreseeable future—there is a third guarantee on all loan-type investments. The textbooks, banks, and brokers don't talk about this guarantee, but you need to know that it exists.

➡ Guaranteed reduction of buying power

---

[4] There is a lot of terminology in this chapter. You will find most of the unfamiliar terms in the Glossary at the end of this book.

In other words, the dollars you get back from the investment will have less buying power than the dollars you invested.

If the rate of inflation over the period of the investment is greater than the interest rate earned on the bond, you will have lost buying power. The jargon calls this a "negative real rate of return." The increased number of dollars you got back from the investment was simply not enough to buy the same goods that you could have bought with the original investment dollars.

The buying power of the principal that you were paid when the bonds matured could be worth one-half or even one-quarter of the buying power you invested. Suppose you invested $10,000 in a government bond and held it for 10 years until maturity. Let's assume that inflation during this 10 years averaged 7.17%. When you made the investment, a loaf of bread cost 25¢. The $10,000 would buy 4,000 loaves of bread. Ten years later, when you got your money back, your $10,000 was still $10,000, but the price of bread had doubled to 50¢. Your $10,000 would buy only 2,000 loaves of bread. Inflation had caused a tremendous loss in buying power.

During retirement, when the generation of cash flow is the key to success, the inability of bonds to generate more income when inflation rises is a serious flaw. The typical retiree probably should have no more money in bonds than they might need to tide them through a stock market correction that might last three to five years.

INTEREST RATE RISK

Interest rate risk means that rising interest rates will cause the value of bonds to fall. Interest rate risk affects all interest-rate-sensitive investments, like bonds. The value of a bond is inversely related to interest rates. The price of a bond rises when interest rates fall and the price of a bond falls when interest rates rise. Think of a teeter-totter with interest rates at one end and bond prices at the other, as in Figure 7-1.

The longer the teeter-totter is, the more the ends will move. Just like the teeter-totter, the longer the maturity of a bond is, the more its price will move. If you hold a high-quality bond to maturity, you can avoid interest rate risk because you are guaranteed to get face value at maturity. Interest rate risk affects your investment only if you have to sell before maturity.

Say you invest $10,000 in a 5% bond that has a 20-year maturity. After 10 years, you need to sell the bond and interest rates have risen to the point that 10-year bonds (there are only 10 years remaining on your bonds) are now yielding 10%. You will receive only about $6,900, because at that price, the yield-to-maturity will equal the same 10% that an investor could get by purchasing a newly issued 10-year bond with a 10% coupon. If you hold them 10 more years, you will get your $10,000 back, but in the meanwhile you will be getting only $500 per year. If you sell the bonds for $6,900 and buy the new 10% bonds, you will get the same benefits from the new bonds that you would have gotten from the old bonds. In other words, after you bought those 5% bonds you were effectively locked in for the duration of the bonds. In a world where the interest on 30-year U.S. Treasury bonds has been more than 15%, bond holders have learned that the value of their bonds can be as volatile as the value of their stocks.

CREDIT AND BUSINESS RISK

Credit risk is the danger that the value of a bond may fall if the creditworthiness of the issuing company declines. Business risk means that the issuing company may fail and then the bond would become worthless. The default of a bond is the ultimate credit risk. The enormous dislocations of the economy over the last 50 years—the switch from a manufacturing economy to a service-and-information economy—has changed the creditworthiness of many companies. Bonds that were bought years ago

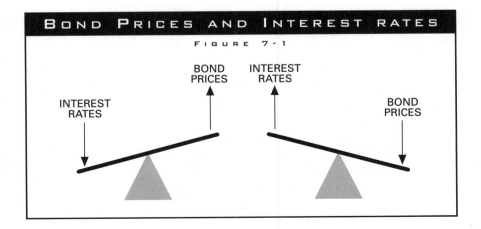

BOND PRICES AND INTEREST RATES

FIGURE 7-1

INTEREST RATES

BOND PRICES

INTEREST RATES

BOND PRICES

with excellent credit ratings gradually may have turned into "junk" bonds, and some of them even lost their value. The lesson to be learned is that bonds have a stable value only if they can be held to maturity and the issuing entity maintains its ability to redeem the bonds. Bond ratings are the key to making judgments about credit and business risk, but as judicious as these services are, no one has a crystal ball.

CONVERSION RATE RISK

Conversion rate risk is the chance that an investment denominated in a foreign currency may lose value if the exchange rate between the foreign currency and the U. S. dollar changes. If the rate of exchange between the dollar and the currency in which the investment is denominated deteriorates, you may lose money even if the investment performs as guaranteed. Say you buy a bond denominated in Thai Baht that pays 14.9% per year. Looks pretty attractive. You hold it for 5 years and get twice as many Baht as you invested. Unfortunately, during this period, inflation in Thailand has been raging, the conversion rate between Baht and U.S. dollars has declined by 60%, and instead of doubling your money, you lost 10% of your capital when you convert it back into dollars.

There are often attractive interest rates available in foreign countries, but Caveat Emptor! It would not be entirely inaccurate to say that the exchange rate mechanism by which conversion rates are set is reasonably accurate, but far from predictable. The truth of it is that picking winners in the foreign exchange market is about as easy as picking winners in a horse race. If you want to pursue this sort of speculation, it is best done in the form of a mutual fund or hedge fund where you have diversification, professional management, and the ability to liquidate on any day that you decide to get out.

Years ago, I had a client whose mother decided to live out her retirement years in Mexico. She asked my opinion about taking her bank accounts to Mexico and depositing them into accounts denominated in pesos. The interest rate was 25% per year and she could live on less than that. Bank rates in the U.S. were paying about half that, and she still could earn enough income to live. She felt that since she was going to live in Mexico and purchase all the necessities there, she would simply float on the value of the peso. It seemed too good to be true, and I advised against it, but she took her life savings south—in more ways than one. Prices soared, the peso was devalued, the exchange rate dropped dramatically, and she became terminally ill. She came back to the United States to seek medical assistance and to be near her family, but her life savings had been decimated. Fortunately, there was financial support available, but she had lost her financial independence in an ill-advised attempt to predict the course of an economy that she did not understand.

BOND BARGAINS

As a rule, you generally get what you pay for. There are very few bargains in the bond marketplace. Your chances of finding a bond that is seriously undervalued are about the same as finding a dust-covered painting by a famous artist in the corner of a flea market. Thousands of people are constantly at work to make certain that the price of any investment you make is "correct" given the latest information that modern technology can put on their computer screens.

When you buy a bond or other debt investment, you are paying a price that reflects the quality of the guarantees that you are getting. Generally, the price of a bond is a function of its quality, maturity, and yield. If a bond seems like a bargain, look again. There could be a call feature that may pull the bond away from you before the maturity date if interest rates fall. Dark clouds may be looming over the credit rating of the issuer, which is not yet reflected in the rating. There may be something strange concerning the taxation of the income. Keep looking until you figure out why the market is valuing the bond the way that it is; the market almost never makes mistakes. Some bond-like investments in today's marketplace defy explanation. They may carry yields that look very attractive compared to the alternatives. Read the fine print, if you can find it. If not, steer clear.

TREASURY OBLIGATIONS

The United States Treasury issues bills, notes, and bonds in the name of the U.S. government. These obligations, backed by "the full faith and credit" of the United States, are considered to be the safest investments in the world in terms of the certainty that they will pay the stated interest and return the principal at maturity. This does not mean that they are fool proof. Treasury bills are obligations with maturities of one year or less. Treasury notes mature in 10 years or less, and Treasury bonds have maturities longer than 10 years. The longest Treasury bonds currently have a 30-year maturity. The government and various governmental and quasi-governmental agencies issue a variety of other obligations that are not Treasury obligations. Many of these obligations do not carry "the full faith and credit" guarantee, but offer slightly higher yields than Treasury obligations. In addition, derivative products based on Treasury obligations exist that do not pay current interest. These are called by the generic name of "zero coupon bonds." These bonds sell at deep discounts based on interest rates and maturities. The difference between the discounted purchase price and the maturity value is the reward for buying these bonds. One disadvantage of these bonds, if held in a taxable account, is that each year the IRS imputes "interest" to these bonds based on the gradual accrual of value. This annual accrual is called the "OID factor" (Original Issue Discount factor).

Recently, the government has issued bonds that will be adjusted for inflation. These inflation-adjusted bonds are sold with a relatively low interest rate. If inflation rises, the value of these bonds will be adjusted. I'm uncomfortable with the fact that the government could change the system for determining the rate of inflation and this could adversely affect the future value of these bonds.

MUNICIPAL BONDS

A very important sub-category of bond investments is municipal bonds. These bonds are issued by states, municipalities, and other governmental and quasi-governmental agencies. The principal advantage of municipal bonds is that the interest on them is free from federal income taxes; some bonds also are free from state income taxes. Brokers are fond of saying that municipal bonds are second in safety to Treasury issues. That may be true, but it leaves a lot of room for trouble. In recent years, we have seen defaults and near-defaults on hundreds of millions of dollars in municipal bonds. Quality is definitely a consideration, and the quality of an issuer can change—think of Orange County, California. I recommend that you buy "A" rated or better bonds if you are buying them directly. The slightly better yields of lower-rated municipal bonds would not compensate you for a default unless you had a very large, well-diversified portfolio of municipals. Many advisors recommend that investors give preference to general obligation bonds, which have the entire tax authority of the issuer behind them, rather than revenue bonds, which depend on revenues from a specific source. The yields on municipal bonds are lower than the yields on taxable bonds of comparable quality. The difference varies from time to time, and you can easily see if it is to your advantage to own the taxable bonds or tax-free bonds. If an A-rated corporate bond yields 7% taxable and you are in a 35% income tax bracket, you are better off buying municipals if you can get better than 4.55% [.07 x (1–.35) = .07 x .65 = .0455].

If you are going to buy individual municipal bonds, questions concerning call features, discounts and premiums, and maturities dictate the need for expert advice. Your financial advisor may or may not understand these subtleties. You should buy municipals in lots of at least $10,000 because larger amounts carry lower commissions and can be bought at better prices. If you cannot afford to own at least 5 to 10 different issues, you may be better off in a mutual fund or a closed-end investment company, or in a unit investment trust that invests in municipal bonds.

"REAL BONDS" VERSUS "DEBT-BASED ASSETS"

If debt investments turn out to be part of your investment strategy, my advice is to stick with "real bonds" that have fixed interest rates and maturities and which have established credit ratings for the borrowers. If you decide to use mutual funds that invest in bonds, be aware that these are not "real bonds." They have no fixed maturity, no guaranteed return of principal, and no guaranteed rate of return. Bond mutual funds are investments that derive their value partly from the bonds they own, but also from the skill of the fund manager who is trading bonds, hopefully, to make a profit for your account. These mutual funds are not true debt investments, but a cross between a debt investment and an equity investment. These bond mutual funds have a role to play in retirement investing, but I call them "debt-based assets" to distinguish them from real bonds.

HYBRID INVESTMENTS

A number of investments represent a cross between bond investments and equity investments. Vehicles such as convertible bonds and preferred stocks are a kind of cross between stocks and bonds. There are many different kinds of these investments, but the bottom line is that they tend to have less risk than straight stocks and more appreciation potential than straight bonds. Some of these may have a potential role to play in your retirement. This is a category of investments that is not wildly popular, but which may deserve your attention or the attention of your financial advisor. Some mutual funds invest in this type of securities, and there are also many individual issues of high-quality companies that carry a high current yield and some potential for price appreciation. When buying these hybrids, remember that you are paying a premium for the guarantees that they carry. Give careful consideration to the creditworthiness of the issuer.

EQUITY INVESTMENTS FOR RETIREES

The world of equity investments is enormous and complex. It encompasses all investments that represent ownership of an interest in some business or asset. If you own a share of AT&T, you are part owner of the company. If you own a share of a mutual fund that owns a share of AT&T, you are still part owner of AT&T. If you own a piece of real estate that you rent, this is a business interest. If you own a gold coin, you have an ownership interest in gold. There are three major categories of equity investments:

1. Stocks
2. Real estate
3. Direct investments

STOCKS

Stocks and stock-related investments are a huge part of the equity investment universe. Recent reports tell us that more than 50% of all American families own stock or mutual funds that invest in stock.

Market Capitalization

There are many different ways to look at stocks. From one dimension, stocks are classified according to the size of the issuing company as rated by their "market capitalization." Market capitalization is simply the number of shares of the company that are outstanding (available to investors) multiplied by the market value of the shares. If a company has one million shares outstanding and the shares are valued at $5 each, the market capitalization of the company is $5 million.

The definition of large capitalization, small capitalization, and medium capitalization companies has varied over time, and it varies from one authority to another. In today's marketplace, companies with capitalization of more than $5 billion are large. Companies with capitalization of less than $1 billion are small, and companies between $1 billion and $5 billion are medium.

Over a long period of time, the stocks of smaller companies have shown more appreciation, on the average, than the stocks of large or medium-sized companies. The disadvantage of smaller company stocks is that they are more volatile than the stocks of larger companies. Their price tends to rise and fall more rapidly than the price of the stock of more well-established companies. Many of these small companies have a limited product range, slim finances, shallow market penetration, and are subject to technological changes. Larger companies generally are more diversified, better financed, and less subject to change because they have a broader market position. On the other hand, larger companies are more mature and less likely to experience dramatic growth. The stocks of larger companies also are closely followed by many analysts, which means that few of these stocks are truly undervalued in the marketplace. The stock of medium-sized companies, so-called "mid-cap stocks," are a useful compromise between the volatility of smaller companies and the limited growth potential of larger companies. It makes sense to have a portion of your assets in the stock of small companies, but small-cap mutual funds, with their ability to diversify among a number of small capitalization stocks, are certainly the smartest way to do it.

Industry Groups

Another cross section of stocks would divide them according to their business. Auto stocks, banks, drug stocks, steel stocks, and airline stocks, to name a few, represent some of the industry groups. The industry groups then are categorized according to their economic characteristics. For example, Ford is an auto stock and automobiles are considered consumer durables. Seen in this light, Ford and Maytag are in the same category because they produce goods that are sold to the consumer (as opposed to "producers") and their products are not consumed as they are used.

Domestic Versus International

Stocks also can be categorized according to where they do business. Many American companies derive a substantial part of their revenues from their overseas business activities. When prospects for the U.S. economy look dim, the stock of companies with major overseas business tends to show more strength than the average stock.

Growth Versus Value

Another cross section of stocks that gets a lot of discussion is "growth stocks" versus "value stocks." Stocks generally can be divided in two groups: value stocks and growth stocks. Thus, the combination of these two groups tends to encompass the whole market. Having said that, it doesn't take a lot of imagination to see that when one group is doing better than the market, the other group must be doing worse than the market. There is no universally accepted definition of a "value" stock or a "growth" stock.

Value stocks are the stocks of companies that have a lot of worth in their business relative to the market capitalization of their stock. If you were going to buy the business, this is the kind of company you would look for: a company whose price is cheap relative to the things that the company owns.

Growth stocks, on the other hand, are the stocks of companies that are growing rapidly and are showing a rapid increase in earnings. Generally, a growth stock has a high price-to-earnings (P/E) ratio, which reflects the market's enthusiasm for the company's prospective growth. The market is hungry for the shares of these rapidly growing companies and the market capitalization of such companies is high relative to the "value" of the company.

Sometimes the market is eager to buy growth stocks, and, in those periods, growth stocks outperform value stocks. In other periods, the market is not so optimistic and is not willing to pay a big premium for future growth. In such periods of muted optimism or downright fear, value stocks tend to outperform growth stocks. The debate about whether growth stocks or value stocks are the better investment tends to lead to a dead end. If the market goes up, both categories will go up—if you hold them long enough. Generally, however, the famous stock market geniuses, like Warren Buffet and John Templeton, have been value investors. "Buy low, sell high" is their credo and they have made billions doing it.

Not everyone agrees on how to define "growth stocks" or "value stocks," and not every mutual fund that calls itself a "growth-oriented fund" or a "value-oriented fund" will stick with its discipline. It is, for example, possible to evaluate the value of a company using "book value" or "price to sales" or "price to earnings" or a variety of other ways. Each of these screens would come up with a different list of "value stocks," and each would be correct. Some value investors get very creative in finding value in a company that others may not see or may not even agree is value. Growth investors also can use various screens. They may look at past trends in earnings, predictions about future earnings, revenues, or sales trends. Some growth-style investors will buy a stock just because the price is rising—this is called momentum investing. As a result of these differences, it actually is possible to see a stock in a list of growth stocks and the same stock in a list of value stocks. Theoretically, this should not be possible, but in practice it happens frequently. As a result of the vagaries of these definitions, treat studies that try to answer questions like, "Is growth investing better than value investing?" with some considerable skepticism. A famous academic study by Fama and French is widely cited as concluding that value investing is better than growth investing, but there are a series of reasons why this renowned academic study probably is not great practical advice.[5]

You may have heard the joke about the rich man who asks the bell boy if he would like to have a nice tip or, instead, learn the secret of the man's great wealth. The bell boy opts for the secret. The man says, "The secret is that there is no secret. Get up early, work hard, and be lucky." In the investment world, the secret is that there is no simple answer.

---

[5] Fama, Eugene and Kenneth R. French, "Cross Section of Variation in Expected Stock Returns," *Journal of Finance*, June 1992.

Today's correct answer is more likely than not to be wrong tomorrow, but keep reading because there are answers that are almost never right.

Stocks and the Business Cycle

The business cycle goes through periods of expansion and periods of contraction. The economy grows well for a period and then it reverses. Various stocks have different relationships to the phases of the business cycle. Some stocks are considered cyclical stocks, and they tend to move with the economic cycle. Other stocks—for example, food stocks—tend to show great strength when the economy is not doing well. This kind of stock is called "counter-cyclical." Some stocks move quite independently of the business cycle.

The typical retiree needs to assess his or her ability to ride through economic cycles in making stock purchases, but the fundamental issue is still the classic, "buy low, sell high." If you are buying a cyclical stock at a low point in the cycle, what are the odds that you will be able to hold it until the cycle turns? If you make a mistake, will you have both the wisdom to see the mistake and the strength to correct it? If the answer is no, do not feel too badly, because many mutual fund managers have the same shortcomings. The mutual fund manager, unlike most individual investors, will keep examining her or his decisions and is more likely to correct a mistake before it gets out of hand. The business cycle is a big reason why there are so few "buy-and-hold" stocks and why professional management is important.

Utility Stocks

The stocks of companies that provide electricity, water, gas, and other services to homes and businesses traditionally have been popular investments for retirees. These stocks were thought to be safe investments because they generally had a government-regulated monopoly and a steady demand for their services. As a result, many of these companies had very long records of steadily increasing dividends—a great kind of investment for anyone, but particularly retirees. In addition, because of their relatively high dividends, these stocks tended to be less vulnerable to market declines. If the economy looked poor and demand for services was not likely to increase, the high dividend still looked attractive to potential investors. Most of these stocks are classic examples of how social, political, and economic change can affect not only companies, but whole industries. Regulators have changed the rules for most electric utilities and the telephone industry has become a free-for-all. This trend toward deregulation of the utility industry is likely to continue until the utility industry is just another business sector. There are still a few utility companies that appear to have a secure position, but it takes more than the wobbly dart throw that it used to take to find the quality investments in this economic sector.

Foreign Versus Domestic Stocks

Another important division is between foreign and domestic stocks. For many years, the stocks of foreign companies were thought to be too racy for the average investor. Even today, mutual fund prospectuses routinely announce that investments in foreign stocks carry a higher risk than investments in domestic stocks. I assess that as a definite "maybe." Certainly, domestic stocks exist that are as safe as any in the world. There are also domestic stocks that are as risky as any in the world. If I were investing for safety, I would prefer a well-established foreign company from a country with a stable economy over a struggling domestic company.

Unquestionably, foreign stocks are more complicated than their domestic counterparts. Accounting standards vary from country to country, and the financial reporting of many foreign corporations leaves a lot to be desired. The standards of disclosure also vary. What might be a required disclosure for U.S. corporations may be a mystery in a foreign company. As foreign corporations aim to compete more actively for U.S. investment capital, their accounting procedures, reporting, and disclosure are improving, making these risks less than they were years ago.

A risk associated with foreign stocks that has not lessened is exchange rate risk, discussed earlier in this chapter. Say you buy shares of a foreign company that sells electricity in its homeland. Say the company has a billion IMUs[6] of revenue from its business activities and profits of 5 IMUs per

---

[6] IMU stands for imaginary monetary units.

outstanding share of stock. At the time you buy the stock, 5 IMUs equals $1.00. The stock is selling for a price-to-earnings ratio of 20:1, so you pay $20.00 for each share. Over the next year, the company does well. Revenues are up 20%, the earnings per share increases 20% to 6 IMUs per share, and the price-to-earnings ratio remains constant. Did you make money? Maybe yes and maybe no. It depends on the exchange rate. If the exchange rate stayed the same and the price-to-earnings ratio is still 20:1, you made 20% plus any dividends. It is not inconceivable that the exchange rate might have changed by 20%. If it went down, you broke even and if it went up, you made 40%. That should make it clear why many authorities see a lot of risk in foreign investments. But it is not quite that simple.

In the last 20 to 30 years, it has become apparent that many foreign stock markets do not fluctuate on the same cycle as the U.S. stock market. The statistical relationship between things like this is called its "correlation." If cycles move together, they are said to have a "positive correlation." If they move opposite of each other, they are said to have a "negative correlation." If they ignore each other, they have a "neutral or zero correlation." When you are worried about the U.S. market going down, it would be nice to know that some other markets have a negative correlation. In the next chapter, we will talk more about how blending investments with negative correlations can reduce the risk in the overall portfolio. This is the fundamental premise of "asset allocation." The bottom line here is that, while foreign stocks may be riskier than domestic stocks, the artful addition of foreign stocks to a portfolio can reduce the overall risk in the portfolio. Amazing but true. In my view, every retirement portfolio should have some foreign stocks in it.

REAL ESTATE

No discussion of equity investments would be complete without mention of real estate. Real estate is the favorite investment of most Americans, because they believe it is highly productive and very safe. Most people who hold this view came to it through their experience with their own homes. Two factors go into this broadly held judgment that need to be clearly understood. First, the experience of the last 50 years has been unprecedented in terms of the rising demand for homes. I feel comfortable making a flat statement that this will not be repeated in the next 50 years, as demand for homes begins to decline because of demographic factors. Second, the success of the typical investment in a home is heavily dependent on the use of leverage—borrowed money. Virtually everyone buys a home using a mortgage. In some cases, a home can be bought with no money down, but a more typical scenario is probably 20% down. Even with 20% down, the leverage is 4:1—one part investment to four parts borrowed money. That is 1.6 times the maximum leverage that an investor can legally use in the stock market. Given the long period of rising demand, the price of real estate has gone up about 5% to 6% per year for the last 45 years. A house that was bought in 1950 for $15,000 might be worth $135,000 to $200,000 45 years later. The stock markets during that period have done much better, but the real estate probably was bought with only $3,000 down. To turn $3,000 into $200,000 over 45 years represents only a 9.75% rate of return and this ignores the monthly mortgage payments. During that same period, the Standard and Poor's 500 has returned an average of about 13.5%. Looking at our 1950 house purchase, $3,000 compounded at 13.5% for 45 years is almost $900,000! The beauty of the home as an investment is that most people will go to great lengths to make certain that they meet their obligation to pay the mortgage and avoid foreclosure. That mitigates the risks in the use of leverage and gives a great feeling of comfort that is not always justified.

Other real estate investments have had widely varying results. Many people lost not only their shirt, but their hat and socks in the 1980s as real estate values tumbled following the 1986 Tax Reform Act. Prior to that change in the law, certain kinds of real estate investments had enormous tax advantages. When the Tax Reform Act stripped away those benefits retroactively, the value of real estate fell. Many properties were worth less than the remaining balance on the mortgage, and the savings and loan crisis ensued. There was a great joke in those days: "Do you know the difference between a pigeon and a Houston real estate tycoon? The pigeon can still make a substantial deposit on a Mercedes."

Real estate can be a great investment, but, like all investments, it has its risks. I will talk about the home as an investment in Chapter 9. The short version of that discussion is that the home is not part of your retirement capital unless you plan to sell it. Other kinds of real estate can be wise investments or not so wise.

Real Estate as a Retirement Investment

Generally, the quality of real estate as a retirement investment is a function of three things:

1. The ability of the real estate to generate a reliable stream of income.
2. The amount of leverage to be used, and your ability to service that debt if the property is vacant.
3. Management issues.

Remember to consider the impact on your retirement of a real estate project that is vacant. It could be a major financial obstacle to enjoying The Prosperous Retirement. Any real estate asset should either lend itself to professional management or it should be a very simple management project. Even a rental house can be a problem if you plan to take a long vacation.

My favorite idea for a retirement real estate investment is a duplex, or a pair of townhouses, in an up-and-coming neighborhood, one that is likely to remain strong for the rest of your life. You live in one unit and rent the other to a reliable family. While you are off enjoying The Prosperous Retirement, you have a source of income and a built-in caretaker for your home—if all goes as planned.

Other Forms of Real Estate Ownership

Another way of owning an interest in real estate is by owning stocks or limited partnerships that invest in real estate. The words "limited partnership" can ruin the day for a lot of investors. In the 1970s and early 1980s, limited partnerships were thought to provide a vehicle for smaller investors to own interests in a variety of attractive assets. They were used to acquire interests in oil and gas properties, real estate, cable television systems, various leasing programs, and other more exotic assets, such as farms and commodity pools. The failure of limited partnerships was so wide spread in the late 1980s and 1990s that many people became convinced that limited partnerships were a fundamentally flawed form of investment. In my opinion, the jury is still out on partnerships as a class of investments. A major factor in the failure of the numerous real estate limited partnerships was the Tax Reform Act of 1986. In that legislation, Congress abruptly reversed course and retroactively withdrew the tax benefits that were the carrot that had lured many investors into highly leveraged real estate ventures (I almost wrote "adventures").

In addition to the lesson that tax laws are subject to change, a couple of other clear lessons emerged out of the failure of these old partnerships. First and foremost is the lesson that the quality of management in a limited partnership is clearly the most important factor in the success or failure of the project. Good management can save a mediocre program and bad management can sink the best of programs. Secondly, partnerships are just another form of doing business. To succeed, the business must be built around a sound concept, be well managed, and be adequately financed. Many partnerships have been small businesses pursuing new business ideas with untried management and marginal finances. When you see them in that light, is it a big surprise that so many failed?

Some partnerships have delivered excellent results, notably in the areas of leasing, low-income housing (tax-credit investments), and the ownership of unleveraged or lightly leveraged real estate. Tax credit partnerships will be mentioned in Chapter 12. Leasing programs can be a useful element in a strategy to diversify your income-producing assets away from stocks and bonds and to provide a rate of return that is competitive with other income sources. I believe that any partnership investment needs to be examined with exceptional care because so many are small, new, and inexperienced. I would not exclude them completely from consideration, but the evaluation of most offerings demands more expertise than most investors command—even if they have professional advisors. Do not wander into this neighborhood without an experienced, knowledgeable, and trusted guide.

Real Estate Investment Trusts

Hundreds of real estate investment trusts [REITs] are traded in the stock market like ordinary stocks. In fact, they *are* ordinary stocks, the only difference is that the business is organized as a real estate investment trust rather than a corporation. The trust organization allows the business activity to enjoy certain tax benefits that are associated with real estate investments. Many people who own these stocks see no difference between owning the stocks of real estate investment trusts and stocks that represent an ownership interest in a corporation.

There are many important differences in the way that different REITs go about their business. Some REITs own actual real estate and are called "equity REITs"; others own mortgages on real estate and are called "mortgage REITs." Some own properties for cash, while others use leverage. Some REITs are concentrated in one real estate sector, i.e., apartment buildings, office buildings, retail properties, industrial properties, while others are diversified into various sectors. Some REITs reinvest their cash flow into the purchase of additional properties, while others distribute the cash flow. Like any investment category, there are many choices and it takes considerable expertise to make wise selections. The stocks of REITs that have large and secure dividends are very interesting investments for retirees.

Real Estate Stocks

Hundreds of stocks represent ownership interests in various aspects of the real estate market. There are property developers, construction companies, companies that manufacture products for the building industry, and companies in the business of buying and selling real estate. These stocks tend to ride on the general trend of the stock market. If economic prospects look strong and interest rates are under control, these stocks do well because that is the kind of environment in which real estate activity tends to be high. If the economy looks weak and interest rates are high, these stocks are likely to sink with the broader market. In other words, these stocks are more like stock than real estate.

Real Estate Mutual Funds

Several mutual funds invest in stocks that are connected with real estate. Some concentrate in REITs, while others tend to invest in stocks that are less directly connected with property ownership. The diversification and professional management that these funds offer may be of interest to some retirees, but I would recommend a more direct ownership, either through individual properties or carefully selected REITs.

DIRECT INVESTMENTS

There is one last type of equity investment that is so big and diverse that there is little to be said about it here. This is the category of direct investments. This could be a ranch or a farm, a business, a piece of equipment to be leased, an oil well, a sand/gravel pit, or any other kind of asset that you own directly and which is an operating business. The two biggest problems with investments like this, from the retirement planning perspective, are:

1. They often constitute an estate planning problem.
2. They are operating businesses and require management.

These assets can be valuable—in many cases they are the bulk of a person's wealth—and yet they might be hard to sell. They could comprise a big estate tax burden without the ability to be liquidated to provide the cash to pay the tax bill. This will be discussed in Chapter 11. If you are the direct owner of a valuable asset, one of the members of your retirement management team needs to be a specialist on this subject.

SUMMARY

The structure of the investment alternatives that we have discussed can be summarized in the following manner:

- **DEBT-BASED ASSET**
  - Treasury bonds, notes, and bills
  - Corporate bonds, notes, and paper
  - Municipal bonds
  - Foreign bonds

- **EQUITY INVESTMENT**
  - Stocks
    Market capitalization
    Value versus growth
    Utility stocks
    Foreign stocks
  - Real estate
  - Direct investments

OWNERSHIP ISSUES

This classification of assets is just the tip of the iceberg because assets come in a variety of forms. In discussing various assets, I've mentioned some of the forms, but it's important to have a clear understanding of the forms because they can change or modify the character of the investment.

FORMS OF ASSET OWNERSHIP

There are five basic forms of asset ownership:

1. Direct ownership
2. Investment companies
3. Unit investment trusts
4. Limited partnership
5. Indirect ownership (derivatives)

Most assets can be owned in a variety of forms. For example, common stocks can be owned directly, through a mutual fund or closed-end investment company, through a unit investment trust, through a partnership, or indirectly through American depository receipts (ADRs), options, or futures.

Direct Ownership

Direct ownership seems self-explanatory—you own the asset directly. This might be a piece of real estate, a stock, a piece of equipment you lease out, or the rights to an invention, but you own it.

The various forms have advantages and disadvantages that flow partly from the underlying assets and partly from the ownership form. The main advantage of direct ownership is control. You buy when you want and you sell when you want. The disadvantages generally are associated with cost. The average investor is not buying and selling huge blocks of property, so the costs associated with these smaller transactions can be a significant disadvantage.

Investment Companies

Investment companies come in two forms: open-ended investment companies, which are commonly called "mutual funds," or closed-end investment companies. Mutual funds can issue additional shares to allow them to continuously take in new money and make new investments. There is no fixed limit to the number of shares that they can issue[7], so they are called "open-ended." The closed-end investment companies have a fixed number of shares outstanding and they are not allowed to issue new shares.

Closed-end investment companies trade like stocks. The price can be more or less than the net asset value[8] of the shares owned by the investment company. The willingness of investors to pay a premium for shares of a closed-end company can be a real mystery, particularly when shares managed by the same manager with the same investment philosophy may be available in a mutual fund for their net asset value. Conversely, when shares of the closed-end investment company are available for a discount, it may or may not represent a bargain. Sometimes the discount simply represents a lack of interest in a particular market sector. Say the closed-end investment company invests in Tasmanian stocks and Tasmania is expected to devalue its currency in the near future. The fund would trade at a discount that reflects the loss of value the market expects from the devaluation. Some funds hold assets that are suspect and the market may discount the shares accordingly.

Investment companies offer a series of benefits: professional management, the ability to buy and sell small amounts, good accounting, and a variety of administrative advantages, such as systematic withdrawal programs. The disadvantages are not insignificant, however. The investor cannot control the timing of sales and purchases within the fund, and tax consequences may be inconvenient. The fund may be very flexible in its management and represent an asset that changes its character outside of the investor's control. There may be significant costs associated with the ownership of some mutual funds. As popular as mutual funds are, they are not ideal for all investors. As always, look before you leap, and if you can't see the bottom of the hole, don't jump in.

---

[7] Mutual funds have a limited number of shares that they are authorized, by the shareholders, to issue, but this limit can be raised by vote of the shareholders.

[8] Net Asset Value (NAV) of a mutual fund share is the value of all the assets and liabilities owned by the fund divided by the outstanding shares.

Unit Investment Trusts

Unit Investment Trusts (UITs) are unmanaged, but professionally selected, pools of assets. They offer the advantages of diversification and professional selection. They have the disadvantages of imperfect pricing and substantial internal costs. In addition, some UITs have dark corners that may hide some surprises. For example, it has become common for UITs of municipal bonds to have relatively short call features. Thus, if interest rates fall, and the investor is theoretically in a position to sell the UIT at a profit, they may find that the bonds in the UIT have relatively short call features that greatly limit the upside potential. Other UITs commonly have zero coupon bonds with which to recoup the distribution costs of the UIT. This changes the investment characteristics of the UIT. All of these features are disclosed in the offering prospectus, but if the UITs are purchased in the secondary market, rather than on the initial offering, the buyer may not receive a prospectus or may not understand the practical implications of details explained in the prospectus. In spite of the disadvantages, UITs are very useful investments for retirees because they offer a convenient way to purchase a diversified portfolio of bonds that have a specific maturity.

Other UITs also may contain a specific portfolio of stocks that offer simple management and a clear investment strategy. UITs are a popular way of implementing strategies like "Dogs of the Dow," in which the investor buys a portfolio of the highest-yielding Dow stocks. When you buy a UIT, insist on seeing the offering document and get an explanation of anything you do not understand. Better yet, take your trusted guide along. It's a jungle out there.

Limited Partnerships

Limited partnerships are a way of owning specific types of assets without having to own the entire asset. It is a method by which investors pool their investments and place the funds under the management of a General Partner, who selects, purchases, and manages the asset. The investors are limited partners and have little voice in the management of the business—and therein lies the rub. A joke of the not-long-ago past held that a limited partnership was a form of business in which the limited partners started out with the money and the General Partner started out with the experience. Over time, it was said, they exchanged positions. I have commented earlier about the dangers of these partnerships and counseled that they be dealt with cautiously, if at all. The dangers are the disadvantage. The advantage that they offer is the opportunity to own classes of assets that would not otherwise be available to any but the largest investors.

Indirect Investments

There are many indirect investments. In general, they derive their value from some relationship with another asset. This relationship makes them derivatives, and derivatives, like limited partnerships, have gotten a not-entirely-undeserved bad reputation. The main disadvantage of derivatives or indirect investments is that the relationship between the derivative and the asset may not be fully understood. Many of these derivatives are new and have not weathered a full market cycle. As a result, no one—literally no one—knows exactly how they will fare.

A type of indirect investment that became popular with retirees in the 1990s was CMOs (collateralized mortgage obligations). These investments are secured by pools of mortgages on real estate. Sounds like a pretty safe investment. Unfortunately, the complexity of the offerings were mind-boggling, and a lot of unexpected consequences exploded on the marketplace. Predictions about how these investments would work in various market situations were based on computer models that were based on certain unproved assumptions. Would you be surprised if I told you that the results differed from the predictions, sometimes dramatically? CMOs are just one group among thousands of derivatives.

In general, derivatives are created to allow investors to focus on specific opportunities in the marketplace. Their specificity makes them questionable as investments for conservative investors who are interested in preservation of capital. In other words, retirees generally should steer clear of derivatives unless they are risking a very small portion of their investable assets. Most responsible financial professionals will be reluctant to intermediate in risky investments for retirees. The liability risk to the financial professional is greater than any potential fee or commission. If a financial professional offers you a risky derivative, you might well wonder about two things: first, how responsible is the professional, and second, how expert are they? In my view, many derivatives are pot-holes that can potentially break the axle of your retirement wheel.

TAX-DEFERRED INVESTMENTS

Tax deferral can add bonus performance to an asset. Let's assume that you are in a 31% tax bracket and that you own a mutual fund that appreciates 10% per year. Let's further assume that the mutual fund has a 100% turnover every year and that, as a result, all the gains are fully taxable each year. The after-tax result, after 20 years, is that a $10,000 investment would be worth $38,697. If we could somehow postpone those taxes until the twentieth year, the mutual fund account would be worth $67,275. After paying the 30% taxes on the appreciation, the tax-deferred account would still be worth $47,092 after taxes. The tax deferral resulted in additional after-tax value of $8,395, an improvement of almost 30%. Figure 7-2 compares the after-tax, terminal value of a tax-deferred account to an account that is taxable each year on its growth.

THE VALUE OF TAX DEFERRAL					
at Various Rates of Return for Various Periods FIGURE 7-2					
Holding Period	Rate of Return				
	5.0%	**7.0%**	**9.0%**	**11.0%**	**13.0%**
5	100%	101%	101%	102%	103%
10	102%	104%	106%	109%	112%
15	105%	109%	114%	121%	128%
20	109%	116%	125%	136%	148%
25	113%	125%	139%	156%	175%
30	119%	135%	155%	179%	207%
35	126%	147%	175%	208%	247%
40	133%	161%	197%	242%	296%

This chart compares the value of the tax-deferred account after paying taxes on the withdrawal, compared to the value of the taxable account after paying taxes on the growth each year.

An example may help to understand this table. Assume that investor A had $10,000 invested at 9% for 20 years in an account on which he or she had to pay 30% in taxes each year on the gain. Investor B had $10,000 at 9% in a tax-deferred account and paid 30% taxes on the gain only when the funds were withdrawn after 20 years. Investor B would have 25% more money, after taxes, than Investor A.

The pattern of the table seems clear. Tax deferral is more beneficial the longer it lasts and the higher the rate of return. This seems to indicate that it is more important to have equity investments in a tax-deferred account than bonds. In addition, tax deferral for periods of less than about 10 years is not that important. It is also important to recognize the cost of tax deferral. The typical methods of getting tax deferral are through the use of tax-sheltered retirement accounts or insurance contracts. The cost of maintaining a tax-deferred retirement account typically is quite nominal. An IRA account may have $100,000 in it and still cost only $5 or $10 per year as an administrative charge. The impact of that cost on total return is trivial.

In the case of insurance contracts, the comparison is more complicated because there are significant internal costs in the insurance contracts. For example, if you are getting tax deferral through the use of a typical variable annuity contract, the internal cost might well be 1.5% per year of the value of the contract. This is a significant burden and pushes the break-even period out to about 12 years before the benefit of tax deferral overcomes the burden of the added cost, and that is assuming an equity investment with a good rate of return. It does not make good sense for retirees to use variable annuities unless they plan to invest the funds in the annuity in an equity investment. If retirees want to use more conservative investments with fixed or guaranteed rates of return, they should seek tax deferral through the used of a fixed annuity that has significantly lower internal costs. The internal costs of variable life insurance contracts tend to be even higher than the internal costs on variable annuities. It makes sense to use the variable life insurance to provide income in the earlier years of retirement and allow the variable annuities to continue to accumulate because the cost of the variable annuity does not rise significantly with age.

CONCLUSION

There are many opinions about investments. Years ago, I used to pick wild mushrooms in Germany with a Russian friend. She would direct me toward certain kinds of mushrooms and away from others. Several times, I noticed that Germans who were picking mushrooms along side us avoided the ones we were picking and instead gathered the ones we were avoiding. I never did get a good explanation of this, but I saw the same Germans more than once. We also never got sick, so I guess we were both right. I suppose that it is true that one man's meat is another man's poison, but I also believe that there really are deadly mushrooms out there. Stick with what you know and understand. If you cannot figure it out, or if the explanations seem tendentious, remember that the main investment objective in retirement is to use your capital to produce the cash flow you need with the minimum risk of loss. That kind of goal should keep you out of the potholes and help keep your retirement wagon wheel rolling smoothly through the years of your retirement.

8.

INVESTMENT STRATEGY

"The social object of skilled investment should be to defeat the dark forces of time and ignorance which envelope our future."
—JOHN MAYNARD KEYNES, 1936

SYNOPSIS: An investment strategy is a plan for using financial resources. It combines the best science and art available to subdue the emotional elements. In this century, there have been a variety of investment strategies recommended to retirees. Fashions in investment strategies change with the times and reflect the mood of a period, as well as the means available for implementing the strategy. Early in this century, it was believed that only the safest bonds were suitable for retirees. By the middle of this century, the "classic" investment strategy for retirement was a portfolio balanced between cash, stocks, and bonds. Since the Second World War, a discipline called Modern Portfolio Theory (MPT) has developed, which seems to rationalize the selection of an investment strategy. MPT has led to the use of additional investment categories assisted by a technology called "asset allocation." Asset allocation continues to evolve, but it is the basic tool for defining an appropriate investment strategy for today's retiree.

S TRATEGY IS THE BROAD PLAN for winning a war. If you view the task of achieving The Prosperous Retirement as a kind of war, investment strategy is a key element in the overall plan. Unfortunately, many retirees view investment strategy as the principal task in retirement management. Other elements, such as selecting a life-style, savings, risk management, longevity planning, and all the non-financial issues, also play important roles in achieving the overall goal. It is true, however, that when careful planning has led to wise choices about the other issues, the key to paying for The Prosperous Retirement is a well-designed investment strategy. The right investment strategy can rescue a marginal retirement just as the wrong strategy can sink an otherwise promising retirement.

The strategic question for a retiree is this: "How can I best employ my retirement capital to provide the cash flow I need during retirement?" There are two risks. On one side, an overly cautious investment strategy may not provide the cash flow needed. On the other side, an overly aggressive investment strategy may result in the loss of principal and lead to inadequate cash flow. There is no simple answer to this ageless dilemma, but here are several fairly simple guidelines.

- First, invest in accordance with your goals and your risk tolerance.
- Second, diversify.
- Third, use a consistent long-term investment strategy based on a "forward-looking" asset allocation.
- Fourth, review your investments periodically, but be patient and restrained in making changes.

The rest of this chapter explains why I believe in these principles, what I think they mean, and how you ought to go about investing your retirement capital. On the way to that conclusion, it will be necessary to explain some background issues. If you don't want to go through all of that background, just skip ahead and read the section called, "So What's a Prosperous Retiree to Do?" When you have read that section, I hope you will be sufficiently interested to go back and read the background information.

THE OBJECTIVE

The "right" investment strategy must be capable of employing your retirement capital base to produce the cash flow that you need to live the life-style that you want. The "right" strategy also must be able to achieve that result without exposing your capital to unacceptable risks. You can see immediately that the "right" answer is a very subjective judgment. One person's "right" answer could easily be unacceptable or illogical for another person. One of the mistaken ideas of the old retirement planning model was that you could ask a person his or her age, then recommend an appropriate investment strategy. Nothing could be sillier.

Most of the time, a tug of war rages between the desire for a little more income and the fear of a little more risk. The resolution of that tension is a question that involves a lot more than just investment strategy or asking someone their age. A central truth is that you should never assume more risk than you need to achieve your goals. A corollary to that rule is that you must guard against the tendency for your goals to grow just because bigger goals seem achievable. That kind of growth is called "greed." A second important rule is that knowledge should guide your fear. If your investment goals lead to a portfolio that makes you uncomfortable, examine the alternatives, but, in the end, make certain that your fears are based on knowledge, not ignorance.

THE OBSTACLES

In the opening quotation, Lord Keynes reminds us that ignorance of the future is the main obstacle along the way to investment success. In addition to ignorance, there are also two permanent and powerful features of human character that are obstacles to investment success. They are fear and greed. Most of us are greedy enough to want a little nicer life-style, but we know that risk and reward are Siamese twins that will wrestle with us on every investment decision.

AN OVERVIEW

The basic choices in investment strategy are amazingly simple. You can choose what to own and when to own it. As simple as that. Unfortunately, the very next question sends us on a multi-stage rocket into intergalactic space. The question is, of course, "What shall I own and when shall I own it?" That question launches us into a rarefied atmosphere of statistics, academic theories, endless alternatives, and the seductive urgings of America's most persuasive people. Just as you cannot go to the moon with baby steps, you cannot make any significant progress on this important question with simple ideas. For every simple idea, there are a host of alternatives that seem to contradict and invalidate the original idea. If it were easy to be a successful investor, more people would be billionaires.

The process of answering the question, "What shall I own and when shall I own it?" begins with another question: "What am I trying to do?" There are many possible choices, but four basic compass points. Your choice from among these alternatives needs to be reflected in your retirement model.

1. I want my assets to meet my needs and those of my spouse.
2. I want my assets to meet our needs and those of our heirs.
3. I want my assets to be as productive as possible.
4. I want my assets to be invested in a way that exposes them to minimal risk of loss.

Your choice from among these alternatives is an individual decision, but I have an opinion. My opinion is that most retirees should seek a comfortable compromise that promises to meet their real needs, while it tries to find some balance between risk and reward. Concerns about heirs and abstract concepts like "productivity" or "good stewardship" are properly viewed as secondary to the basic quest for financial security.

The rest of this chapter will make just three points:

1. Advice on investment strategies for retirees has changed from time to time. There is no perennial "right" answer.
2. The current state of the art, Modern Portfolio Theory, has developed a technology called "asset allocation" that brings a degree of science to the process.
3. The eternal wisdom of knowledge, patience, and diversification is likely to serve a retiree better than any other strategy.

HISTORICAL VIEW

The entire question of managing funds to support retirement is relatively new. The very concept of retirement is only about 100 years old, and for about half of that period, most people retired only briefly and with very limited means. As a result, for most retirees in those early days, the issue of investment strategy was a moot point. Few retirees had enough assets to make the topic interesting and those who had a few dollars were urged to invest them with the utmost care.

Prior to the Second World War, "utmost care" meant only the very safest kinds of bonds. There had been enough bank failures during the 19th Century that advisors generally did not recommend bank deposits. There was no Federal Deposit Insurance Corporation (FDIC) to insure against losses, so investors were directed not to banks, but to the bonds of the very best corporations. In the second half of the 19th Century and early years of the 20th, those "safe" corporations generally were railroads or utilities. Among the bonds that were thought to be particularly safe were equipment bonds, secured by specific equipment that was essential to the corporation's operations.[1] The investor was competing with banks and insurance companies for these very highly regarded securities and the yields were very low. "Safety first" was the motto because there seemed to be so little room for error.

In the first half of this century, stocks were considered to be pure "speculation." Investors were urged to place their investment funds in bonds and risk only their "speculative capital" (in other words, their gambling funds) in the stock market. Washington Irving, in the second half of the 19th Century, captured the essence of this contempt for stocks when he wrote, "Speculation is the romance of trade, and casts contempt upon all its sober realities. It renders the stock-jobber a magician, and the exchange a region of enchantment." Clearly, stocks, in those days, were not something that the average investor would use to pursue important goals.

The Stock Market Crash of 1929, and the resulting Depression, cut a wide swath in this thinking. It demonstrated that stocks, bonds, and banks all were subject to failure. In the wake of the Depression, impor-

---

[1] Seen any equipment bonds recently?

tant reforms were made in the nation's financial institutions, causing all three types of investments to rise in prestige. In addition, the massive economic failure spurred a wave of thought about investment fundamentals. In the 1930s, the science of securities analysis was born. In the 1940s, when pension plans became an important part of the investment landscape, their trustees generally espoused a philosophy of investing in a balanced and diversified portfolio. A balance was achieved between stocks and bonds. In both categories, an attempt was made to invest in a variety of high-quality companies and a variety of solid industries. A typical balance might be 40% stocks and 60% bonds. A large portfolio might include several hundred different issues in 20 or more industries.

THE FIDUCIARY BURDEN

The manager of a pension fund was acting as a "fiduciary," a person who exercises authority over other people's money. The courts had long held such fiduciaries to a high standard of care. That standard was defined in the "prudent man rule," which states that a fiduciary must act "with the care, skill, prudence and diligence under the circumstances then prevailing that a prudent man acting in a like capacity and familiar with such matters would use in the conduct of an enterprise of a like character and with like aims."[2] With that sharp, legal blade hanging over the heads of the trustees, an investment portfolio containing 40% stocks seemed risky enough.

As individuals began to command their own retirement savings, this kind of conservative advice spilled out of the boardrooms. The balanced, diversified portfolio became the "right answer" for retirement investments in the 1940s, 1950s, and 1960s. Toward the end of that period, in the middle 1960s, people saw the terrific results that had been achieved in the stock market in the first half of the 1960s and greed began to overcome fear. Thinking shifted, and, along with it, the advice to people planning retirement. The advice shifted from the 40/60 balanced portfolio to the "Rule of 100." According to the Rule of 100, investors were supposed to subtract their age from 100 and the remainder was the per-

---

[2] In recent years, the burden for pension trustees has been raised to the so-called "prudent expert rule" in which the fiduciary is expected to have expertise beyond that of an ordinary person.

centage of the investor's assets that were to be invested in stocks. Thus, a 55-year-old investor was to have 45% in stocks and 55% in bonds. For people under the age of 60, the result was a small increase over the old 40/60 rule in the percentage of their portfolio that would be in stocks. For people over 60, the result was more bonds.

THE MARKET AS MECCA

The market correction of 1969, in which the Dow Jones Industrial Average declined more than 15%, seemed to demonstrate why people approaching retirement needed to be cautious. The hammering that the market took in 1973 and 1974, during which time the Standard and Poor's 500 declined more than 40%, seemed to be proof positive that people approaching retirement could not afford to have too much of their retirement capital invested in the stock market. In 1975, the tide turned. Over the next 22 years, the S&P 500 averaged more than 15% returns per year. There were only three years with negative returns, and the worst year in the period was down less than 7.5%. By 1998, many investors, particularly those under 40, are wondering why anyone would want to own anything but stocks.

It was not just investment returns that drew investors and their advisors to the stock market like moths to a flame. In the last 50 years, enormous changes have occurred in the financial markets. Brokerage houses have invested hundreds of millions of dollars in advertising to attract the average investor. Think of all the slogans: "The Rock," "the old fashioned way," "one investor at a time," and numerous others. Commissions have plunged and you now can place trades by telephone, fax, and over the Internet. The names of some no-load mutual fund managers have become as well-known as sports stars.[3] Mutual funds have proliferated and their advertising dollars have spawned a magazine rack full of financial journals. Stock market investing—either through stocks, mutual funds, or more exotic derivatives—has become not just cocktail party conversation, but talk around the dinner table and the chatter of every barber, beautician, and cab driver.

In addition to the advertising and the increased-ease-decreased-cost of investing, another important factor underlies the current popularity of

---

[3] There are no trading cards—yet!

stock market investing. Many more people believe that they know how to participate in the stock market without getting burned.

THE ILLUSION OF CLARITY

In the last 50 years, the general level of knowledge about investments has greatly increased among the populace, but two factors in particular have helped to create the illusion that a useful understanding of the market is accessible to anyone who wants it. The first factor is the development of Modern Portfolio Theory (MPT), a series of studies that has led to the widely held belief that it is possible to optimize the risk/reward relationship in a portfolio of investments. Second is a body of data compiled by Ibbotson Associates, which seems to make a strong case for equity investments in preference to bond investments for long-term investors.[4] These two developments have encouraged millions of new investors to launch themselves into the rarefied air of the investment world in the fervent belief that they really know how to fly. The practical test of this mass migration will be to see how many arrive at their desired destination.

SECURITIES SELECTION AND TIMING

During the 1930s and 1940s, the art of securities analysis began to take form. It helped advisors give guidance that was a little more sophisticated than "buy low, sell high." In the wake of the Great Crash of 1929, it was clear that the ancient wisdom of "Don't put all your eggs in one basket," was not entirely adequate.[5] In the 1930s, the kind of advice that investors heard was more likely to be Henry Loeb's elegant paraphrase of Pudd'nhead Wilson's famous quip[6], "The greater safety lies in putting all your eggs in one basket and watching that basket." The sense of that

---

[4] There are many sources of tabulated data about investments: Morningstar, ValueLine, SEI, Lipper, Chase, Morgan Stanley, and others, but in my view, no one has done as much as Ibbotson to popularize investment data.

[5] The Talmud—a book of ancient Jewish wisdom—urged people to divide their wealth into three parts and invest a third in land, a third in business, and hold a third in reserve.

[6] "Put all your eggs in the one basket and—WATCH THAT BASKET!" *Pudd'nhead Wilson* by Mark Twain.

more contemporary wisdom roughly translates into the idea that there are times to be in the market and times to be out.[7] You don't have to be a great economic historian to know that there were times to be in the market and times to be out. There were times to buy gold and times to sell it. There were times to own real estate and times to rent. The idea that it is possible to make judgments about these cycles is called "market timing." There is no question that if anyone could really do market timing consistently, they would not have to work for a living. One of the persistent illusions of the financial marketplace is that it is possible to study the movement of asset prices to determine the underlying factors that cause these movements. From this study, so the theory goes, it is possible to predict the movement of asset prices and to time the purchase and sale of assets to profit from the price changes. There are people who claim to have benefited from these so-called timing services. There probably also were people who claimed to have benefited from snake oil potions in the 19th Century. It is, of course, possible that there really were benefits, but no one has been able to make a convincing proof for either snake oil or market timing.

GRAHAM CRACKERS ARE NOURISHING

The modern science of securities selection took a giant stride in 1934 when Benjamin Graham and David Dodd published a book called *Security Analysis*. In this book, which has been so influential that the 1934 edition was recently re-published, Graham and Dodd spelled out the process for evaluating securities as investments. The basic sense of the book was that investors should examine the value of the company issuing a security. If the market value of the company's securities was less than the value that an investor might pay to buy the whole company, the securities are undervalued and should be bought. The ideas in this book, now more than 60 years old, are still fundamental to the selection of

---

[7] A well-known study by the University of Michigan revealed that in the 1,276 days of the bull market from August 12, 1982, to August 25, 1987, about 85.6% of the gain came in 3.1% of the time. Forty days out of the 1,276 days of the rally produced 22% of the total 26.3% gain. Other studies for other rallies show similar results. Missing just a few days out of a big rally can be very important.

individual stocks and bonds. It may not be entirely fair to say that the science of securities analysis has not changed in the last 50 years, but the basics certainly have not. Analysts still pore over corporate reports, looking for clues about which securities are undervalued so they can buy low and sell high. Today, electronic data bases and computers make it possible to screen and analyze vast quantities of data, but the basic process is largely unchanged.

In 1949, Benjamin Graham wrote another book called *The Intelligent Investor*, intended for lay persons. In this book, he spelled out a series of practical rules for investment selection. Two things about Graham's second book seem particularly striking from today's perspective. First was his recognition that the "truth" about investments has changed from time to time and that today's "truth" may be irrelevant or worse at some time in the future. The second point was that the seeds of investor ruin typically are sown when, in good times, investors assume imprudent risks. The trap he says is to ". . . assume that prosperity is synonymous with safety."[8]

He talks of the "margin of safety" that investors always should maintain. Margin of safety is the idea that even if there is an economic "twitch," the value of the company will still be more than the price you are paying for its securities. I am certain that, at some point in the future, Graham's chapter on "Margin of Safety" will be widely quoted, but currently it is not very popular.

PORTFOLIO MANAGEMENT

While the fundamentals of security selection have not changed much in 60 years, the science of putting together a portfolio of investments has undergone dramatic changes from a variety of sources. Academicians have done a lot of interesting work that has percolated through to financial professionals and, in some cases, even to the public. The markets have soared, carrying with them the hopes and dreams of millions of new investors. Data about securities performance has become ubiquitous and easier to understand. Communication about investment strategy has become unavoidable. You would have to live in a cave to avoid hearing, reading, seeing, and being questioned on investment strategies. The level of financial informa-

---

[8] Graham, Benjamin. *The Intelligent Investor*, NY, Harper & Brothers, 1959, p. 257.

tion and expertise has changed as radically and dramatically as other areas of science and technology.

MODERN PORTFOLIO THEORY

Modern Portfolio Theory (MPT) currently is the predominant model used by investment managers and financial professionals. The theory has evolved over the last 50 years, and it gives us the following guidance:

- ➥ The portfolio, not the individual security, is the appropriate focus of investment management.
- ➥ The prices of various asset classes do not move together, but tend to have a dynamic relationship that is somewhat predictable.
- ➥ It is necessary to use a variety of different kinds of assets to structure a portfolio that optimizes risk and reward.
- ➥ The selection of individual securities is less important than the selection of investment categories.
- ➥ It is not possible to add significant value to an investment portfolio by timing the purchase and sale of securities.

EVOLUTION OF MODERN PORTFOLIO THEORY

Modern Portfolio Theory began to emerge in the mid-1950s after the publication of an article by Harry Markowitz entitled, "Portfolio Selection." This article in the March 1952 *Journal of Finance* began the evolution of MPT. At the time, Markowitz was a 25-year-old graduate student at the University of Chicago. His work ultimately earned him the Nobel Prize in Economics in 1990. The importance of Markowitz's work was that it shifted the focus from the selection of individual securities to the process of structuring a portfolio of securities. Markowitz assumed that investors are always trying to get the highest return that they can for a given level of risk. As a result, the market is constantly repricing individual assets to reflect their risk/reward relationships. He reasoned that, since there was little inefficiency in the pricing of individual securities, the more interesting challenge was to develop a methodology for optimizing risk and return in a portfolio of securities. He theorized that, by considering the relationship of asset returns—one asset category to another—it should be possible to devise a portfolio that optimized risk and return more efficiently than any one asset or asset category. In other words, a portfolio of well-selected assets had a better risk/reward relationship than any one asset. It seems obvious today that a portfolio in which some assets go up when others go down is a lower-risk portfolio than one in which all assets move together. Fifty years ago, this was a revolutionary thought, and the revolution has not yet ended.

Markowitz derived an equation that allows a statistician—or even a lay person using the appropriate software—to calculate the risk and reward potential of a portfolio. The equation considers the rate of return and the risk[9] of the individual assets, the weighting of the assets in the portfolio, and the way that the asset categories move relative to one another. The technical term for the movement of asset categories relative to one another is "covariance."[10] By studying the rates of return, the risk, and the covariance of various asset categories, it is possible to assess the historical risk and reward of any portfolio. It also is possible to compare the returns of various portfolios with the same risk level and determine the most efficient portfolio combination. Conversely, it is possible to compare the risks of various portfolios with the same rates of return and determine the most efficient. It is clear that, for any given level of risk, there is a portfolio that gives the highest possible return.

By plotting the optimized returns of portfolios with various risk levels, Markowitz derived a curve called "the efficient frontier," as seen in Figure 8-1. This curve reflects the highest return available at each level of risk. Each point along this curve represents a unique combination of asset categories. It is possible to compare the risk and return potential of a portfolio with the efficient frontier and determine the extent to which the portfolio can be optimized. By studying these combinations, an

---

[9] Typically measured by standard deviation of investment returns over time.

[10] Covariance is the tendency of the returns of various asset categories to move in consort with or independently of one another. The measure of covariance is the "correlation coefficient," which is the statistical probability that asset categories will move together or separately. A correlation coefficient of +1 means they move identically. A correlation coefficient of 0 means that they are totally independent, and -1 means that they move in opposite directions.

investor or financial consultant can find important information, but the truth about the future is not to be found on the efficient frontier.

The reason that Markowitz's methodology does not predict the future is obvious. The mathematics are based on past history, and as every mutual fund prospectus reminds us, "Past performance is no assurance of future results." [11] If the future is exactly like the past, this methodology will allow you to position your portfolio perfectly to achieve an optimum risk/reward relationship. If, however, the future were predictable based on past history, there would be still better ways to devise your investment strategy. [12] Since it is not, we need to keep thinking and looking.

ANOTHER MPT PROBLEM

It is essential to note that, in 1952, there was only one computer in the world that could process alphanumeric data—UNIVAC. As a result of this limited computational horsepower, Markowitz chose to use the standard deviation of investment performance as a surrogate for risk. Standard deviation encompasses both positive volatility and negative volatility. It would be a rare investor who thought that positive volatility (an increase in price) was a risk that was to be avoided. The more intu-

---

[11] It is amazing that, while the SEC requires mutual funds to include this warning on their advertisements, they do not require it on asset allocation presentations.

[12] Pick the winner and bet the bundle.

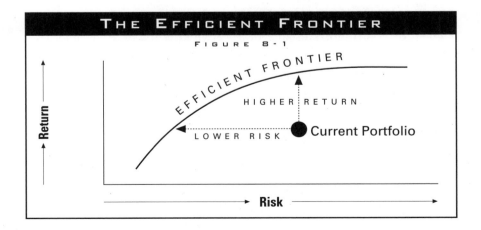

THE EFFICIENT FRONTIER

FIGURE 8-1

itive step would be to use only negative volatility by measuring something called "semi-variance." In 1952, the computing horsepower just did not exist to focus on negative volatility. The implications of this choice are very significant because they help lead to the conclusion that the market is efficient. It is hypothesized that gains above some norm will be recaptured by losses sufficient to bring the average back to the norm. This is dogma, and I stand to lose my finance merit badge by telling you that I find this slightly counter-intuitive.

PORTFOLIO PERFORMANCE

The next major piece of MPT was placed into the puzzle with the development of the Capital Asset Pricing Model (CAPM) by William Sharpe, a student of Markowitz's. This work is considered so important that Sharpe was the co-recipient with Markowitz of the Nobel prize for Economics in 1990. One of the important insights that flows out of Sharpe's work is the idea of "diversifiable risk" and "non-diversifiable risk." To make this as simple as I can, the idea is that it is possible to diversify a portfolio so that the risk to the portfolio of a single business failure is greatly reduced. This is diversifiable risk. If the portfolio is composed only of stocks, and the stock market suffers a broad decline, no amount of diversification among stocks will protect the value of the portfolio. This is non-diversifiable risk.

Sharpe also contributed something called the "Sharpe Ratio," which is a measure of the additional return that a given portfolio will achieve by assuming an additional measure of risk. It is a measure of the "efficiency" of a portfolio. This all sounds very impressive in terms of moving forward toward a more scientific basis for structuring a portfolio of investments, a topic near and dear to the heart of any retiree with assets to invest. Again, we are dealing with dogma and I am in danger of excrutiation when I confide to you (soto voce) that this magnificent contribution to financial management is an academic work based on some pretty unrealistic assumptions, namely:

- ➔ There are no taxes or transaction costs.
- ➔ All investors have the same time horizon.

➽ All investors have the same expected return.

➽ All investment decisions are rational.

➽ Investors can borrow funds at Treasury bill interest rates.

A house may offer good shelter without having a perfect foundation. There is use in Sharpe's work, even though it does not offer the perfect answers that many would like. It is also good to remember that the higher the structure is built, the more important is the quality of the foundation. As other academicians base their post-graduate studies on Sharpe's CAPM, there is more and more danger that the arbitrary assumptions at the base will produce results that are not very reliable.

BRINSON ET. AL.

The next piece of the MPT puzzle was placed on the table with the publication of the article, "Determinants of Portfolio Performance," in the July/August 1986 issue of *Financial Analysts Journal*. The article was co-authored by Gary P. Brinson, L. Randolph Hood, and Gilbert L. Beebower. For better or for worse, this article changed the world of investment management forever. The article reported the results of a study of the investment performance achieved by 91 large pension plans over a 10-year period, 1974 to 1983. The study examined the variations in the returns achieved by the pension plans in terms of three variables:

1. Market timing
2. Security selection
3. Asset allocation

The study came to the startling conclusion that almost 94% of the variance in performance could be explained by asset allocation. A relatively trivial 1.7% was added by market timing and about 4.2% was added by security selection.

In 1991, Brinson and Beebower, with a new associate, Brian D. Singer, published, "Determinants of Portfolio Performance II: An Update." This study updated the original report by examining 82 large pension plans during the period 1977 to 1987. The second study generally confirmed the findings of the first study. The selection of individual securities and the timing of purchases and sales added little to performance. The chief determinant of the performance of these portfolios was the choice of asset categories. In other words, they concluded that the choice of stocks or bonds was far more important than the choice of which stock or which bond or when they were bought or sold.

In the fractious world of investment managers, it is surprising that these studies have won such wide acceptance, which is not to say that there has been no criticism. One study from the prestigious Frank Russell research organization argues that if the Brinson studies had started from an assumption that the portfolios were invested as an average pension plan is and not from the assumption that the pension plan was invested in cash, the difference attributable to asset categories—while still important—would not have been so overwhelming. Another criticism that can be made is that not every individual investor operates within the narrow constraints of a pension plan. If the analysis had included a wider variety of portfolios, the conclusion might have been different and more generally applicable.

Again, my financial merit badge may be at risk, but I have a slightly different opinion about the significance of these widely quoted studies. I believe that these studies are instructive on the importance of asset allocation, but it is clear to me that the selection of individual assets carries a much greater risk and reward potential in the real world than it does in these studies. It is, for example, possible in real life to go bankrupt by an inappropriate selection of investments. Individual investors and even mutual fund managers can select from a much broader range of assets than the managers of large pension funds, and in that broader range, some real dangers and some real opportunities exist.

THE PRACTICAL SIDE OF ASSET ALLOCATION

In addition to the theoretical problems underlying asset allocation theory, a number of practical problems crop up as well. Many practitioners use an asset allocation model that they buy from a supplier. They know how this "black box" works, but they are not prepared to analyze the data on which the model is based. Most are surprised to find that the indexes which simulate the performance of various asset categories may not have much to do with the actual asset. Still others find that the period covered by the data distorts the results. I recall a practitioner who, some years ago, complained that his asset allocation model was recommending a very high percent of fixed annuities. When he looked into the "black box," he found that the data on which these recommendations were based was the yield of fixed annuities from 1975 to 1985, a period of very high yields. In the early 1990s, when this question arose, yields had fallen below the lowest point in the 10-year data sample. A perfect example of what computer people call GIGO, "garbage in, garbage out."

A skilled practitioner can overcome these deficiencies, but more challenges lay ahead. The task of translating the asset allocation recommendations into an investment portfolio is immensely complicated. It is essential to understand that the process of "optimizing" a portfolio using asset allocation is a very delicate matter. Small changes in the portfolio and in the data that describe the various asset categories often will cause unexpectedly large changes in the recommendations. It is, for example, conceivable that an asset allocation program that recommends 35% "growth" based on the performance data of the S&P 500 might change that recommendation dramatically if the program were informed that the performance of the growth asset would differ slightly from the S&P. If the program knew that it was going to get one point less performance from a sluggish S&P 500 index fund, or 2% more variance from a "quasi-index fund" that is trying to outperform the S&P, it might shift the allocation from 35% to 20% or 50%.

If you truly believe in asset allocation, it is hard to argue for anything but index funds, if the indexing is "real." Unfortunately, as soon as you get beyond the S&P 500, the notion of index funds gets a little hazy. Funds that are trying to index the Morgan Stanley Capital International (MSCI) Europe/Australasia/Far East (EAFE) have their work cut out for them. The EAFE index covers 1,125 companies in 20 different countries. Some funds attempt to emulate this index with representative stocks in the various countries rather than with all 1,125 stocks. Every asset category has similar problems, so it is not easy to find investments that actually mimic the data on which the asset allocation recommendations are based. To make matters worse, some mutual funds try to beat the averages by various strategies within the fund. For example, some funds increase their cash positions when the market looks dangerous. Others will go completely to cash. Some funds have considerable flexibility in their investment policy. While they call themselves "growth funds," they may be in bonds or small companies or foreign stocks, which means that they are not entirely suitable for implementing an asset allocation strategy.

While I believe in asset allocation, I'm not a "true believer." I prefer the use of managed funds rather than index funds in the asset allocation process. The management of the funds attempts to use intelligence to beat the index and add value to the process. At the same time, these funds must have a statistical similarity to the data used in the asset allocation model. Various sources provide information that allows the advisor or the investor to monitor the statistics.

The investor being guided by asset allocation has one more principal hurdle to clear. Asset allocation is based on the historical performance of various asset categories. We all know that, while history does not repeat itself, the study of past events is our only guide to the future. Past patterns of investment performance are unlikely to repeat themselves exactly, but future patterns are expected to be similar to the past. What happens if you or your advisor sense a sea change, the end of one trend and the beginning of another? Are you to ignore this because the data in the asset allocation model does not reflect what has yet to occur? Remember my story about the fixed annuity yields. Is the investor supposed to assume that interest rates are going back up to the high levels that they were at a few years ago? Another apt illustration of this problem is in the area of emerging markets. The emerging markets index began in 1987, so it is just 10 years old. For many practitioners, it does not make sense to include an asset category with less than 10 years of data in their asset allocation modeling. Now that the index is 10 years old, they are including this category complete with the fact that, in 3 of the 10 years, the category was up more than 50% for the year. Is that likely to occur again as the growth cycle of the emerging nations moves to a higher level? No one knows, but I think it would be foolish to let the data override logic. In my opinion, an informed observer may well have a vision of the future that is a suitable basis for adjusting the recommendations of the asset allocation model. I call this a "forward looking asset allocation." It uses statistics based on expectations about the future rather than statistics about the past to model an "optimized" portfolio. Past performance must guide our expectations, but we must not let it guide us off the cliff.

The bottom line on implementing an asset allocation strategy is that the advisor needs to understand the data on which the model bases its recommendations. The advisor then must select investments that truly emulate the categories selected and which will be guided by that investment strategy over time. These funds are rarely in the headlines, and for some investors the idea of investing in "mediocre" funds does not seem very attractive. Personally, I really believe the tale about the tortoise and the hare.

This variation on the idea of asset allocation, which I call "forward looking asset allocation," is a lot like the old way of creating a diversified portfolio. The financial advisor makes a recommendation for a portfolio based on an understanding of the investor's needs, the past performance of assets, and the advisor's expectation about the future. The advisor then uses an asset allocation model to test the efficiency of the recommended portfolio against the model's ideal portfolio. If the results seem reasonably efficient, the advisor implements the recommendation. If the recommendation proves to be inefficient in the model's analysis, the advisor can try to make adjustments or simply can understand the source of the inefficiency and use the recommendation in spite of the model's frown.

THE IBBOTSON DATA

Another major cause underlying the current popularity of stock investments has been the work done by Professor Roger G. Ibbotson and his associates. For a number of years, Ibbotson Associates has produced information about the risks and returns of various classes of investments and compared these data to inflation. In addition to the data on investment returns and the volatility (standard deviation) of those returns, they also have provided important information about the correlation coefficients of various investments—their statistical tendency to move in conjunction with or independently of one another. The translucent clarity of this data has given academics, investment advisors, financial planners, stock brokers, and other advisors a new ability to explain the historical realities of the investment world. It also has given portfolio managers the ability to use mathematics, based on Markowitz's work and the Ibbotson data, to structure optimized portfolios using the asset allocation methodology. What had previously seemed like a tangle of arcane theories has become transparent and seemingly obvious to anyone.

The basic data that Ibbotson Associates produces is contained in a yearbook called, *Stocks, Bonds, Bills and Inflation*.[13] This has become the SBBIble (Sorry, I couldn't resist) of investment advisors. The yearbook presents a series of data that shows the month-by-month results accrued for various investments since 1925. Now, more than 70 years of pristine data allows us to see clearly the results that were achieved by investments in large companies, small companies,[14] corporate bonds, Treasury bonds, and Treasury bills, including how those results compared with inflation and with one another.

Year after year, the Ibbotson data have chronicled the consistent long-term rise of the stock market. The power and clarity of these num-

---

[13] *Stocks, Bonds, Bills and Inflation Yearbook*, Chicago, Ibbotson Associates, 1996. (312) 616-1620.
[14] Small company stocks were added to the data in 1981.

ANNUAL TOTAL RETURNS	
For Various Asset Categories, 1926-1996	
FIGURE 8-2	
Small Company Stocks	12.6%
Large Company Stocks	10.7%
Long-Term Corporate Bonds	5.6%
Long-Term Government Bonds	5.1%
Intermediate-Term Government Bonds	5.2%
U. S. Treasury Bills	3.7%
Inflation	3.1%

Source: Ibbotson Associates–*SBBI 1997 Yearbook*. Returns are arithmetic mean for the period.

bers, which scream that stocks consistently outperform cash and bonds in any intermediate and longer-term period, has become the mantra of every broker, financial journalist, and financial planner. People who know little else about the stock market can tell you that stocks have averaged annual returns of more than 10% since 1926. The story of investment returns is summed up in Figure 8-2.

THE IMPLICATIONS OF THE IBBOTSON DATA

The basic story is simple. On a quite consistent basis, common stocks have yielded total returns (dividends plus capital appreciation) approximately twice that of bonds. Common stocks and the stocks of small companies are the only assets in this universe that have significantly outperformed inflation—after taxes. The differences in the yields of the various classes of assets are very significant over longer periods of time. Figure 8-3 shows the mathematical results of compounding $10,000 at various rates of return over various periods of time. While the rates of return are those achieved by the Ibbotson asset classes over a 71-year period, they do not represent the actual results of any investment because the actual investment results varied from year to year.

VALUE OF $10,000 COMPOUNDED						
Over Various Periods–at Various Rates of Return						
FIGURE 8-3						
Year	3.7%	5.1%	5.2%	5.6%	10.7%	12.6%
5	$11,992	$12,824	$12,885	$13,132	$16,624	$18,101
10	$14,381	$16,445	$16,602	$17,244	$27,636	$32,763
15	$17,246	$21,088	$21,391	$22,644	$45,942	$59,303
20	$20,681	$27,043	$27,562	$29,736	$76,375	$107,342
25	$24,801	$34,679	$35,514	$39,048	$126,967	$194,294
30	$29,741	$44,471	$45,759	$51,276	$211,071	$351,683
35	$35,666	$57,029	$58,959	$67,334	$350,887	$636,566
40	$42,771	$73,132	$75,968	$88,421	$583,317	$1,152,221

This is only a table of mathematical calculations. It uses the 71-year arithmetical mean return for the various asset categories reported in Ibbotson Associates, SBBI 1997, but it does not represent the actual investment results achieved by these asset categories over time.

In other words, the timing of returns can cause results to vary even if the average returns are the same.[15]

It almost seems like a mistake that the difference between 10.7% and 12.6% can make a $568,904 difference in the growth of $10,000 over 40 years, but it is not an error. Minor differences in rates of return can make enormous differences over long periods of time. Given these enormous differences in the long-term performance of various asset classes, you might well ask, "Why would anyone want to own bonds?" Good question. Post-Depression retirees were told that their retirement savings should be invested only in the highest-quality bonds. More recently, retirees have been told that they should subtract their age from 100 and the resulting number was the percentage of their portfolio that should be invested in stocks (the so-called "Rule of 100"). The remainder was to be in bonds. In the face of increasing life expectancies, some advisors have started saying, "Subtract your age from 110 and the resulting number is the percent of your portfolio to invest in stocks." The "truth," as you would expect, is more complicated.

DEALING WITH VOLATILITY

The Ibbotson data say if you buy stocks and hold them long enough, you will be well rewarded. In the short term, however, you may lose money, in some cases "big money." There have been four years since 1926 when you would have lost more than 20% with investments in the stocks of large companies. In that period, there were seven years when investments in the stocks of small companies lost more than 20%, including two years when they lost more than 50%. The risk is that if you cannot[16] hold the stocks long enough for the averages to work their magic, you may suffer a loss. This seems to make it clear that holding assets for the long term is the way to reduce the risks associated with volatility.[17]

---

[15] $1,000 compounded at an arbitrary 10% per year for 10 years equals $2,593.74 and the average return is 10%. The same $1,000 compounded at 100% the first year and zero percent for another 9 years is worth $2,000 at the end of 10 years and has an average yield of 10%. Aren't numbers fun?

[16] Either emotionally or practically.

[17] Some experts, including Paul Samuelson, take exception to this view on technical terms that do not, in my view, invalidate the practical conclusion.

There is no question that the volatility of investment categories increases as the potential gain increases. The statistics bear out the belief that there is no free lunch. In other words, if you want the best possible returns, you also must accept the possibility of the worst possible returns, at least in the short run. In the long run, along with the expectation of high returns, comes the increasing likelihood that you will participate in a down market. Figure 8-4, however, shows that in the last 71 years—the period of the Ibbotson data—the longer you held stocks, the more likely it was that your investment return would exceed the rate of inflation.

Conversely, the longer you held long-term bonds, the more likely it was that your return would not exceed the rate of inflation. Among the bond investments, intermediate-term government bonds clearly have offered the best chance of betting inflation, but there was still a 30% possibility that over a 20-year period the yield on your intermediate bonds would not have exceeded the rate of inflation.

In today's world, where many retirees can expect to spend 20 or more years in retirement, these observations have important practical implications. Retirees should plan to maintain a consistent investment strategy for a long period. If their holding period is sufficiently long, their strategy should emphasize stock and real estate investment over bonds and cash.

A study of the data underlying Figure 8-4 shows that in the 1940s and 1950s, interest rates lagged behind the rate of inflation as the gov-

PROBABILITY OF OUTPERFORMING INFLATION

Various Investment Assets over Various Holding Periods, 1926-1996

FIGURE 8-4

	1-Year	5-Year	10-Year	15-Year	20-Year
Common Stock	69.0%	79.1%	88.7%	93.0%	100.0%
Small Company Stock	73.2%	82.1%	90.3%	98.2%	100.0%
Long-Term Corporate Bonds	64.8%	58.2%	53.2%	57.9%	51.9%
Long-Term Govt. Bonds	60.6%	53.7%	46.8%	40.4%	25.0%
Intermediate Govt. Bonds	60.6%	65.1%	66.1%	66.7%	69.2%
U. S. Treasury Bills	64.8%	60.3%	56.5%	64.9%	61.5%

Source: Ibbotson Associates–*SBBI 1997 Yearbook,* Chapter 2 and Figure 4-1.

ernment struggled to finance the Second World War. The yields on bonds also were slow to respond to rising inflation during the 1970s. The lesson to be learned is that bonds are not a good investment option when inflation starts into an upward trend.

There were two general periods when stocks were underperformers. First, of course, was the Great Depression just after the Crash of 1929. You may find it counter-intuitive, but stocks bought just after the Crash, in the early 1930s, were among the best buys ever. The other period when stocks underperformed both bonds and inflation was in 1973 and 1974, following the shock of the OPEC Crisis, which increased the price of oil from under $2 a barrel to over $10 a barrel in two years.

No one knows when or from where the next shock will strike, but it seems likely that well-selected stocks, held over long periods of time, will continue to outperform bonds and inflation.

SMALL COMPANY STOCK STRATEGY

The Ibbotson data seem to sing a seductive song about the stocks of small companies. If rates of return were the entire story, every investor would be invested 100% in the stocks of small companies because the data tell us that, over long periods, those stocks outperform other investments. In thinking about this data, it is supremely important to remember that the Ibbotson data are not about the stocks of just any small company. They are about the stocks that comprise the smallest 20% of the companies on the New York Stock Exchange and, since 1981, the stocks of equivalent size from the American Stock Exchange and the Over-the-Counter Market. This currently includes companies with a median market capitalization of about $165 million, which is much smaller than the holdings of a typical small-cap mutual fund (which Morningstar defines as $1 billion).

When you look at the data closely, you will see that the stocks of small companies have delivered wildly inconsistent results over the years. In 1929, 1931, and 1937, they were off 50% or more. In 1933, they were up more than 140%. In the years since 1940, returns have varied from minus 30% in 1973 to gains of more than 50% in 8 years. While the average return is the highest of any of the investment categories, the year-to-year deviation from that average also is the highest of any of the investment categories.

Think through those two facts: highest return in the long term, greatest variation year-to-year. The question that comes to mind is, "How long is long term?" "How long do I have to hold on to these small company stocks to achieve a return that beats the other investment categories?" This is a great question, but like most great questions, the answer is not so clear. Looking back to 1925, we can see that over the last 71 years, the stocks of small companies have been the top performing investment category in more than 30 of those years. There have been 12 periods of 15 years when the stocks of larger companies outperformed the stocks of small companies. One of those periods still is running, although the recent returns on small companies have been high and rising. No one can predict the future course of the market. It is possible that the internationalization of markets and the demand for large stocks in retirement plans have altered the fundamentals. On the other hand, the stocks of small companies may be overdue to perform better than the stocks of larger companies. "You pays your nickel, and you takes your chance."

SO WHAT'S A PROSPEROUS RETIREE TO DO?

Here is the bottom line. It is an eight-step process:

1. Use the retirement modeling process to determine the rate of return you will need to make your retirement capital base provide all the retirement cash flow you will need. Use the retirement planning model to determine the first year in which your capital base will decrease—this is called "the first year of capital withdrawal." Add this number of years to the number of years you expect to live. Divide this sum by two and you have the "average time to capital withdrawals" (ATCW).
2. Use the ATCW to select a basic asset allocation recommendation. This is an overall recommendation of the allocation between equity assets (stocks and real estate) and debt assets (bonds and cash).
3. Select a detailed asset allocation that has the potential to deliver the required rate of return. If the asset allocation is more aggressive than recommended based on the ATCW, give special consideration to the selection of asset categories.

4. Adjust the recommended basic asset allocation to reflect your personal, subjective risk tolerance and any other factors that may influence your thinking.
5. Implement the asset allocation.
6. Monitor the results.
7. Make changes from time to time as needed.
8. Make a comprehensive reassessment every 2 to 3 years.

What Rate of Return Do You Need?

Chapter 6 should have made it clear that determining this is not as easy as it looks. You can easily add up the income expected from all sources: Social Security, pension, retirement earnings, and other sources. Then you can look at your current budget, add the expenses that will be new in retirement, and subtract the expenses that will end in retirement. The difference between income and expenses (I assume that expenses will exceed income) needs to be made up by cash flow generated from your retirement capital. That is the easy part. The hard part is modeling the future of your income needs. I have explained in other parts of the book that income in the early years of the active phase of retirement will be increased by the expenses associated with realizing your "retirement dreams." Then, I think your income needs will tend to be an inflation-adjusted continuation of your pre-retirement budget. In the passive phase of retirement, I believe your expenses will tend to dwindle over time to a subsistence budget. Then, lastly, in the final phase of retirement, I expect your medical and nursing expenses to be largely covered by insurance and your living budget to be an inflation-adjusted continuation of the subsistence budget. For many retirees, this means that the retirement capital base must earn enough "surplus income" in the early phases of retirement so that the retirement capital base can grow large enough to provide the inflation-swollen income required later on. The rate of return that is required to pull all of this together can only be determined by modeling your retirement, as explained in some detail in Chapter 6.

Average Time to Capital Withdrawals

By now you understand that the asset categories with higher rates of return also have more variability in their returns—greater volatility, greater risk. To ameliorate this risk, you must be prepared to hold these more-productive assets for longer periods of time. It would not be wise to invest in the stocks of small companies if you knew that the money was needed in 12 months. It might not be stupid either if you really needed higher returns, but it would certainly be risky. The risk is that these high-ly volatile assets might not produce the high rate of return that you want. In that short time frame, they might actually decrease substantially in value. Thus, the average time to capital withdrawal (ATCW) is a key fac-tor in determining a basic asset allocation.

This is the kernel of truth that was buried in the old rules of thumb about shifting your asset allocation as you approached retirement. A more modern understanding of that concept includes the idea that you are likely to live for many years in retirement. During those many years, you will continue to need inflation protection. As a result, you are likely to require a rate of return that will have your retirement capital base producing more dollars in each of the early years of your retirement than you will need to live. As a result, your capital base is likely to continue to grow in the early years of your retirement. You are adding to your capital base in those years, not digging into your retirement capital. The first year in which the retirement model shows a decrease in your retirement capital base is the first year of capital withdraw-al. It is important to note that just taking income from your capital base is not considered a capital withdrawal as long as the base continues to grow. In many retirements, particularly those that plan to leave large bequests, the capital base may never decrease. In that case, the first year of capital with-drawal is the same as the last year of capital withdrawal—the year in which the last person included in the retirement plan dies. By adding the first year and the last year together and dividing by two we get the average time to capital withdrawal (ATCW).[18] Knowing how long the capital base is going to be in place leads us to a basic asset allocation recommendation.

An example may help make the ATCW concept a little clearer. Herb and Marie retire at 62. They believe that Marie is likely to live to age 94.

---

[18] A mathematically oriented reader will recognize that this is not a precise methodology, because the return on the portfolio is a geometric function. We are just guessing about the future and this simple method is a reasonable basis for planning.

They are both collecting Social Security benefits and pensions. They have retirement capital of $500,000, not including their home or personal property. In the early years of retirement, they are drawing about $1,000 a month from their capital base to supplement their other income sources and allow them to enjoy The Prosperous Retirement. This represents a draw of less than 2.5% on their capital base. Interest and dividends on the capital base are only $10,000 so they are selling a few shares of a mutual fund to generate the other $2,000 of cash flow. The after-tax rate of return on their investment portfolio is 7.75%. According to their retirement model, their capital base will continue to grow in value for the first 18 years of their retirement. In the 19th year of their retirement, they expect their capital base to begin to shrink. Their average time to capital withdrawal (ATCW) is 25 years [{(94–62) + 18 } / 2]. Their investment policy should be based on the expectation of continuing for 25 years.

Select a Basic Asset Allocation

The first step in selecting an asset allocation strategy is to determine the percent of the portfolio that will be in equity assets and the percent in bonds. In a retirement situation, a basic consideration—and therefore a good place to start—is the average time to capital withdrawal (ATCW). Figure 8-5 gives some basic guidelines. There are many reasons why these recommendations are just basic guidelines and not final answers. First, they are not all-encompassing. Retirees with ATCWs of less than 4 years probably should not have more than 10% or 15% of their assets in stocks. Retirees

BASIC ASSET ALLOCATION RECOMMENDATION									
Based on Average Time to Capital Withdrawal and the Related Rate of Return									
FIGURE 8-5									
Average Time to Capital Withdrawal (ATCW) in Years									
	4	6	8	10	12	14	16	18	20
Equity	15.0%	20.0%	30.0%	40.0%	50.0%	60.0%	70.0%	80.0%	90.0%
Debt	85.0%	80.0%	70.0%	60.0%	50.0%	40.0%	30.0%	20.0%	10.0%
RoR	5.5%	6.3%	6.8%	7.3%	7.9%	8.4%	8.9%	9.4%	10.0%

with more than 20 years of average time to withdrawals logically can have any portion of their portfolio in stocks that they want.

What happens if the ATCW is 10 years and the retiree needs a portfolio return of 8% rather than the 7.3% indicated? Given an ACTW of 10 years, it is not hard to see that increasing the equity exposure to 50% or even 60% is not impossible. It also might be possible, within the 40% equity/60% debt recommendation, to use asset categories with higher potential returns. Another alternative is to use a higher proportion of equity assets, but lower-risk assets. For example, rather than using a 40% equity allocation composed of higher-risk stocks, it might make more sense to increase the allocation to 50% but shift to lower-risk categories. Rather than 10% small company, 15% foreign, and 15% large company stocks, it might make sense to go to 5% small company, 10% foreign, 20% large company, and 15% mid-cap value stocks. Using an asset allocation model will tell you how this shift in strategy has affected risk and reward in the past.

This seems like the appropriate time to make the point that not all 50/50 portfolios have the same risk and reward characteristics. It should be obvious that a portfolio with 50% small company stocks has a higher risk and reward potential than a portfolio with 50% stocks of large companies. Likewise, a portfolio of high-yield bonds or foreign bonds has higher risk/reward characteristics than a money market portfolio or intermediate-term government bonds. It is conceivable that a 100% stock portfolio might have less risk than a 100% bond portfolio, depending on the nature of the actual assets.

Adjust the Asset Allocation

The retiree, working with the financial advisor, should adjust the basic asset allocation recommendation to reflect the retiree's needs, subjective risk tolerance, and other unique factors that may influence this decision. If the required rate of return is higher than indicated for the basic recommendation, some changes must be made. An increased commitment to equities or the use of higher risk/reward asset categories may be appropriate. In other cases, it may force the process back to the modeling phase to see how to increase retirement earnings, lower the budget, postpone retirement, or find some other way to lower the required rate of return.

Implement the Asset Allocation

Once the basic asset allocation is determined, it is necessary to select the asset categories to be represented in the portfolio. Then, select specific investments to represent these asset categories in your portfolio. This is where the rubber meets the road. Anyone who does not feel nervous when making these decisions probably is not paying close enough attention. There are endless reasons for concern. "Have I assessed my longevity properly?" "Is the rate of return that I am shooting for really high enough?" "Is the asset allocation really right?" "Are markets in the future going to be anything like they were in the past?" "Have I selected the right asset categories to consider?" "Are the specific investments that I have selected going to deliver the right results?" There are more ways to get it wrong than there are to get it right. The good news is that you do not have to get it exactly right to get satisfactory results. The decisions that are made can be changed—in fact, they probably will be changed—as we get new information and better insights.

It is very important to stick with seasoned alternatives. Do not select assets or asset categories that represent new ways of investing that have not been through the market cycle. Track records are no indication of future performance, but they are the only basis that we have for selecting assets. Ideas about how an unproven investment may do in the future may be persuasive, but they are also pure speculation.

Monitor the Results

Two basic questions are helpful in monitoring results: "How are we doing?" and "What can we do to improve performance going forward?" There is another question that is more difficult but much more interesting; that is, "Are things unfolding in a way that was encompassed by the range of possibilities that I expected when I made these investment decisions?" This is where I love asset allocation. It sets up a range of expectations. As events unfold, we can compare the actual results with those expectations and see if something unexpected is happening. We are always looking for the unexpected, because it may be a warning sign that the plan needs to be re-evaluated.

Make Changes From Time to Time

It is a good idea to make changes from time to time. Change may even improve the performance of your portfolio, but the bigger benefit is that it gives you a sense of control and increases your confidence when the tides change. It is important to make only small changes and to stick with your basic asset allocation strategy, unless something fundamental changes. You may decide to exchange one mutual fund for another, or to sell this stock or bond in favor of another, but be slow to change the basic allocation. Do not make fundamental changes unless you have a really rational reason for doing it. Do not allow market performance, and the resulting emotions, to push you into a change in asset allocation. Do not chase hot asset categories, and be slow to dump cold ones.

Comprehensive Reassessment Every 2 to 3 Years

Every two or three years, it is appropriate to sit down with your financial advisor and review the entire investment strategy. Look at the capital base, the budget, and the rate of return that you are seeking. Look at the economy and the markets. Review the opinions about the economic tides. Consider your longevity expectations and any changes in your personal situation. It is this type of factor that can properly lead to a fundamental revision of your asset allocation policy. It may be that no change is required, but it is always comforting to know that you checked.

CONCLUSION

There is no certainty in nature, certainly none in the investment world. Smart people have preceded us, though, and the legacy of their work should command our respect. Modern Portfolio Theory and asset allocation are important tools. They do not provide the perfect answer to the question, "What shall I own and when shall I own it?" but they give us a reasonable basis for making a guess. They also give us a basis for evaluating the results we get from our choices. The method of considering the period over which you will be holding your investments gives you a logical starting point for selecting a basic investment strategy. The process of picking the individual investments puts the plan into motion. Once the strategy is implemented, you need to keep comparing the results with your needs and expectations to see if or when changes are required. Like all great commanders, you follow the best strategy you can, you implement the strategy with all the skill you can command, you make adjustments as required, and you hope for the best outcome. Eisenhower really did understand about planning.

9.

MANAGING THE PROSPEROUS RETIREMENT

*"Some great men owe most of their greatness to the ability
of detecting in those they destine for their tools the exact
quality of strength that matters for their work."*
—JOSEPH CONRAD, *Lord Jim*

SYNOPSIS: Managing The Prosperous Retirement serves two purposes. First, it keeps your affairs up-to-date and on track. Second, it gives you the comfort and peace-of-mind that comes from knowing that important matters are in good order. Management begins with the establishment of objectives. These objectives help to define the activities that are necessary. The goals and activities point to the advisors who will be helpful in keeping your retirement wheel rolling smoothly. Some activities in the management process are repeated weekly, others quarterly, and still others annually. Some activities require assistance, while others can be done by yourself. The choice of retirement advisors is crucial. You need to be able to place your complete trust in these advisors. Surround yourself with the best advisors you can find, and deal with them in a way that gives you the full benefit of their expertise.

GOOD MANAGEMENT ALWAYS has clear objectives. The management of your retirement has two main objectives. First, you want to keep your retirement on track. Second, you want to build the feeling of confidence, comfort, and peace-of-mind that can come only from knowing that your retirement really is on the right track. It is only with that peace-of-mind that you can experience The Prosperous Retirement.

THE RETIREMENT MODEL

In Chapter 6, we built a model of your retirement. We figured out how much your retirement was likely to cost year-by-year. We estimated the various sources of income. We tried to guess at your longevity and the rate of inflation. Finally, we figured out what your capital base might consist of, and how you could use that capital to provide the cash flow you would need to keep the retirement wheel turning. In Chapter 7, we considered various kinds of investments and the returns that you might expect from them. In Chapter 8, we examined investment strategies to optimize the productivity of your portfolio. Out of these discussions emerged a picture of what it was going to take to build your prosperous retirement. Remember, plans are powerful only if they are used to guide actions.

IMPLEMENTING THE MODEL

Once you have modeled your retirement, you need to take steps to put plans into action and to make certain that plans stay on track. You have to work with your trusted advisors to put the plans into motion. Your financial planner is the quarterback of your retirement management team. The financial planner is a generalist who understands the entire range of issues that affect your retirement. The financial planner helps you to identify the issues in your retirement, and then to find the professionals you need to deal with those issues. The financial planner also ensures that you are getting the support you need from all the professionals on your team. You work with the estate planning attorney to implement the estate plan. You work with the tax advisor to implement the tax management plan. You work with the insurance advisor to implement the various risk management strategies. You work with your financial planner to develop an appropriate asset allocation. You then work with an investment manager to manage your investments in accordance with the asset allocation. There are many details to be taken care of, but you work your way through them one step at a time.

KEEPING THE PLAN ON TRACK

A plan for anything as complex as your retirement cannot possibly be so perfect that it does not need to be adjusted as the future lays down its cards one at a time. To make the necessary adjustments, you and your financial planner need to keep an eye on what is happening and determine what modifications are necessary. The plan to achieve The Prosperous Retirement is based on a number of assumptions. If reality unwinds in a way that is different from the assumptions, it is important to know as soon as possible so that remedial steps can be taken. It would, for example, be important to know that investment returns had fallen behind projections and the capital base was declining. The sooner you saw this trend, the easier it might be to find a remedy. You might decide to increase your retirement earnings, or to reduce your life-style and budget to alleviate the drain on your retirement capital. In other circumstances, the retirement capital may have started ahead of projections because of some earlier period in which investment returns were higher than anticipated. In that case, remedial actions might be unnecessary because the recent decline was just bringing your capital base back in line with the projections in the plan. The important thing is to know what is going on and to think about what needs to be done. Out of the clarity of your understanding comes the comfort of knowing that all the fun you are having is not from adrenaline-induced skating on thin ice.

THE MANAGEMENT PROCESS

The central objective of managing your retirement is to know how your retirement actually is doing compared to the model that you built. To accomplish that goal, at least three levels of financial management are involved:

1. Strategic review
2. Operational oversight
3. Selection and management of advisors

In addition—and this is not entirely separated from financial management—there is the management of all the non-financial issues that were discussed in Chapter 2.

STRATEGIC REVIEW

The strategic review deals with the big-picture issues and probably should be done once a year. It comprises three steps. First, spend a little time asking yourself about the big-picture questions that were discussed in Chapter 3. A full stomach and a glass of port seem to help with this big-picture thinking. The one question to keep asking in your annual strategic review is, "What important facts do I know today that I did not know when I made the retirement plan?" You are not rethinking the plan, you are just comparing reality with the assumptions.

- Have your life-style and budget gotten ahead of themselves?
- Have your expectations about the future, particularly the year ahead, changed since last year?
- Have you started slowing down financially?
- Is your health still good or are problems beginning to appear?
- Does it seem more or less important to leave money to your heirs or charities than it did last year?
- Have your investments done what they were supposed to have done?
- Have the tax laws changed in some way that affects your income or estate tax picture?
- Have your insurance needs changed in any way?
- How are your advisors doing?
- If you actually did a financial model—and I really hope you did—how does your current situation compare with the model?
- Are affairs so far out of whack that you may need to redo the plan?

This end-of-the-year review may seem like an enormous amount of work, but if you are doing the operational reviews on a regular basis and keeping abreast of the financial news, the end-of-the-year review is not much work, it is just a change in perspective. Hopefully, this period of reflection will help get your thoughts in order for the next two phases.

The next step is to get together with your spouse and review your thoughts. This raises an interesting point. In many families, one person carries the main burden of managing the family finances. That is fine and good if that person is going to outlive his or her spouse. If there is even a chance that the spouse may outlive the financial manager, it is wise—

in fact, I think obligatory—to include the spouse in the management of the family finances. The spouse should attend meetings with the advisors. He or she should know where the papers are and understand the strategic plan. The less-involved spouse need not be informed about all the details, but do not position that spouse for failure by keeping him or her in the dark on important matters. At this meeting, the managing spouse should explain his or her conclusions about the state of the retirement and suggest a program of activities for the year ahead. The conclusions should certainly include a comparison of the current state of affairs and the plan that was made. The program of activities should include the work that is to be done with advisors and by advisors.

PLANNING THE ANNUAL CYCLE

If the idea of an annual cycle that begins on January 1 makes sense to you, begin your strategic planning session in December of the preceding year. At that time, lay out your management plan for the coming year. Do it in writing on a calendar. Put down a day for the strategic review in December. Put down operational reviews every six months. Some people prefer a review every three months, while, for others, once a year is enough. Whatever makes you comfortable is the right answer. Put down your tax planning in October and your tax preparation in March and April. Put in a risk management review (see Chapter 10) and an estate planning review (see Chapter 11). Put in two hours every week to review the financial headlines and an hour to input your budget data. Does this seem like over-kill? I think not. You are managing a business called "The Prosperous Retirement," and you will be well served to give it your attention. Your retirement may work satisfactorily without your attention, but it will work better with your attention. In addition, you will have the security and satisfaction of knowing that things are in order.

In earlier phases of your life, it probably was possible to get along very nicely without all these controls. In those halcyon days, if things got out of control, you had time and the ability to pour your energy into getting things back on track. If lack of attention led to a loss of capital, there was both time to recover and an active stream of income with which to clean up the mess. In retirement, there is less time and a reduced stream of income, so it is more important that problems be detected and corrected as quickly as possible.

While you have the calendar out, as in Figure 9-1, you might as well add items for the management of the non-financial issues: vacations, exercise, an annual physical exam, your dental check up, a retreat with your spouse to assess "the state of the union," time for spiritual development, and the annual retirement party. I really think that it is entirely appropriate to celebrate your retirement once a year. If this idea embarrasses you, it can be disguised as a Fourth of July celebration. It is, after all, about independence. The annual party helps to keep you focused on your wonderful retirement. It gives you an occasion for complimenting yourself on the terrific job you

PLANNING CALENDAR	
FIGURE 9-1	
Weekly Tasks	Budget Input and Review Financial News Review
January	State of the Retirement Meeting with Spouse Strategic Planning Meeting with Advisor Quarterly Estimated Taxes *(January 15)*
February	Quarterly Operational/Investment Review Annual Dental Check-Up
March	Tax Data to Accountant
April	Review and Submit Tax Return/Quarterly Estimated Taxes *(April 15)*
May	Quarterly Operational/Investment Review
June	Lunch with Insurance Advisor Annual Physical Exam Quarterly Estimated Taxes *(June 15)*
July	Retirement Party *(Can be disguised as July 4)*
August	Quarterly Operational/Investment Review Vacation to Visit Kids
September	Review Estate Plan with Estate Planner Quarterly Estimated Taxes *(September 15)*
October	Year-End Tax Planning
November	Quarterly Operational/Investment Review
December	Annual Strategic Planning Review

and your spouse are doing and then sharing that happiness with others. What a terrific reason for a party. Keep reminding yourself that this life is not a dress rehearsal. Take pleasure in the moment.

The Advisor Strategic Review

The final step of the strategic review process is to meet with your principal financial advisor and review your conclusions. Do this in mid-January. I strongly recommend that you begin the session with a clear statement evaluating the work that the advisor has done for you in the past year. "I have been very pleased with your work in the last year, and I plan to continue our work together in the year ahead. There are, however, some issues that I think it would be useful to discuss. . . ." Alternatively, if you are not happy, "I have decided to work with you again this year, but there are some issues that bother me. I would like to discuss the following. . . ." If your dissatisfaction is prolonged and profound, meet with the advisor in whom you had placed your trust and tell the advisor why you are firing him or her. If you would find this face-to-face meeting too difficult, write a personal note saying good-bye and explaining why you are terminating your assignment. I assume that in spite of the advisor's failings, he or she tried hard and deserves to hear it from you personally. Furthermore, if you discipline yourself to fire the advisor in this way, you are far less likely to do so for frivolous or emotional reasons. This relationship is important, and you do not want to manage your retirement with a team that is changing too frequently. If things are going reasonably well, but not perfectly, come to the meeting with your concerns and questions clearly in mind or even written out. If these are complicated issues or issues which may require some research, you should give the advisor a chance to prepare for the meeting.

There is a tendency for meetings like this to focus on investment results. Do not allow that to happen. This strategic review is not the place to worry about asset allocation, lagging investment results, lost statements, the phone answering system, or other operational matters. This meeting must focus on the big issues. Are you satisfied with the process the advisor has established? Is the advisor demonstrating the expertise that you expect? Is the advisor still committed to a strong relationship?

Have there been changes in your life about which the advisor needs to be informed? Do you need to revise your investment policy statement? Are you satisfied with the service that you are getting from the advisor and the advisor's staff? Are you satisfied with the cost of the service? Are you satisfied with the focus of the advisor's work or is the advisor too narrowly focused on investment issues? Do your operational reviews with the advisor answer your questions? Is the advisor helping you to monitor other aspects of your retirement: tax planning, estate planning, risk management? Is the financial advisor acting like the quarterback of your retirement team (see Figure 9-2) or is the advisor just another player? If you are acting as your own quarterback, you better know it.

Communications

It is best not to let trusted advisors worry about what is going on in your head. It gets in the way of them doing their best work for you. There are many examples, but a fairly obvious one is your investment portfolio. If the investment managers believe that you are not happy with their work, they are likely to change your portfolio to reflect what they think you want rather than what they truly think is best. This may result in an investment posture that is not optimum. You may inadvertently be pushing your advisors in the wrong direction because your communications with them are not frank and clear.

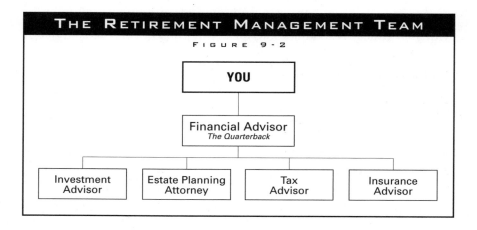

THE RETIREMENT MANAGEMENT TEAM

FIGURE 9-2

YOU

Financial Advisor
The Quarterback

| Investment Advisor | Estate Planning Attorney | Tax Advisor | Insurance Advisor |

OPERATIONAL MANAGEMENT

The next hurdle is to deal with the operational issues: tracking of investments, investment management issues, tax management, risk management, and estate planning. Start with the weekly tasks. I suggest that you devote two hours a week to scanning the financial horizon. For my money, *Barron's* is the best information source. It comes out once a week and, in about two hours, I can cover all the relevant information. It has lots of data, but it also gives the reader a good sense of what currently concerns sophisticated investors and financial managers. *The Wall Street Journal* is a daily invitation to spend a lot of time and to get buried in details. Magazines generally are too focused on the hot topics and encourage you to lose your long-term perspective. I call *Money* magazine the *Cosmopolitan* of the financial world, full of sexy stuff and flashing lights, but not much wisdom. *Forbes* is interesting, but goes for the sensational side. *Business Week* is more a news magazine and lacks the financial details. *Fortune* is a great big-picture magazine, but lacks the tactical detail. *Morningstar Mutual Funds*[1] is considered by many as the last word on mutual funds. Morningstar contains a lot of detailed, useful information, and may draw you more deeply into investment management than you really want. There are many other sources of information, but I don't think you want to get obsessive about following the markets—leave that to your advisors. You want to know just enough to be able to form an opinion about the level of their knowledge. I usually get my *Barron's* on Monday and spend a couple of hours over my Tuesday morning coffee checking on what is in the news.

Budget

The other issue that should be dealt with weekly is the budget. You can try putting data into the budget monthly, but I find that harder and less accurate than a weekly accounting. I recommend that you use Quicken[2] software on a personal computer to keep your budget information. It is the most popular and widely acclaimed personal finance program. It makes it relatively easy to keep track of your budget and will help

---

[1] Trademark of Morningstar, Inc. (800) 735-0700

[2] Quicken is a trademark of Intuit, Inc. (800) 446-8848.

you with other financial tasks, as well. In about an hour a week, you can make your inputs to the program and it will give you reports that will tell you everything that you need to know to keep your budget under control. It used to be that you were busy earning a living and didn't have time for budget control. That was all right then. In those days, it may have made sense to put the extra energy into your work, where it would earn more money. Now that controlling the expense side of the ledger has become your chief financial tool, it makes sense to put the time and energy into tracking your budget as a way of keeping it under control. Knowing the size and composition of your budget is one of the keys to enjoying the full potential of The Prosperous Retirement. Too many retirements that could have been prosperous have been made less enjoyable because the retirees were not certain that they could afford to spend more in retirement. One of the keys to The Prosperous Retirement is knowing that you can afford to spend what you need to enjoy the active phase of retirement. Too many retirees wind up leaving more than they intended to heirs, charities, and the IRS because they weren't certain that their capital base would support their budget. It is easy to know what your capital base is, and, if you know what your budget is, you can easily control the overall flow of your retirement. I know that some people think that "budget" is a swear word, like "golf," but I urge you to track your budget from time to time, even if you are unwilling to do it every week or month.

Operational Reviews

The next step in the management process comprises the operational reviews. These meetings are intended to be a detailed review of your asset allocation, your individual investments, and any other changes in your financial situation. Some people find that quarterly reviews are more than they need. I think that reviews every four months—or even twice a year—probably are adequate. For some people, once a year is all they want, but two or three times per year is my preference, even though there is a danger in any review—and the more often the reviews are, the bigger the danger is. The danger is that you will be disappointed or impatient if too many of these reviews result in no action. I cannot overemphasize the point that "no action" is a perfectly legitimate—even desirable—outcome to a review, even if everything does not appear to be perfectly positioned. There is a famous story about the renowned financier, Bernard Baruch. According to the story, a journalist asked Mr. Baruch, a fabulously successful investor, what the market would do. Mr. Baruch was a person of great reserve and considerable wit. He replied acerbically, "The market will fluctuate." While the market is fluctuating, your investments will not always be in favor. This does not mean that you should move things around in an attempt—all too often in vain—to "catch the wave." Every good surfer knows that if you miss a wave, you cannot catch up with it. Do not expect—in fact, do not *allow*—your financial advisor to change your investments every quarter or even every year. Remember, even a broken watch is correct twice a day, unless you keep changing the hands.

Adjusting Asset Allocation

The periodic review meeting should include a review of your current asset allocation compared to your target allocation. Minor variations should be ignored. Variations above 5% to 10% should be corrected, but there is a controversy over how quickly these imbalances should be corrected. Some advisors recommend quarterly adjustments, others, annual adjustments. There are arguments on both sides, but my preference is for annual adjustments of imbalances under 10%. A larger imbalance probably should be resolved more quickly, but it also can be allowed to run to year end.

Asset Monitoring

A bigger issue in reviewing asset allocation is the classification problem that was discussed in Chapter 7. Let's say that your asset allocation calls for 25% growth. Your advisor selects the XYZ Mutual Fund to represent the growth position. At the time of the recommendation, XYZ is a great growth-oriented mutual fund investing in a portfolio of mid-cap stocks balanced between growth stocks and value stocks. Over time, the fund grows in size because investors are attracted by its outstanding performance. The manager of the fund finds it harder and harder to identify enough mid-cap stocks to fill the investment portfolio and gradually the composition of the fund slides up to larger companies. The total return on the fund is fine, but the dividend yield on the portfolio grows. Soon the fund looks more like a growth-income fund, rather than a growth fund. What should you do? You probably need a new growth fund, but the real point of this story is that your advisor needs to monitor the investment characteristics of the assets in your portfolio to alert you if any of them are sliding out of the asset category that they were selected to represent. It is not enough to monitor total return. It is necessary to watch the internal dynamics of the investments to ensure that they are getting the return in the right way. A publication like *Morningstar Mutual Funds* can help with tasks like this, but even with help, it takes time and expertise. If this were easy to do, you would not need an advisor.

Investment Policy Review

Periodically, your advisor should check your written investment policy and discuss it with you. You should think about whether there is any reason to change the investment policy and the asset allocation that flows out of it. The investment policy is a fundamental document. Everyone with an investment advisor should have a written policy. The investment policy should give details on the kinds of returns you are seeking and the kinds of risks you are prepared to undertake.

The Non-Investment Issues

While focusing on investment and asset allocation issues, the operational review also should touch on other details of your retirement. Is your budget on track? Have there been changes in your family status or health? Are your retirement earnings coming in as projected? Are you certain that you are still bringing significant value to the marketplace, or is it time to really retire? I recommend that you choose a couple of good friends who understand that they are to help you perceive the moment when it is best to retire from the workplace. (If there are several, the advice can come anonymously.)

Are there other issues which have arisen that might lead you to re-examine the suitability of your retirement plan? Your principal advisor, your trusted financial guru, also should make certain that you are keeping in touch with your other advisors: the estate planning attorney, the tax accountant, and the insurance advisor. It is the financial planner's job to make certain that you have the services of any professional that you need.

SELECTING A FINANCIAL ADVISOR

The financial advisor plays such a key role in the management of your retirement that you should select this person with the utmost care. You probably need to exercise more care in selecting a financial advisor than a doctor, a dentist, a lawyer, or a psychotherapist. All these other professions are quite tightly regulated; no one would call themselves a "surgeon" if they were not properly trained and licensed. However, anyone can call themselves a "financial planner" or "financial consultant." If you place your trust in a charlatan, they can deprive you of the benefits of a lifetime of hard work and diligent savings. Under current regulations, anyone who is not a convicted felon and who has $150 and a few minutes to fill out the form can become a "Registered Investment Advisor." So how are you to find the "right person"? Who can you trust? There are recognizable professional credentials in the financial planning business and you would be wise to insist that your advisor has one or more of them.

Certified Financial Planner® (CFP®)

Certified Financial Planner (CFP) is the most widely recognized credential, with more than 32,000 people currently trained and licensed to use this credential. The certification means that the practitioner has passed a difficult, comprehensive examination and they have at least 2 years of professional experience. Most CFP candidates have prepared for the test through a two-year program of self-study. The CFP credential is licensed for use by the Certified Financial Planner Board of Standards, Inc. (CFP Board). Every CFP licensee subscribes to a strict code of ethics and must meet a bi-annual continuing education requirement.

There are good CFP licensees and not-so-good CFP licensees, but the unqualified few will lose their license. The CFP designation is a significant credential. The CFP Board will help you find a CFP licensee in your area.[3]

A CFP is a suitable person to be your financial generalist, the quarterback of your retirement team, but there are other appropriate credentials as well. One point to understand about CFP licensees is that although one part of the CFP course deals with investments, not every

---

[3] Appendix 3, Financial Advisor Organizations, gives contact information.

CFP licensee is an investment expert. If your financial advisor is also your investment manager, you should make careful inquiry about the credentials in this demanding specialization. Your questions might include:

- How long have you been managing other people's investments?
- What is your investment management method?
- What investment vehicles do you use?
- What is the cost of your investment management?
- What kind of results have you been able to achieve?
- Do you have an audited track record?
- Can I have three references with whom you have worked for at least four years?

Advisor Experience

You absolutely want a financial advisor and investment manager who has been through at least one market cycle as a professional advisor. In early 1998, this means that they should have been in the business for more than seven years, because the last decline—a small one at that—was in 1990. What you would really like is an investment manager who went through the fire and brimstone of the 1973-74 decline. Unfortunately, that was 25 years ago, when there were few financial advisors. Those who remain generally are looking at retirement, and you will need to ask about who will advise you when the advisor joins you in retirement.

The Advisor's Process

The advisor should have a clear process that allows him or her to focus on your needs. Regardless of the results, you do not want an advisor who has a one-size-fits-all process, unless the size is truly your size. If the financial advisor has identified a particular investment style that is well suited to your needs, and then recommends an investment advisor who works in that style, it is a reasonable choice. If, on the other hand, the financial advisor informs you that his or her in-house investment management team manages all their client investments, it is time to make careful inquiry about the process, the people, their credentials, and their results. Any ambiguity about these questions when there is not a true arm's-length relationship between the financial advisor and the investment advisor is cause for concern. In my view—and many disagree—being a financial advisor and an investment advisor are both full-time jobs. It would be a rare talent who could handle both of these for a client.

Defining the Advisor's Role

The financial advisor should be prepared to tailor his or her services to your needs in terms of your asset allocation, the frequency of reporting, and the cost of services. The advisor must be prepared to help you identify your goals, assess your risk tolerance, recommend suitable investment strategies, and introduce you to appropriate investment managers. The financial advisor also must be able to advise you on tax matters, estate planning, and risk management. In other words, the financial advisor is a financial generalist, not a specialist.

Risk Tolerance

A complicated question that you need to work through with your financial advisor is your risk tolerance. Most people think they are "conservative investors," and that their advisors should find all the guidance they need in that pronouncement. The truth is more complicated. In the final analysis, risk tolerance is largely subjective and can be altered by education, experience, or having trust in your advisors. There also is an element of objective reality in assessing risk tolerance. The objective factors have to do with age, net worth, sources of income, margin for savings, and the time available before the investment funds are likely to be needed (ATCW). In short, these factors answer the question: "If you were to lose these funds, how difficult would it be to make good the loss?"

The following formula gives the risk tolerance equation:

**Risk Tolerance =
Objective Risk Tolerance x Subjective Risk Tolerance**

The objective risk tolerance could be very high, but if the subjective tolerance is zero, the final answer is zero. I usually try to assess subjective tolerance with a series of questions that attempt to answer one basic question, "How many dollars, invested at what level of risk, will keep you awake at night?" Other variations on this theme are, "How many dollars of loss (or what percentage of decline) in the stock market would motivate you to move from stocks to bonds or cash?" Your financial advisor should go through this process with you, and it should be interactive. You should tell the advisor what you think and feel, and the advisor should tell you what he or she thinks and recommends. From that discussion should flow a mutual understanding of what you are willing to do and what the advisor is planning to do. These two things should be similar.

Conflicts of Interest

A potent source of conflict arises with those financial advisors who are affiliated with an organization that produces its own financial products—so-called "proprietary products." If the advisor has such a relationship, he or she will be under pressure, sometimes in the form of higher compensation, to sell the organization's products rather than competing products. Financial advisors have a hard enough job already without having one hand tied behind their back.

This question of conflict of interest also raises a lively debate among financial professionals. Generally, these discussions or debates among professionals are centered on proprietary products and the form of compensation of the financial advisor. Most sophisticated observers agree that the pressures of proprietary products are difficult to manage. I advise you to stay away from financial advisors who predominately sell products that are produced by a company with which they are affiliated. I would definitely stay away from financial advisors or specialists who sell financial products that they produce themselves. These people cannot be objective about the quality of the products they are selling, and you need that objectivity. Their enthusiasm for their own ideas can be overpowering and unhealthy.

Compensating the Advisor

The question of compensation is more complicated. Every financial professional has to make a living, and if they are really good at what they do, they generally are rewarded quite generously. There are three types of financial advisors in the marketplace from the viewpoint of how they are compensated. Some financial planners are "fee-only" financial planners. They do not make money from the sale or servicing of financial products. They work only with no-load products that do not have sales charges. These planners earn their income from the fees that their clients pay them for their services.

Other financial planners provide their planning services without a fee and are compensated only by the commissions that they collect from the products that they sell to their clients. These planners are called "commission-only" financial planners. The commissions these planners charge are supposed to be fully disclosed in the prospectus or on the confirmation that details each sale or purchase. Some of these costs are detailed more clearly than others. For example, there may be 12b-1 fees, the so-called "trail commissions"—which will be discussed in more detail in a few paragraphs. These can be as high as 1% per year, and they just slide out of your account without a note saying, "You just paid $250 in trail commissions on your account valued at $25,000." These trail commissions are disclosed in the prospectus, but they are not announced when they are withdrawn from your account.

Another subtle cost with some brokers is the so-called "principal trade." The confirmation for such a trade will reveal that the trade was done as a principal transaction, but it will not tell you how much the broker-dealer made—or lost—on the trade. In some stocks and bonds that are not actively traded, the spread between the "bid price" (the price at which someone is willing to buy the security) and the "ask price" (the price at which someone is willing to sell the security) can be significant. In a principal trade, the broker-dealer buys the security on the bid price and sells it to you the next day at the ask price, pocketing the difference. This is perfectly legal even though the difference may be a lot more than the commission that would have been charged if they had just bought the security for you.

A third kind of financial planner is the "fee-plus-commission" financial planner, who charges both fees and commissions. This sounds like "double dipping," but financial planning is a competitive business. Generally, the combination comes out to be about the same or sometimes even less than commissions alone or fees alone.

Asking About the Advisor's Compensation

There is no right or wrong answer to the question of how your financial planner is compensated, but the method of compensation should be clear, fully disclosed, and open for your questions. It is perfectly polite to ask your financial advisor for an accounting of the full cost of their services and other compensation information. Here is a possible script. "I would like to know, on an annual basis, what your services are costing me. This figure should include all fees and commissions—including trail commissions—that you receive, plus transaction costs. I also want to be informed if any product or service I am buying from you has a contest or incentive program in which my purchase will be included and which may help you earn extra commissions, a trip, or a prize. This includes so-called 'due-diligence trips,' which are supposedly educational but are frequently conducted in exotic locations. Such a contest or prize is not a bar to buying the product, but I do want to know about it."

Cost and Value

In today's marketplace, the distinction between fee-only financial planners, commission-only financial planners, and fee-plus-commission financial planners is being blurred by the "wrap-fee programs" and "asset management" programs. These programs typically forego front-end sales charges for a fee that is charged annually for the services received. One typical program offers management of an investment portfolio with no brokerage fee (commissions), but with an annual "wrap fee" that covers the cost of brokerage, management, and reporting. These programs started some years ago with annual fees of 3%, but they generally have come down in price. A fair price might be in the .75% to 1.75% range, depending on the size of the portfolio and the services being offered. Very active management or an exotic strategy might command a higher fee. Less active management or a strategy involving only mutual funds should have a slightly lower fee. It is important to remember that the fee comes right off your investment performance and, in most cases, is tax deductible only to the extent that your miscellaneous business expenses exceed 2% of your adjusted gross income.

I know a joke about a corporate executive who was asked about his retirement plan. "Oh," he says, "I have had a great retirement plan in place for years. My financial planner has retired, my attorney has retired, and my accountant has retired. Me—I'm still working." Don't let that happen to you. It makes sense to have an advisor and to compensate him or her fairly for services, but the services should pay for themselves. The payoff may not come every year, but if your financial advisor helps you to persevere through a bad market cycle, it could easily save you more than 5 or even 10 years of fees. If your financial advisor is helping you to keep your retirement on track, your investments under control, and your mind free of stress, he or she is worth a lot.

Fee-Only Advisors

The National Association of Personal Financial Advisors (NAPFA) is an organization of financial planners who provide services for a fee, but do not receive compensation for any products that they sell or service. This is a relatively small, but growing, organization, with just over 600 members. These financial planners generally are not licensed with a bro-ker-dealer. That means that, while they are subject to the supervision of the Securities and Exchange Commission (SEC) as investment advisors, they are not subject to the supervision of a broker-dealer and the National Association of Securities Dealers (NASD) or any of the major stock exchanges. This is an important issue, since many of these finan-cial planners are intermediating securities transactions. But, since they are not directly compensated for the intermediation, they are not required to be licensed and supervised. The securities business is compli-cated, and it is worrisome that these planners play such a complicated role without any required training, supervision, or licensing. In addition, the members of NAPFA claim to be a source of unbiased advice because they do not sell products for commissions. This position generally is sup-ported by journalists and consumer advocates, some of whom do not have a very sophisticated understanding of the financial services world.

The opposite side of this fact is that these advisors do not use the majority of products available in the marketplace, because most products have sales commissions. (Sales of no-load mutual funds in 1996 com-prised slightly more than 40% of all mutual fund sales, and there are only a few insurance products available without commission.)

There are three categories of membership in NAPFA. Any affiliation with NAPFA requires a commitment to provide advisory service compensated only by fees. To be categorized as a Member, advisors must have a bachelor's degree and specialized education in financial planning. They must have at least three years of experience. They must offer comprehensive financial planning services. A plan that the member has written is reviewed by the membership committee. They must complete 60 hours of continuing education every two years, and their compensation must be only from fees. Two other categories, Provisional Member and Sustaining Member, vary slightly in their requirements. The Provisional Member does not yet meet the experiential requirement. The Sustaining Member is specialized in some way and does not provide comprehensive financial planning.

Using No-Load Mutual Funds

A good deal of research indicates that in the long term (10 years+), there is no significant difference in performance between load mutual funds, which charge a sales commission, and no-load funds, which do not charge a sales commission. The full-page advertisements in *The Wall Street Journal* and *Money* magazine are expensive and the bulk of them are from no-load mutual funds. Too many investors and journalists seem to think that "no-load" means "free." Far from it.

Recent studies by Dalbar and Associates, an independent research organization based in Boston, have demonstrated that the presence or absence of an advisor is more important than the structure of the mutual fund's distribution system.

All mutual fund management companies make money by managing investments. They all charge a management fee. In the load funds, in addition to the management fee, there is a sales charge. Part of the sales charge goes to the broker-dealer, which retains a portion of the commission and passes the rest along to the person who recommended the fund to you. In addition, many funds have a so-called 12b-1 fee, which is paid quarterly to the registered representative whose name is on your mutual fund statement, and who is supposed to be providing regular service. A typical 12b-1 fee is 25 basis points (.25%) annually. In other words, if you have $10,000 in the fund, the fee is $25 per year. A million-dollar account would pay $2,500 per year.

The no-load funds generally do not have 12b-1 fees, but some do. There is a cost to distribute (sell) mutual funds, regardless of the system of distribution. A load fund pays a commission but does less media advertising, while a no-load fund does not pay commissions but spends more on advertising.

There are other reasons why the long-term results of load and no-load funds are so similar: The average investor in a load fund holds the fund for about 41 months, while the average no-load investor holds the investment for only about 32 months.[4] The higher turnover in no-load funds adds to their costs, forces managers to keep a larger part of the funds' assets in cash, and adds to the risk of the funds. In addition, the no-load fund manager sells his or her fund with performance. As a result, the no-load fund manager is more likely to pursue short-term performance at the risk of losing the long-term race. The choice between load funds and no-load funds is largely meaningless for the long-term investor. Unfortunately, the "fee-only" advisors make this their principal point of differentiation in the marketplace. It is not a significant benefit; instead, it prevents these advisors from using the majority of mutual funds because they are load funds. I regard their bias against load funds as a handicap, but there are many fine planners in NAPFA who produce outstanding results for their clients. You should understand the limits of their position, but it should not be a bar to having a NAPFA member as a financial advisor.

Mutual Fund Expense Ratios

Financial journalists, regulators, and consumer advocates urge investors to pay attention to mutual fund expense ratios. What percent of the funds under management are spent each year for the mutual fund's expenses? It seems obvious that the lower the overhead, the more profit there is for the investors. Like most obvious truths, there are serious prob-

---

[4] Based on the 1996 update of the Dalbar, Inc., study, *Quantitative Analysis of Investor Behavior*, aggregate numbers for both equity and fixed-income funds.

lems with this idea. First, expense ratios tend to decrease as funds increase in size. Funds that pursue investment goals which will suffer as the fund grows in size—like small capitalization funds—always will have higher expense ratios. Funds investing in foreign stocks tend to have higher expense ratios. The obvious advice is to compare apples-to-apples, but, as we have noted in a previous chapter, this is easier said than done. My advice is to pay attention to expense ratios relative to similar funds, but don't get carried away. If a fund is a few tenths of a percent higher in expenses, but has delivered good, consistent performance, the extra expenses could be a real bargain. Long-term performance, not expenses, are the bottom line in selecting mutual funds.

Mutual Funds Without Sales Charges

Before I leave this topic, I need to note that, among the services that are proving popular in the marketplace, a service which allows you to buy both load funds and no-load funds without a sales charge has emerged. This sounds like a free lunch, but we all know that the free lunch is a mythical beast. I noted earlier that all advisors must be paid. You pay advisors who use this service an annual fee for their services. The good news is that you avoid paying the advisor a big charge up front. The bad news is that you may pay them a smaller fee over a longer period of time. The typical numbers go something like this. Say you are investing $100,000 with an advisor. The advisor says, "I can sell you a front-end loaded fund with a 5.5% commission or I can sell you the same fund with no sales charge. Which do you prefer." Sounds like a "no-brainer," but wait for the punch line. In response to the obvious question, the planner continues. "The 5.5% commission is a one-time event. The purchase without a sales charge must be done via our management program, which charges 1% per year for our services." That sounds like the no-sales-charge version is better for about 5 or 6 years. Actually, it is better for about 6 or 7 years, but after that the front-end sales charge actually may be the better deal if all you wanted was the investment and not the advice.

If you are planning to take my advice and buy the services of the advisor, you are probably better off buying the investments without a sales charge and agreeing to pay the annual service fee. Normally, these arrangements require you to pay at least one year's fee, but if the service is not satisfactory, you can leave after the year with no further obligation. When discussing an arrangement like this, remember two points. First, re-read the paragraph on "Asking About the Advisor's Compensation." Second, the fees on these arrangements are normally negotiable. A polite question might be, "Is there any way in which I might get these services for a reduced fee?"

Chartered Financial Consultant (ChFC)

Another meaningful credential for a financial advisor is the Chartered Financial Consultant designation—ChFC. This credential is awarded by the American College in Bryn Mawr, Pennsylvania, to candidates who have successfully completed their 10-part course. The designation requires continuing education, and all ChFCs subscribe to a code of ethics. The American College is an outgrowth of the insurance industry, so their training tends to emphasize insurance matters more than other courses. The course covers all areas of the financial planning process, including investments.

The American College code of ethics differs from the CFP code in one significant respect. While both codes enjoin their licensees to deal fairly, honorably, and professionally with the public, only the CFP code of ethics specifically requires its licensees to provide services within their area of competence. This could be worrisome if the financial advisor is also the investment manager, but may not have advanced credentials in asset management. The ChFC designation is a full-fledged professional designation suitable for your financial advisor.

Personal Financial Specialist (PFS)

The American Institute of Certified Public Accountants (AICPA - the CPA organization) has a sub-specialty called the Personal Financial Specialist (PFS). The PFS, in addition to being a CPA, has specialized training to work with individuals on the management of personal finances. There are about 7,000 CPAs who have this additional accreditation. This is a very serious credential and a great background if your needs are heavily oriented toward tax management.

Something to be aware of, however, is the tendency of some accountants to be conservative in their approach to personal financial management. If your retirement is solidly anchored on a substantial asset base and you are looking for a conservative advisor, a PFS could be a great choice. If you are trying to stretch for the best possible retirement, this person may not be the right choice. One issue to ask about is whether your particular PFS has any sort of a relationship with a service provider that will be providing investment management services. Some accountants have arrangements by which they share in the portfolio management fees charged by the investment managers that they recommend. If such an arrangement exists, you should be fully informed about it in advance of any agreements being signed.

Chartered Financial Analyst (CFA)

Another credential that is seen in the marketplace is the Chartered Financial Analyst (CFA). This is a very prestigious credential that focuses on financial analysis. A CFA is more likely to be managing a mutual fund than working with individuals as a financial advisor. Some CFAs, however, do work directly with individuals. If your retirement concerns are weighted in the direction of investment management, a CFA could be just the right choice. If you are looking for a financial quarterback who is well versed in all aspects of personal financial management, this may not be the right credential unless it is held in conjunction with other designations.

Master's Degrees

Several fully accredited institutions, including the College for Financial Planning and the American College, offer master's degrees in financial services/planning. This advanced degree is a sure sign that the bearer is a serious student of financial services and has been willing to spend a lot of time to enhance their professional knowledge of the many issues in financial planning. Normally, an advanced degree is seen in combination with other professional credentials. These people typically are the most highly credentialed practitioners of financial planning, and there are not too many around.

Specialized Retirement Credentials

A relatively new program from the College for Financial Planning results in the award of two new credentials that are likely to become prominent. One is the Chartered Retirement Planning Counselor (CRPC) and the other is the Chartered Retirement Planning Specialist (CRPS). Both credentials are awarded only after the successful completion of a comprehensive study program and a monitored examination on the materials. The CRPC is trained as a retirement counselor for individuals, while the CRPS is trained as an advisor to the organizations that sponsor retirement plans. The CRPC credential demonstrates that the advisor is truly specialized in retirement planning. There is no supervising organization and no continuing education requirement for holders of these credentials. As a result, if your advisor is a CRPC, he or she also should hold some other credential or membership that subjects them to continuing education requirements, a code of ethics, and some kind of organizational oversight.

Other Credentials

There are a number of other credentials that can be seen in the marketplace, but they generally are not broad-based financial planning credentials. They indicate that the financial planner has completed some specialized course of instruction and commands some specialized expertise. There are Certified Divorce Planners, Certified Mutual Fund Specialists, Certified Investment Management Consultants (CIMC), and others. When you see these designations, it is appropriate to ask exactly what they mean. What does it qualify you to do? What did you have to do to get this designation? How long have you held it? Does it require continuing education?

Cost

This process of employing a management team to help guide your retirement probably sounds like it will cost a lot of money and take a lot of time. It probably will, but if you get what you are paying for, it will be worth it. There is really no way to tell you what these services are going to cost. Costs will vary by the services provided, the credentials and expertise of the practitioner, the area of the country, and your individual requirements. If your affairs are enormous and complicated, they will cost more. It is fair to ask professionals what their services are going to cost. It is fair to shop around for professional services as long as the service being offered is truly comparable. It is fair to ask the professional if there is anyway you can change your situation or your requirements to lower the cost of services. As a general rule, you can probably expect to spend between 1% and 2% of your investment net worth per year for professional services. The benefits you can expect are:

✔ An efficient investment portfolio that truly reflects your investment needs and your risk tolerance
✔ The ability to move from investment to investment without additional costs
✔ The ability to determine the very best retirement life-style you can really afford
✔ The knowledge that you are managing complicated areas of taxes, estate taxes, risk, and investment management in the best possible way
✔ The comfort of knowing that, when you are no longer able to manage your affairs, they will be in good order and professional help will be available

Trust

Credentials are important and your financial advisor should have them, but they must have one other thing—your undivided trust. Fancy offices and strong staffs are wonderful and give you confidence that you are working with a successful person. Slick materials are enticing. Successful people are powerful. Great presentations can be very seductive. Even recommendations from satisfied clients are very attractive. All of these can lead you toward the decision to engage a financial advisor, but reserve the final decision until the day after you have heard all the facts and listened to their presentation. The final question must be, "Do I feel that I can trust this person with something as important as my retirement?"

Trust must be the final screen, because it is the one characteristic that can make financial advisors worth whatever you are paying. You must be able to trust their advice to stick with your strategy when your instincts are telling you to run. You must have enough confidence in their advice to let them guide you through the periodic crises that engulf the markets and our lives. If they fail to command your trust and confidence, there is little that they can do to justify the fees you are paying them. If, at any point in your relationship, a shadow falls across the trust that you have placed in your financial advisor, resolve it or find a new advisor. There is no room in this relationship for doubts. It does not matter how the advisor is paid—how much or how little, fees, commissions, or both—if you trust him or her, you have the right advisor. If you do not trust him or her, you have the wrong advisor. An advisor of marginal competence and extreme diligence will recognize his or her own weaknesses and, out of loyalty to you, will bring in the specialists required to ensure that your interests are protected. If you find a financial advisor acting outside his or her competence, failing to live up to the representations, or taking compensation from sources that were not fully disclosed, it is time to fire them. Make no compromises on the trust issue.

THE FINANCIAL MANAGEMENT TEAM

In addition to your principal financial advisor, who should be a generalist financial planner, you will need an estate planning specialist attorney, a tax accountant, and an insurance advisor, possibly two insurance advisors. As your quarterback, the financial advisor should be given the option of recommending people to you. If you already have specialists with whom you enjoy working, ask your advisor if he or she is willing to work with them. Arrange a meeting and let them evaluate each other. Generally, your advisor should be flexible enough to work with your other advisors. If the financial advisor identifies problems in their work, listen carefully and take the appropriate actions.

The Estate Planning Specialist

Most attorneys can do simple estate planning. Your estate planning is likely to be more complicated than "simple." Accordingly, you should work with an attorney who specializes in estate planning. This is not your business attorney who helps you with routine legal problems. I schedule a meeting with the estate planning attorney once a year. I call well in advance and make certain that we meet when the attorney is not pressed for time. The meeting will be brief. I tell the attorney when I schedule the meeting that I would like to review my estate planning and get any recommendations he or she may have for modifications. Have the laws changed? Have there been court cases that impact our planning? Have our family affairs changed or are there better ideas for doing what we want to do? I expect to pay for an hour of the attorney's time and I say that up front. The attorney's review should take 30 minutes and the meeting about the same, unless there are changes to be made. I also know that, in addition to the changes in my affairs or in the world, there have been changes in the attorney's knowledge. There may be new ideas from which my family and I can benefit. I want to give the attorney a chance to discuss these ideas with me. I do not begrudge the attorney the fees because I know that good advice in this area can save me and my family a great deal of money.

Tax Advisor

The selection of a tax advisor is not a simple matter. Everyone who is in the business community probably knows an accountant or someone who "does taxes." The tax code is too complicated to entrust your retirement to someone who "does taxes." This is not the weekly laundry, where if it doesn't come clean, we can just run it through the machine a second time. One of life's little blood-pressure raisers is getting a notice from the IRS that something is not to their liking. I do not advocate giving the IRS their way on everything—in fact, they frequently are wrong. The tax code is so complicated that literally no one knows the right answers on all the questions that might come up. It has always been my policy to recommend that clients have their taxes prepared by a Certified Public Accountant (CPA). (See Chapter 12 for some useful advice about taxes.)

I generally recommend that, in selecting a CPA, people take the time to interview several candidates before entrusting anyone with your tax work. Obviously, the interview should be done during a slack time of the year. The summer usually is a good time for CPAs. Ask them about their policy of dealing with "gray areas." I advocate that everyone should pay the IRS exactly what they owe them and not one penny more. I advocate giving yourself the benefit of any reasonable doubt. Your accountant should share this attitude. I recommend that you allow yourself to be guided by the words of Judge Learned Hand,[5] "Anyone may so arrange his affairs that his taxes shall be as low as possible. He is not bound to choose that pattern which best pays the treasury. Everyone does it, rich and poor alike, and all do right; for nobody owes any public duty to pay more than the law demands."

You should plan some time in October or early November to gather your preliminary tax information and schedule a brief meeting with your tax advisor. You need to highlight the changes from the preceding year and ask if there are any recommendations for actions before year-end. This is the time to ask your tax advisor if there are strategies that you can put in place to help control your taxes.

No later than early March, gather all the documentation that you need to give the accountant and schedule a meeting to turn that information over. Try to have the information as organized and processed as possible. If there are capital gains, gather the facts and figure the capital gain. Gather all your papers into groups: income sources together, deductions together, dividends together, interest together, capital gains together. Have everything as organized and clear as possible. You will pay for it if you turn your papers over to the accountant in a shoe box. Give yourself and the accountant a break by having everything well organized. If your accountant gives you a tax questionnaire, as most do, make a conscientious effort to fill it out. Plan to spend a few minutes explaining any ambiguities or questions that you may have, but remember this is the crazy season for accountants. You do not want your taxes back on April 15th, so get the information to the accountant as quickly as you can. You want at least a day or two to look over the tax return and discuss it with your spouse before you have to sign and submit it.

---

[5] Judge Learned Hand, a New York jurist sometimes called "The Tenth Justice of the Supreme Court," died in 1961, innocent of political correctitude.

Insurance Advisor

You will need at least one insurance advisor, but possibly two or even more. The insurance world, like everything else, has gotten complicated in recent years. Insurance agents tend to be divided into two main groups, although there is considerable overlap. One group of agents works in life, health, and disability insurance. These agents typically have a license to sell "life and health insurance." Another group of insurance agents are called "property/casualty agents," and they sell auto and homeowners' insurance as their primary business. Seldom does a life and health agent sell auto or homeowners' insurance because they are complicated areas requiring special expertise. Property/casualty agents, on the other hand, frequently sell life insurance, particularly simple life insurance policies. The other insurance policies discussed in Chapters 10 and 11 should be bought from specialists who fully understand the complexity of the issues involved.

All of these specialty areas have credentials and you should inquire about the qualifications of your advisor. You really want an advisor, not just a salesperson. Your insurance advisor may be the same person as your financial advisor. Most financial planners are trained to recognize the risk management issues and tell you when you need help. I recommend that you ignore Woody Allen's comment and call your insurance advisor for lunch once a year. (Woody Allen said, "There is one thing worse than death—lunch with an insurance agent.") Try to bring a friend who might profit from meeting "your insurance person," because you know that your advisor makes a living from referral business. Ask the advisor to review your file and be prepared to make any recommendations that seem in order. I think it is a good idea to express your appreciation for the review by paying for the lunch. If you have to discuss financial details or fill out papers, skip the lunch and meet with the advisor in his or her office.

MANAGING THE FINAL PHASE

I have left for last the most difficult problem in managing your retirement. I call this "the end game," an expression I have borrowed from chess. In chess, the end game is the last phase of the game when most of the pieces have been removed from the board. In terms of retirement, it is the final phase where most of the issues have been managed, but there is a need to continue to provide adequate financial means for the surviving spouse while not leaving so much in the estate that taxes will be a problem.

I have noted, in working with older clients, that money tends to be the last reality. When people can no longer remember their children's names or whether their spouse is alive, when food is of no further interest and even television is unfathomable, money still seems real. If you ask people in this state if they want to make gifts to their heirs, all too often they will balk because the idea of giving away money seems to expose them to unacceptable risk. Plans must be made, documents signed, the idea firmly planted to allow the management of this final phase in some rational way. The person who is going to make those final rational decisions for you probably will not be you.

KEEP SMILING

The proper management of your retirement should be a matter of pride. You worked long and hard, planned wisely, saved diligently, and now your retirement can be a living monument to the wise way in which you have lived your life. Even if everything else in your life was not so wise, here is a final opportunity to show yourself and the rest of the world what a competent person you are. Plan your retirement carefully. Implement the plan diligently. Be patient—do not be quick to change your arrangements. Keep smiling and make them all wonder what you are up to.

10.

MANAGING RISK IN THE PROSPEROUS RETIREMENT

"Only the unknown frightens men. But once a man has faced the unknown, that terror becomes the known."
—ANTOINE DE SAINT-EXUPÉRY, 1939

SYNOPSIS: Risk is the possibility of loss. There are risks everywhere that we routinely ignore. The transition to retirement is an appropriate time to examine the risks in our lives, some of which are new or changed. When we can identify the risks, we can make decisions about how to deal with them. We can try to avoid the risk, reduce the risk, or retain the risk. We also can use insurance to transfer the risk to others. The principal sources of risk in our lives are: home, vehicles, personal property, personal liabilities, health and accident, and investments. The specific risks vary, but identifying them allows us to make rational choices about dealing with them and increases the probability that The Prosperous Retirement actually will be realized.

Life is a risky business. Most of the time, we keep our mind focused on the task in front of us and we don't notice the risks all around. Years ago, I used to jump out of airplanes. The first few times I jumped, it took enormous preparation, concentration, and force of will to go out the door of a perfectly good airplane flying about 1,500 feet above the ground. Gradually, the experience became less terrifying, and pretty soon it didn't seem risky at all. So it is with much of life.

I work with a concept I call "the Sphere of Consciousness." I can't deal on a daily basis with nuclear war, entropy, children starving, ethnic cleansing, and the possibility of a meteor hitting earth. I have to shrink my sphere of consciousness to include only those matters that are likely to have a practical effect on my life. I worry about putting gas in the car, remembering my wife's birthday, avoiding bicyclists, setting the alarm clock, and other things that will probably have an impact on my life. I'm not really thinking about all the risks in my life on a daily basis, and you probably aren't either. Just for a few minutes, I want you to focus on the perils that surround you and think about how you can avoid them, deal with them, or transfer as much of their risk away from you as possible.

RISK MANAGEMENT TECHNIQUES

"Risk" is defined as the possibility of a loss. The cause of the loss is called a "peril." An auto accident is a peril because it may cause a loss. A fire in your home is a peril. A workman working in your attic is a peril. A motorcycle under a tarp in your backyard is a peril, just like a swimming pool in your backyard. Anything that can cause a loss is a peril. There are four basic techniques for dealing with these perils and they are called "risk management techniques."

1. Risk avoidance
2. Risk reduction
3. Risk retention
4. Risk transfer

Driving is a peril. You can avoid the risk in driving by not getting out on the road. You may be able to reduce the risk by taking a bus or traveling less frequently. You can decide that the risk is manageable and do nothing about it, thus retaining the risk. You can transfer some of the risk—the possibility of loss—to an insurance company by buying auto insurance. The same alternatives generally exist for every peril.

RISK MANAGEMENT PRINCIPLES

Some general principles exist to guide you through the risk management process. First, remember that insurance is not a lottery ticket. It is not good news to receive an insurance benefit. Insurance is purchased to protect against catastrophe, not to eliminate minor risks. Never take a risk that is more than you are prepared to lose. Do not retain risks for losses that could be ruinous. Be aware of perils, and never take the attitude that "it can't happen to me." Murphy's Law in the area of insurance says, "Losses do occur and generally on the day after your coverage has lapsed."

IDENTIFYING RISKS

To reduce the possibility of loss, it is necessary to identify the risk. The sphere of consciousness comes into play here. We want to focus on only those perils that have a reasonable probability of affecting your life. For the time being, let's forget about the meteor. You need to think about the specifics of your circumstances and decide if there are special dangers in your life that may need risk management. For example, if your hobby is welding, you might want to consider not doing it in your basement, so that—in case of a fire—it won't threaten everything you own.

The principal dangers of everyday life are related to home, vehicles, personal property, personal liabilities, health and accident, and investments. Those are the primary factors that can be damaged and snarl your life. You have gone through an entire lifetime dealing with these risks, but you may not have noticed the subtle changes in the risks as you got older and went into retirement.

PROTECTING YOUR HOME

Your home has become more valuable over the years, and it may comprise an important part of your retirement capital. It is of paramount importance to make certain that it is properly insured. Make certain that your property and casualty agent (your home and auto insurance person) is fully informed about additions, changes, and improvements. Do you have a recent market value appraisal for your home? Is the residence insurance amount adequate to provide the necessary coverage? If your home is located in an area where it might be exposed to damage from earthquakes, floods, or other natural hazards, does your coverage extend to these risks? Does your policy reflect any new uses—like a home office? Does it reflect a new ownership form that may have resulted from your estate planning? If you have moved a business into your home or built an extensive shop, are these still covered under the homeowner's policy? If you have acquired new property—something like a stamp collection or an antique—are they properly covered under your policy?

Over the years, you may have acquired some personal property that has become valuable. Rugs, porcelain, crystal, silver, paintings, collections, or antiques may represent significant value. There is a dilemma in this: Your homeowner's policy has "internal limits" that may well exclude these valuable items from full coverage. The typical "floater policy" that extends coverage to items that exceed the "internal limits" of the basic homeowner's policy is not cheap. Depending on the insurance company, your location, and the nature of the property, the premium may be .5% to 1% of the value of the property covered, each year. Wow, that painting you bought 35 years ago for $500, which is now worth $10,000, is costing $100 per year to insure!

If the painting were lost through fire or theft would you replace it? Is it necessary to have it covered? Good questions. It seems to me that the answer lies in three additional questions: First, is the value of this item part of your retirement capital? Are you thinking that, at some point, it may be sold to pay for a part of your retirement? If so, the object needs coverage. Second, if the object is lost, would you replace it? If so, insure it. Third, is the object of such value that you would just feel terrible if it were lost and there was no protection? If so, insure it. If the object is irreplaceable or largely of sentimental value, I would be inclined to retain the risk of loss and not pay the insurance premium. If the property is family jewelry or some other small object, consider keeping it in a vault or safe deposit box when you are not using it. It is your property, so it is your call, but do give it some thought.

Home Inventory

This raises another interesting point. You know that you should have a record of the valuable items in your home. Some people have elaborate inventories that they have maintained for years. Others use one of the new computer programs for making their home inventories. Some people suggest taking photos or videos of your home to help jog your memory in the case of a loss. Retirement might be the time when there is finally an opportunity to do these wise things. In the process, you can think about what needs to be covered, which items you can allow to be uninsured, and what should go to the safe deposit box.

PROTECTING YOUR VEHICLES

Vehicles raise interesting complications in retirement. Is there a boat in your life? Is it properly insured? A canoe or a small boat typically is covered automatically under your homeowner's policy, but as they get larger and the motor exceeds certain limits, you need separate coverage for the boat. If the boat is rarely used, you may be reluctant to insure it. The issue here typically is not the potential loss of value if the boat is lost or damaged, but the liability that you might incur if someone is injured. If the boat is loaned to another party, or even if it is removed without your permission, you may be responsible for any damage. This raises the question: If the boat is rarely used, would you be better off to sell it and rent a replacement for those few times you would like to go boating?

The same argument may pertain to automobiles that are rarely used. It may be great to have a pickup truck or an old four-wheeler for those rare occasions when you need it, but ask yourself if there is a disproportionate risk in having it around. Do friends ask you to use it? Is it possible that some teenager might "borrow" your vehicle and get into trouble with it? Years ago, we worked with a woman who was a psychiatrist. She had a 1940 Harley Davidson motorcycle that she called "the psychiatrist's psychiatrist." When her life got stressful, she would take the tarp off the Harley and cruise a country road until the wind blowing through her hair had cleared her mind. Unfortunately, one of the neighborhood kids knew about the "hog" and the fact that it was not locked or secured. The kid "borrowed" the bike and banged it up—and himself along with it. It could have been worse. A lawyer might have claimed that the unlocked antique motorcycle was an "attractive nuisance" that represented an unreasonable temptation. The moral of the story is that if you have antique cars, motorcycles, high performance bikes, a swimming pool, or any other object that might be considered an "attractive nuisance," make certain that it is well secured when not in use. If it is seldom or never in use, consider getting rid of it.

Another risk management issue pertains to your automobiles. As people get older, they slow down mentally and physically. If you continue to drive as you get older and slow down, give yourself all the help you can. Take enough time to get where you are going without rushing. Better to be late than. . . . Reconsider a trip if the weather is bad. If you find night driving hard, confine yourself to daylight hours. Bring your vehicle in regularly for maintenance or maintain it yourself, but make certain that your car is in good mechanical order and that all the safety features are up to par. No one who has spent a lifetime enjoying the independence of driving their own car wants to think about giving it up. Remember that it is not just your life that is at stake. When the time comes, be prepared to face the facts.

It is a common practice among the owners of older cars to drop their collision damage coverage. The notion is that, as the replacement value of the car declines, it no longer makes sense to pay a premium for that minimal protection. Instead, you might consider reducing the cost of the collision damage coverage by increasing the deductible. If you are a careful driver who seldom suffers a loss, it might make sense to retain some of this risk by having a $500 or even a $1,000 deductible. Insurance protects against catastrophes, not the trivial. The idea of reducing collision damage coverage may be fine and good, but don't let this line of thought carry over to the other coverages. You still need the full liability coverage, even if your car is very old. This protects against an accident victim trying to attack your other assets. Another coverage that may not seem important is the so-called "uninsured motorist coverage." This coverage protects you from the damages that might occur through an accident with an uninsured motorist. It is not protection for the uninsured—the protection is yours. This usually is not expensive coverage, and you should protect yourself with the same liability limits that you extend to others.

PERSONAL LIABILITY

If you are happily living The Prosperous Retirement, people may perceive that you are "well off." If something goes wrong and they are seeking restitution, they may see you as the "deep pocket" who can set things straight financially. You probably know that there is something called "umbrella coverage," or "extended personal liability insurance," that gives you more protection and slightly broader coverage than your homeowner's and auto policies. It is not expensive, and you should probably check into buying a policy, if you do not already have it. Insurance agents frequently are not quick to recommend this coverage because they feel they need to be as price-competitive as possible, and this is an extra cost that the competition may not be showing. Further, it is a low margin product for them and not one that everyone is willing to buy. In spite of all these factors, mention it to your agent and see if the agent recommends it in your circumstances.

LIFE INSURANCE

You might well think that one of the blessings of retirement is that you will never again have to speak with a life insurance agent. Another surprise! Life insurance may play several key roles in your retirement planning.

Pension Maximization Strategy

An important use of life insurance is to protect your dependents against the possible loss of pension dollars that are based only on your life. Usually, a pension gives the retiree an option to have a "joint-and-survivor benefit" or a "single-life benefit." The joint-and-survivor option will pay the pension to you as long as you live, then all or part of the benefit to your designated beneficiary for as long as they live. The single-life option will pay a larger amount to you as long as you live, but it stops when you stop. Sometimes you are better off electing the larger single-life option. If your potential beneficiary is not in good health, and if you would still collect the reduced benefit even if the beneficiary dies before you, it might make sense to examine the use of life insurance instead of the joint-and-survivor pension option. It works like this: You determine the difference between the single life and the joint benefit. You then check to see how much life insurance you can buy with that annual amount. If the death benefit to your beneficiary is enough to replace the pension benefit, you buy the insurance and elect the single-life option. In the event that you die, and the single-life benefit is stopped, the insurance proceeds replace the pension for the survivor. If the numbers work, you buy the insurance, and then, in the event that your beneficiary dies before you do, you stop paying the premium and let the insurance lapse. This strategy sometimes is called the "pension maximization strategy." It does not always work. Your life insurance agent may need to shop hard to find a policy that will make it work.

Insurance in Estate Planning

Life insurance can be used in other ways that revolve around the fact that life insurance benefits are not subject to income tax and can be arranged to be outside your estate and, therefore, immune from estate taxes. These applications are highly technical and usually are associated with estate planning. Don't be surprised if your estate planner or your financial planner suggests that you consider the use of life insurance as a method of maximizing the wealth that you can pass to your heirs.

Tax-Free Exchange of Old Policies

Another question that arises is what to do with old, cash-value life insurance policies. The retiree may have accumulated enough wealth that the death benefit of an old policy may no longer be very meaningful. You might examine the possibility of making a tax-free exchange (IRC Section 1035) of the cash value for a variable annuity contract. The variable annuity may prove to be a more productive asset. You can roll the cost basis of the policy into the new contract and eventually get a withdrawal that will be partially sheltered from income taxes. This represents another fairly complicated issue, but a great way to salvage some of the premiums that you paid over all those years for an insurance policy that may no longer be relevant.

Variable Life Insurance

Another popular vehicle that connects life insurance with retirement is the use of a variable life insurance contract to create a "private pension plan." The idea behind this product is that a person can make unlimited contributions to a variable life insurance contract, and like a pension plan, it will grow on a tax-deferred basis. Unlike the pension plan, the contribution is not tax deductible, but the contribution does not require a matching contribution for other employees. For some small business owners, this is an attractive alternative.

The problem is that at older ages—above 55—the cost of the insurance part of the contract may impede the flow of funds into the investment part of the plan. It is possible to present a plan like this in a very favorable light, even if it is really not the best solution for your circumstances. You need a trusted advisor to evaluate this kind of a proposal.

HEALTH INSURANCE

Health insurance is a key issue for retirees. Many people retire at ages that leave them years and years before they will be eligible for Medicare at age 65. The Consolidated Omnibus Budget Reconciliation Act (referred to as COBRA) obligates an employer to give a retiring employee the opportunity to buy "continuation coverage" on their health insurance. Employers are not required to continue the coverage beyond 18 or 36 months, depending on the situation. You have to pay for this coverage, but it may be just the ticket if you have only a short time until you turn 65.

Another option may be to switch to the health coverage available through your spouse's employment. Another alternative may be to look for health insurance through some professional association or through a group like the American Association of Retired Persons (AARP). Another alternative that is cost competitive and becoming increasingly popular is a Health Maintenance Organization (HMO). The press reports that the services offered by these organizations vary greatly. You should make a careful investigation before you sign up. It is too late to worry about your HMO when you need medical services and discover some problem in the system. The typical allegation is that some HMOs restrict the treatments that their doctors can use in order to increase the HMO's profitability. This kind of a problem is not easy to detect unless you interview a number of the HMO's members. You know that you need health insurance, but you may be used to having it provided and, thus, not be prepared to do the research to make the best possible election. It pays to spend a day or two to get this right.

Medicare Supplements

Even after Medicare takes over at age 65, it still is important to have supplemental coverage to cover the gaps in Medicare. For this reason, these Medicare supplemental policies are sometimes referred to as "Medigap" policies. Medicare's financial situation is causing the gaps in coverage to get wider and wider, so supplemental coverage is essential.

In 1990, the federal government forced the providers of Medicare supplements to standardize their offerings into 10 standard policies, referred to as type A through type J. In my view, the "right answer" for a Medicare supplement is designated "F." The F supplement covers all the basic benefits, plus the hospital and doctor deductibles. In addition, it covers 100% of excess doctor bills for covered treatments. That gap seems to be growing and it is important to have it closed by insurance. Type F also covers skilled-nursing co-insurance and coverage abroad. Type F does not cover prescription drugs (H, I, and J do), at-home care, or preventive care. Type I and type J are more complete coverages, but are much more expensive. If you need expensive prescription medicine, type I or J should be considered.

HMO Versus Medicare

Some HMOs have started taking Medicare assignment; in other words, they are accepting Medicare's payment and not charging the patient anything extra. This is worth examining if it is available to you—in fact, it may be your best alternative. In an attempt to lower the cost of Medicare, the Medicare providers have become very strict. It is difficult to submit a claim, it is difficult to understand their negative responses, it is difficult to respond to their requirements. If you decide to go the HMO/Medicare assignment route, it costs you nothing and you have an organization that will take care of dealing with Medicare. The same comments pertain to HMOs as a substitute for Medicare, as we discussed above. Check the HMO very carefully, because it will be too late when a problem actually arises. A reasonable question to ask the HMO representative during the evaluation process is, "Under what circumstances would I be better off dealing directly with Medicare and a Medicare supplement?"

It is worth investing some time and energy in finding the "right solution" for your medical care needs. This is likely to be a major issue at some point in your retirement. When it does become an issue, you will want to have the right support in place and not have to worry about changing, if changing is even a possibility.

LONG-TERM CARE INSURANCE

I've made the argument in Chapter 9 that long-term care insurance is a very important piece of the retirement management puzzle. There is a reasonably high probability that you will require nursing home care or home health care at some time during your retirement.[1] The cost of nursing homes continues to rise, like all medical expenses, at a rate that exceeds the general rate of inflation. We see statistics that suggest the current cost of nursing home care is about $40,000 a year in many parts of the country. The two coasts are higher, and there are places where nursing home care is cheaper. Long-term care insurance is the only kind of insurance that will cover the cost of this very expense, long-term custodial care, the kind that people need when they simply can't take care of themselves anymore. If you are hospitalized and need nursing home care to give you a chance to recuperate, your medical insurance probably will cover expenses, and Medicare will cover skilled nursing care for up to 100 days as long as it is part of a recuperative process. However, neither Medicare nor Medicare supplements will pay for long-term custodial care.

Medicaid, the government program that pays for medical care for indigent people, will pay for nursing home care, but to qualify, you have to be poor. The states set the eligibility standards for Medicaid, but in all cases, the criteria include two standards: First, you must use up virtually all of your assets. Second, you have to have income that is below the maximum set by the state. If you have a pension of $2,000 per month and spend all your assets, you will still not qualify for Medicaid because your income is too high. Regardless of the fact that $2,000 a month will not pay for a nursing home in most parts of the country, your income is too high to qualify for Medicaid.

---

[1] The most recent statistics available are from the 1985 *National Nursing Home Survey.* More recent data may be too politically sensitive to be released. It is almost certain that nursing home stays are getting longer.

This is a complicated matter because standards vary from state to state, but let me point out some of the problems. First, there are still some states in which it is necessary for a couple to spend virtually all their wealth before either of them can qualify for Medicaid. Most states have enacted laws allowing one spouse to spend down his or her share of the family's wealth to qualify without impoverishing the other spouse. These generally are called anti-spousal impoverishment statutes and it is important to know if your state has such a statute. Most states also have rules that say a certain small amount of assets—say $15,000—can be retained and still allow you to qualify for Medicaid.

In addition to the assets, Medicaid generally exempts the home and an automobile. The home exemption may seem like an opportunity, but many states have enacted laws that allow the state to place a lien against the home for any Medicaid paid on behalf of the owner. Thus, when the owners die and the property is liquidated, the state can recover any funds they have paid in Medicaid benefits.

In many places, there has been a lively traffic in lawyers advising older people on how to qualify for Medicaid. Their basic strategy is to give away all your non-exempt assets, generally to family members, and thus qualify for Medicaid. This creates another potential problem. In the process of qualifying for Medicaid, the proposed recipient of benefits will be asked if he or she has given away any assets in the last 36[2] months. Gifts during that period are not allowed. Thus, the advice generally is to give away the assets, leaving enough to live on for 36 months. Then you can apply for aid when the 36-month look-back period will not show any gifts. This strategy has been called "the Great Middle Class Fraud," and the government gradually is closing this loophole. If you decide to go this route, make certain that your advisor is well versed in the latest information to prevent this loophole from turning into a noose.

Early in the first Clinton Administration, it appeared that the government might be preparing to broaden government support for long-term care. However, the evidence showed that such support would be an unbearable burden for the government, and the proposals were rebuffed. The Health Insurance Portability and Accountability Act of 1996 (HIPAA '96) was a clear signal of a reversal in the government's direction. The Act offered tax

---

[2] 60 months in the case of irrevocable trusts

deductibility, as a medical expense subject to the 7-1/2% threshold, for insurance premiums paid for long-term care insurance. Policies issued after January 1, 1997, will have to meet specified standards to be "tax qualified" and have the premiums be deductible. The standards address five issues:

1. Benefits must be based either on severe cognitive impairment (generally Alzheimer's disease) or the need for substantial assistance with at least two Activities of Daily Living (so-called ADLs). (Most policies recognize five ADLs: dressing, transferring, toileting, continence, and eating. Some policies add a sixth, bathing.)
2. Loss of the ability to perform ADLs must be certified by a health care practitioner to last at least 90 days.
3. Benefits cannot duplicate those available under Medicare or fill in Medicare deductibles or co-insurance.
4. A nonforfeiture option must be offered, but purchase is not required.
5. The policy must include consumer protection standards based on the North American Insurance Commissioners' Model Act and Regulation.

You can count on the fact that most long-term care policies will meet these standards. In fact, many of the earlier policies had more liberal provisions. Fortunately, any policy issued before 1997 is considered "tax qualified."

Because long-term care insurance is not an insurance coverage that most people understand or have any experience with, I will go into some details. More than 100 companies offer policies that provide benefits for long-term care. Several different forms exist. One form provides payments for the cost of care up to the limit of the benefit purchased. Other policies provide the benefit amount, regardless of the cost of care, if the insured meets the qualifications for benefits. Other policies are structured like annuities or life insurance contracts, which allow benefits to be paid for long-term care from the cash value of the policy. This kind of insurance has changed a great deal in the last 10 years and it continues to evolve, but it is my current view that policies which are simply long-term care insurance are the most effective way to protect against the costs of long-term care.

The cost of long-term care insurance is based on the following factors:

- ➡ The age of the insured at the time the policy is issued. Generally, policies will be issued on standard terms up to age 80. Policies with reduced benefits are available for issue up to age 90 from some companies. Premiums will not go up as your age increases. In fact, my investigations indicate that the earlier you buy long-term care insurance, the lower its cost will be if held to your life-expectancy or longer. You do need to be aware, that while the insurance company cannot increase your individual premium, they do have the right to increase the premiums of all persons in your classification. Generally, this means that, if their loss experience in your state is above their projections, they can increase premiums for everyone in your state.

- ➡ The next cost factor is the amount of daily benefit. Generally, companies offer daily benefits ranging from $50 a day to $250 a day. The cost of the policy is directly related to the benefit level. HIPAA '96 provided that benefits up to $175 per day (to be indexed) would not be taxable regardless of the cost of care. Benefits above $175 per day will be taxable to the extent that they exceed the actual cost of care.

- ➡ The next cost factor is the so-called "elimination period." This is the period during which you must receive care before the benefits start. Typical elimination periods range from 0 days to 365 days. The longer the elimination period the less expensive the coverage will be. I recommend at least a 90-day elimination period, and even a longer period if you are comfortable bearing the cost.

- ➡ The next cost factor is how long the coverage will last. All companies offer lifetime coverage as their most expensive option. This will cover you for an unlimited period of time. All companies also offer shorter periods of coverage. These shorter periods range from 1 year to 6 years. I recommend lifetime coverage if you can afford it, but the statistics suggest that shorter periods may be adequate.[3] If you feel that you must control the cost of this insurance, consider 6 years of coverage for females and 4 years for males. The statistics indicate that men generally last about 2 years in a nursing home

---

[3] Remember, the statistics are now 13 years old.

and women about twice that long. There is no way of knowing if these statistics will persist in the future, but it appears likely that they will be extended.

●◆ Another cost feature is home care. Some policies provide home care as a standard feature. You can opt for nursing home only, home care only, or both. Other policies allow you to choose the level of benefit for home care separate from the nursing home benefit. There is no doubt that most people would prefer to stay home as long as possible, but you must understand that, in most cases, the disability will progress to a point where the only sensible place for care is in a nursing home. If you must economize someplace, this is the place. On the principle that insurance is to protect against cat-astrophe not against inconvenience, I recommend that you econo-mize by selecting a policy that provides only nursing home care. Interestingly, there is a new concept making an appearance that interjects a "care manager" in this process. The care manager decides the most effective way of caring for you. If they say "home care," you get home care. If they say "nursing home," nursing home it is. In some cases, these policies are less expensive than a straight nursing home policy. This presents another reason to find a trusted insurance advisor.

●◆ The last cost factor is whether the policy has inflation protection. There are typically three options. The first option is no inflation protection. If you select a $100 per day benefit, that is what you will get. If you need the benefit in 15 years, and costs have dou-bled, you still will get only $100 per day. This is a reasonable option only for people who are older than 75 or 80 years of age when they take the policy. The second option is compounding inflation protection. This mirrors the way that inflation works and it makes sense, particularly for people who are taking the insurance at an early age—say less than 65. Be certain to ask if the inflation protection is "capped." Some policies cap the increase in benefit at two times the original benefit level, while others have no cap but cost more. The third option, is simple inflation protection. An amount is added each year to the benefit level, but it is a fixed percentage of the original benefit. For example, a 5% simple inflation protection would add $5 per year to a $100 original benefit. After 10 years, the benefit has increased to $150 rather than the $162.89 that it would have increased to if the 5% were compounded. This is a reasonable choice for people between the ages of 65 and 75. The best protection, regardless of age, is uncapped inflation protection on a compounding basis. The cost, however, may prove to be more than you want to spend, so some compromise may be in order.

There are other points of differentiation between various long-term care policies. Do not assume that they all have the same features. Some companies offer a discount if both spouses are covered. Some have a life-time exclusion and others have a new exclusion for each confinement. Some companies waive premiums if you are in a nursing home for a certain period, while others also will waive premiums if you are on home care. Some companies are easier to work with if you make a claim, while others will be less cooperative. Long-term care insurance is a new and complicated area. You should work with a trusted insurance advisor, and he or she should use a long-term insurance specialist if needed. A long-term care insurance specialist should be able to compare your policy options among at least three or four different companies. Work with a trusted advisor, read the materials, ask good questions, think about this carefully, but do not go without long-term care insurance.

INVESTMENT RISK

It may seem strange to have a section in the risk management chapter that deals with investments, but there is method to this madness. I want you to focus on the risk side of investing without thinking about the benefits, the attractions, the complications of the process of portfolio management, the many alternatives, or the prejudices that you bring to the process. In the context of expanding our sphere of consciousness, let us examine the perils in investments. There are three main perils. First, and typically foremost in people's minds, is the loss of principal. Second is the loss of buying power. The dollars invested are eroded more quickly by the abrasive force of inflation than they can grow. Third is the failure to meet your needs. If assets are invested so conservatively that they do not meet your needs, it will be hard to enjoy The Prosperous Retirement. You can see that this is a gangplank across a deep chasm, but please note that there is a safety net on one side. If your assets fail to meet your goals, you will not be destroyed. You may have to reassess your plans, but life goes on after disappointment. This is true even if your assets fail to keep pace with inflation. Yes, that will expose you to a declining lifestyle, but life will go on. Only the loss of your capital base threatens you in a fundamental way and then only if the loss is substantial. Even a substantial decline in the value of your capital base may not affect your retirement in a significant way. The lesson from these observations is do not be greedy, do not try to maximize the return on your portfolio at the expense of safety, and—most of all—do not allow yourself to indulge in the ego trip of taking unnecessary risks so you can leave a larger legacy.

Having said that, let me ask you a question that may help to keep you in balance. "Would you rather be poor in a world where everyone else is rich, or would you rather be poor in a world where everyone is poor?" The answer is obvious for most people, and it reminds us that we don't want to be so conservative that we fall behind the great mass of our contemporaries. The middle road is the safe way to get almost anyplace.

It seems to me that some operational rules also flow out of these observations. First, never risk more than you are prepared to lose. Retirement investments should be invested in proven investment vehicles. Real estate may be a proven investment vehicle, but a new office building that is not yet leased is not a proven vehicle. Venture no more than you can afford to lose. New investment vehicles are not to be trusted until they have been through a cycle or two.

Not every financial advisor really understands every vehicle that is in the marketplace. Your trusted advisors should have the integrity to deal with what they understand and steer you away from the rest. Do not be tempted to change advisors because your advisor is not prepared to risk your assets on the "latest and greatest."

I recall a client who called and asked what I thought of an investment that returned 5% a week. I giggled and said that I dreamed of such things, but unfortunately they didn't exist. The client was miffed and asked how I could be so certain when I hadn't heard the deal. I said, "Because my calculator tells me that if I invest $1,000 for 5 years at 5% per week, it will turn into $300 million and that is not real." If an investment offers benefits that are too good to be true, don't get sucked in.

In recent years, many of the mutual fund companies have gotten into the "fund of the month" mode. They create new fund categories as a method of marketing. Remember, market research still shows that the word "new" is the most powerful selling word in the advertising vocabulary. The problem is that these investments represent untested concepts. Risk no more than you are prepared to lose.

The principal wisdom in the world of investments is still diversification; it is the way to keep risks in your portfolio at a manageable level. I have noted earlier that this does not mean having a $1 million dollar portfolio split among 100 investments. A manageable diversification is about 20 assets that represent truly diverse investment categories. This doesn't mean 20 different stocks or 20 different bonds. It means a variety of stock-type investments, a variety of bond-type investments, a reasonable diversification between domestic and foreign assets, and a diversification between financial assets and so-called "hard assets." Remember we are betting that the economy will continue to follow the "80% channel" in which it has muddled along for the last 70 years. While we have our consciousness expanded, we must note that it could fall into depression or hyper-inflation. If you can afford it, it makes sense to hedge against those contingencies, but not at the expense of missing out on The Prosperous Retirement.

An important protection in managing your investments is to pay attention. Keep informed about what is happening in the markets and the thinking that is driving them. You need to keep your head level and look forward, but you also must be aware of what is happening with others. Their panic or their euphoria could affect your future. The bottom line is to be informed, but stay calm. Don't be greedy. Tread the middle road, and stick with proven investment vehicles.

OK! It is time to shrink our sphere of consciousness back to the size that allows us to enjoy our lives and experience The Prosperous Retirement.

11.

ESTATE PLANNING IN THE PROSPEROUS RETIREMENT

*"In this world nothing can be said to be certain
except death and taxes."*
—BENJAMIN FRANKLIN, 1789

SYNOPSIS: Estate planning deals with issues that are connected to death and dying. The original concept of the term concerned the disposition of assets left by a person who had died. Today, estate planning includes instructions about the disposition of assets, but it also includes planning to avoid estate taxes, income taxes, and excess expenses, as well as instructions about dealing with health-related questions, disability, and incapacity. Estate planning is heavily marketed by attorneys, insurance agents, and financial planners. It is an important reason that retirees seek the services of these professionals. An understanding of the issues and alternatives will help keep fees under control and also help avoid the purchase of unnecessary services and products. An understanding of estate planning also will help you to manage your retirement in a way that allows you to squeeze out the maximum measure of prosperity.

IF YOU LOOK UP "estate" in the dictionary, you will find that one of the definitions is, "the assets and liabilities of a dead person." From this, you might guess that "estate planning" consists of instructions for the disposition of a person's earthly possessions. That was the principal meaning of estate planning for a long time, but in today's complicated world, it includes a much wider range of issues. Today, estate planning also includes questions concerning the income and estate taxes due to the state and federal governments from the estate of a deceased person. It includes several insurance factors, and the use of certain legal devices to avoid or postpone taxes. Estate planning also concerns issues connected with disability, incompetence, incapacity, and medical treatment. As unpleasant as it is to think about these matters, it is vitally important to your well-being. Leaving your affairs in good order is not only a way of denying the government an excessive claim on your assets, but it is a sign of your respect and consideration for your heirs, the people who will be forced to sort out any untidiness that you leave behind. Estate planning is a highly technical subject. There are many books on the overall subject, and even volumes on many of the subtopics. The purpose of this modest chapter is simply to alert you to some of the key estate planning issues, to urge you to get professional assistance in doing your estate planning, and to keep your planning current.

DISPOSITION OF ASSETS

The first issue to be considered is the disposition of assets. There are four basic methods in current use to leave instructions about the distribution of assets.

1. Wills
2. So-called "will substitutes"
3. Living trusts
4. Intestacy

Intestacy

There is disagreement in the legal and financial planning community over the "best form" of estate planning. In truth, none of the methods is the undisputed champion, but intestacy generally is regarded as a loser.

Intestacy is the condition of dying without a will—intestate. In the event that a person dies without a will, the state of residence imposes rules concerning the disposition of assets. It would be a rare person who would want to dispose of assets in exactly the way the state directs. In addition, if you have considerable assets and die without leaving instructions, the process of untangling your affairs could burden your heirs for a considerable time. Clearly, you do not want to die intestate.

Wills

The classic estate planning document is a will: a legally binding set of instructions about what is to be done with a person's assets and liabilities at death. For a will to be legally enforceable, it must meet certain standards for format and documentation, which vary from state to state. In general, the will needs to be made by a competent person, without duress. The will must be in a form that is clear and be properly signed and witnessed. A holographic will, which is written by hand, does not need witnesses in most jurisdictions. It is, however, just a curiosity, because you do not want to write a will without the benefit of professional legal counsel.

Will Substitutes

The next alternative employs "will substitutes." A will substitute refers to a form of ownership that transfers property automatically on the death of the owner, without going through probate or any other legal process. A common form of will substitute is Joint Tenancy with Right of Survivorship (JTWROS), in which two or more persons are listed as joint owners of the account. If one person dies, the account transfers to the survivor. There are other will substitutes: "Payable on Death" (POD) accounts; retirement plan accounts with designated beneficiaries; life insurance contracts, including annuities, which have beneficiaries other than your estate. All assets owned in the form of a will substitute are included in the deceased person's taxable estate, but they are not included in the probate estate for purposes of qualifying for simplified probate. (See below.) Many people, without the benefit of a qualified advisor, see will substitutes as a convenient way to avoid probate. They may not understand all the ramifications, including the estate tax consequences. These ownership forms can play a role in smaller estates, but they should be used with caution in larger estates, if at all.

Living Trust

The last basic method for the disposition of property is the so-called "revocable living trust." A trust is a legal form in which one person (the grantor) places property in the care of a second party (the trustee) for the benefit of a third party (the beneficiary). A living trust is an arrangement by which a living person transfers ownership of assets to the trust. A revocable trust can be revoked by the grantor. There are testamentary trusts, in which the property transfer is made by the estate of a deceased person, and irrevocable trusts, which cannot be revoked. While normally there are three parties to a trust, that does not mean that the trust must involve three different people.

You may be amazed to discover that it is perfectly legal, and actually useful, to make a trust in which all three parties are the same person. This is not even a taxable event because it is only a change in the form of ownership and not a change of owner, but it may be a great help in dealing with your estate. The point of such an arrangement is to make your death an event that does not affect the ownership of the assets. The trust—not the beneficiary, nor the grantor, nor the trustee—"owns" the assets. The trust continues to exist even after the death of any of the three parties. The trust document sets up a successor trustee to take over the management of the trust assets in the event of the death or incapacity of the trustee. With only minimal paperwork, the new trustee takes over management of the assets, and this change does not have to go through probate or any other judicial process.

PROBATE

Many people are concerned about probate, particularly the expense of probate. Technically, the probate process is simply a judicial process of "proving the will." The process establishes the validity of the will and provides supervision for the execution of the will. The probate process is a matter of state law and the will is probated in the state of residence of the deceased. For many retirees, the question of legal residence can be difficult. It is not impossible to have two or even more states claiming their share of your estate. In fact, if you own real estate in another state, your estate definitely will have to go through "ancillary probate"—an additional probate process—in the state where the real estate is located.

Some states have very high costs of probate because the lawyers have succeeded in getting laws adopted that allow them to charge fees based on the value of the estate rather than on the work involved. In such states, it is common for probate costs to exceed 10% of the value of the estate. In other states, where "fair fees" are mandated, the cost of probate may be just a few percent, say 3% to 4%. Let's note, however, that 3% of $1 million is $30,000. In those states where probate costs are high, wills typically are not the right answer for large estates.

Public Process

Another disadvantage of the probate process is that it is a public process. A will is "published" and any interested party can be informed of the provisions of your will. Let's say that you decide to leave more money to one child than another. This would become public knowledge in the probate process, while it could be concealed with a living trust arrangement. There are other important benefits to the living trust, and it has become the preferred vehicle for sophisticated estate planning. Among the other advantages of the living trust is the fact that it takes much less time to transfer an estate that is held in trust form. There is no need to wait to set up probate. There is no wait to get a personal representative appointed. There is no delay in making interim distributions out of the estate. The estate can be closed more quickly than an estate that goes through probate. These advantages make the transfer of closely held assets, like a family-owned business, simpler with a trust.

MANAGEMENT OF ASSETS

The trust also can—and this is a very big benefit—make it much easier to manage your assets when you are no longer able to do so because of infirmity or incompetence. The trust form makes it very easy for your heirs to turn the management of the assets over to a professional investment manager. The principal disadvantages of the living trust are that it generally is more expensive to set up than a will, and there is work to be done in transferring your assets into the trust name. For the kind of estate that most prosperous retirees own, the living trust probably is the "right answer."

POUR-OVER WILL

It is not necessary to have absolutely all your assets in the living trust. Generally, some assets—like your personal bank accounts—are not in the trust name. A provision normally is included in the living trust documentation which is called a "pour-over will." In essence, the pour-over will says "any property that I own at the time of my death that is not in my living trust will be 'poured over' from my personal ownership to trust ownership at the time of my death." Sometimes, a pour-over will can be enormously important because some advisors recommend the use of an "unfunded living trust." Generally, I view this arrangement as self-defeating, but we see it more often than you might think.

SIMPLIFIED PROBATE

Most states have provisions for simplified probate for small estates. As a result, a person with a small estate may elect to use a low-cost will even in a state with high probate expenses. The estate sometimes can be kept under the limit for simplified probate by the use of will substitutes. There may be disadvantages to this style of estate planning. For example, it may lead to an unplanned, unequal distribution of assets and unexpected taxes.

USING AN ESTATE ATTORNEY

Inexpensive computer programs and handbooks abound to guide you to the correct format for a will, but I recommend that you avoid them. These computer programs can give you the easy information, but they cannot ask you the pointed questions, give the wise advice, and keep you from making bad elections. Skilled estate planning attorneys can do all these things and their services are worth every dollar that they typically charge for basic estate planning documentation. If your estate planning is more complicated, their services will cost more, but bring a lot more benefit. There is, of course, the potential danger of being lured into a complicated estate plan when a simple plan might do just as well. Like any other expensive purchase, you need to examine the benefits and costs of all the alternatives. Do not let a trivial benefit drive you to spend a lot more money on estate planning. It is acceptable, even smart, to ask an attorney what various alternatives will cost and to make clear the benefits of each alternative.

When you select your estate planning attorney, make certain that you get a true estate planning specialist. If you have taken my advice and established a trusting relationship with a financial advisor, the recommendation of that advisor can be very helpful in finding the right attorney. The key question to ask the attorney is, "What portion of your practice is estate planning?" Unless the answer is something like, "the overwhelming percentage," keep looking. This brings us to the controversy about wills and trusts. A second question to ask the attorney is, "How many of your estate planning cases result in wills and how many in living trusts?" The answer should be that there is some balance and the decision is made on the specifics of the client's situation, not on the lawyer's prejudice. Some estate planning attorneys tend to use living trusts for everyone. Others tend to use wills for everyone. Neither is the universal right answer. The right answer is that the attorney should evaluate your particular situation before recommending either solution. The basic trade-off between a will and a living trust is that the living trust usually is more expensive, but it avoids the public probate that is required for a will. A major question in making this choice is the cost of probate in the state of your legal residence. An estate planning attorney, possibly your financial advisor, can give you a good idea of the cost in your state based upon your assets and goals.

BENEFITS OF A LIVING TRUST

Here are 10 reasons why a funded, revocable living trust arrangement may be preferable to a will.

1. Avoids legal and administrative expenses of probate.
2. Reduces the time to transfer the estate.

3. Ensures privacy.
4. Provides a simple way to manage your assets in case of your incapacity, preferable to a power of attorney.
5. Can serve as a receptacle for death benefits.
6. Allows continuation of family income upon death, disability, or incompetence.
7. Avoids ancillary probates in other states.
8. Allows a smoother transition of closely held assets.
9. Provides a flexible tool for complex estate planning.
10. Is easier to amend than a will.

Another benefit sometimes claimed for living trusts is that they provide for estate tax benefits. While this is true, it is equally true for a properly drawn will. Everything a living trust can do about taxes can be done with a will. Tax savings are a potential benefit of any estate planning and do not depend on the form used.

FEDERAL ESTATE TAX SYSTEM

The basic scheme of federal estate taxation is simple. All persons, when they die, are allowed to pass $625,000[1] to anyone they want without federal estate taxes. They can pass an unlimited amount of wealth to their spouses without estate tax.[2] A person also can make an unlimited number of gifts each year. The only limit is that each individual must receive no more than $10,000 per year.[3] Thus, if your estate is no more than $625,000, federal estate taxes are not a problem. If your estate is a little larger than $625,000, you can use gifts to lower it to $625,000. If you are married, you can just leave it all to your spouse. If your estate exceeds $625,000 and it is not left to a spouse, the taxes begin at 37% of the excess and rise to 55%.

---

[1] Beginning January 1, 1998, this exemption gradually increases until, in 2006, it will be $1,000,000 (*See Appendix 5*).

[2] Assuming that the spouse is a U.S. citizen, or in the case of non-U.S. citizen spouse, that a Qualified Domestic Order Trust (QDOT) is used.

[3] The Taxpayer Relief Act of 1997 provides for indexing of this amount. It is to be increased annually by the rate of inflation, but the indexed amount will be rounded down to the next lower $1,000. It is likely to be several years until this increases to $11,000.

Figure 11-1 shows how quickly the gift and estate tax rates rise from 37% to 55%.

I have worked with these numbers for years, and I still find it shocking that the federal government can be so covetous of my hard-earned wealth. A recent estimate says that, over the next 20 years, something like $8 trillion (that is a "t") will be passed from one generation to another. Both the government and the Generation Xers are eyeing that wealth transfer as a solution to their financial challenges. The federal government is not likely to give up its claim on this enormous transfer of gifts and bequests.

ESTATE PLANNING TRAPS

If you were paying attention as I described the three ways that you could avoid estate taxes, you probably noted that each of these situations raised other questions. Your estate includes everything you own: financial assets, insurance proceeds, home value, personal possessions, art, antiques, and jewelry. If you have less than $625,000 in assets, you may have trouble enjoying The Prosperous Retirement, so this is a trap in itself. Giving away large sums of money when you are old, insecure, possibly in need of medical care, and not at all certain how long medical science can keep you going is

GIFT-ESTATE TAX RATES

FIGURE 11-1

Taxable Estate (after deductions)	Tax	Marginal Tax Rate (Tax on next dollar*)
$625,000	–	37%
$750,000	$55,500	39%
$1,000,000	$153,000	41%
$1,250,000	$255,500	43%
$1,500,000	$363,000	45%
$2,000,000	$588,000	49%
$2,500,000	$833,000	53%
$3,000,000	$1,098,000	55%

*The benefits of the graduated estate and gift tax rates and the $600,000 exemption are phased out for estates/gifts over $10 Million.

very difficult. If you are planning on using gifts when you are "old"[4] to avoid estate taxes, this also may turn out to be a trap. The biggest trap of all is the unlimited marital deduction. It seems like such a nice, easy, loving solution. You just die first, leave it all to your spouse, and let her or him spend it. If you do this, you waste $202,050,[5] because, as I explain in the next section, that was the value of the tax exemption that you did not use on your death.

UNIFIED CREDIT SHELTER TRUST (BY-PASS TRUST)

The smart way to avoid estate taxes on estates up to $1.25 million is to use your $202,050 tax credit to create a $625,000 trust that does not become part of your spouse's estate. This kind of a trust generally is called a "unified credit shelter trust," because it uses the $202,050 credit to create a $625,000 trust without paying any estate taxes. Sometimes this also is called a "By-Pass Trust," because it by-passes the estate of the surviving spouse.

This trust can have any restrictions or directions that you want, but the point of keeping the money in the trust, rather than just giving it to your children or other heirs, is that you can give the trustee the ability to use the income from the trust to support your spouse or any of your other heirs who need support. Typically, on the death of the surviving spouse, the trust is collapsed and the assets are distributed to the heirs.

QUALIFIED TERMINAL INTEREST PROPERTY TRUST (QTIP TRUST)

The remainder of the estate of the deceased goes into another trust for the survivor. The format frequently used for this trust is called a Qualified Terminal Interest Property (QTIP) Trust. The assets in the QTIP trust qualify for the spousal exemption from estate taxes in the estate of the deceased. To qualify for this exemption, the trust must provide that the income from the trust is paid to the surviving spouse. On the death of the survivor, the value of the trust is included in the estate of the second spouse to die. When the second spouse dies there is another $625,000 exemption, which allows the couple to pass a total of $1,250,000 plus the appreciation on the by-pass trust to their heirs without estate taxes.

---

[4] One of my heroes, Bernard Baruch, said "A person is 'old' if they are 15 years older than me."
[5] . . . or more, depending on when you die.

In essence, the first spouse to die uses the Unified Gift and Estate Tax Credit to put $625,000 into a "By-Pass Trust" without paying any estate taxes. The By-Pass Trust does not "belong" to the surviving spouse and is not included in that surviving spouse's estate. The trust may provide for the income on the trust assets to be paid to the surviving spouse or it may have other provisions. There is complete flexibility in the provisions of this trust. The picture of this strategy is illustrated in Figure 11-2.

One variation on the By-Pass Trust is called a "Family Trust." The Family Trust may give the trustee the authority to distribute income to family members other than the surviving spouse.[6] If the children or the parents of one of the spouses needs income, the trustee may be able to pass the income along to them if the trust authorizes such a distribution. This may be a way to pass income from the trust to a family member who needs the income and is in a lower tax bracket than the surviving spouse. The trust also may give the trustee the authority to invade the principal of the trust (sometimes called

---

[6] This often is called a "sprinkling provision."

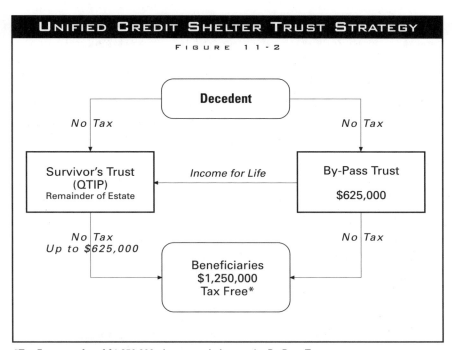

*Tax-Free transfer of $1,250,000 plus appreciation on the By-Pass Trust.

"the corpus") if one of the designated beneficiaries has a need that is recognized by the trust and which exceeds the income available.

This is not simple stuff. It takes close cooperation between you and the estate planning attorney. It also may be helpful to have your financial advisor involved in this process if the advisor is familiar with your family situation and may be able to pose some useful "what if" questions. It is important to get your estate planning documents in good order, because you will not be around to correct them when they come into effect.

A couple can leave $1,250,000, plus the appreciation in the By-Pass Trust, to their heirs without estate taxes. If there are many years between the death of the first spouse and the second spouse, it is possible that the By-Pass Trust can grow to be much more than $625,000. There are two problems, however, in allowing the By-Pass Trust to retain "income." If the income comes in the form of interest, dividends, capital gains distributions, or realized capital gains, and is not distributed to the beneficiaries in the year that it is realized, the income will be taxed at the tax rate for trusts, which goes up much more rapidly than individual rates. For example, a trust with income of only $7,500 is in the very highest federal income tax bracket—39.6%. If the "income" in the trust is in the form of unrealized capital gains, there is no "stepped-up cost basis" (see Chapter 13 or the glossary) on the assets when the trust is dissolved. If the trust liquidates the assets, the capital gains are taxable at capital gains rates and, if the assets are distributed to the heirs, they inherit the trust's cost basis. There is no general bottom line to this discussion. The decision about investing the By-Pass Trust assets for growth or income should be based on the overall situation of the surviving spouse and the heirs. The same is also true of the decision about distributing income or retaining it in the trust.

LARGER ESTATES

Using the techniques that we have described, a couple can leave $1,250,000 to their heirs without estate taxes. If the estate is larger than $1,250,000, other techniques are in order. No estate is too large to avoid estate taxes, but the more complicated techniques generally result in a loss of control over some of the assets. Really big estates, say larger than $5 million, may require the use of multiple trusts, foundations, partnerships, or other techniques that are the realm of a select circle of estate planning specialists and which are well beyond the scope of this modest effort. Between $1,250,000 and $5,000,000 (a lovely neighborhood, by the way), there are a number of techniques for keeping your money out of the hands of the Washington establishment.

THE LIQUIDITY ISSUE

In these intermediate-sized estates, taxes may need to be paid. Consideration must be given to the source of cash with which these taxes are to be paid. This is called "the liquidity issue." The liquidity issue affects everyone, but comes down hardest on the owners of large illiquid assets. Assets like farms, ranches, family-owned businesses, and non-income producing real estate can be valuable, causing taxes to be due, but they are not readily converted into cash. Special provisions in the estate tax laws are designed to provide some flexibility for the owners of assets like these, but the programs are restrictive and may not prove to be the best solution. Expert analysis of your situation and objectives will help you decide the best course of action.

LIFE INSURANCE

One alternative may be to just pay the taxes out of the proceeds of a life insurance policy purchased for this specific purpose. A typical way of doing this is for each spouse to leave the interest in the illiquid asset to the surviving spouse. The couple takes out a special form of life insurance called "second-to-die" life insurance. This policy pays benefits only on the death of the second spouse.[7] This kind of insurance is significantly cheaper than two separate policies.

Irrevocable Life Insurance Trust (ILIT)

Obviously, if the proceeds of the life insurance policy go into the estate of the second spouse, they will greatly increase the estate taxes to be paid. The typical way to keep the life insurance proceeds out of the estate is to place the insurance policy in an irrevocable life insurance trust (ILIT—pronounced like "eyelet"). The ILIT allows the insurance

---

[7] Some second-to-die policies pay a benefit on the first death, such as converting to a paid-up policy, to which no further premiums are payable.

proceeds to pass to the heirs without income or estate taxes. The second-to-die life insurance policy is owned by the ILIT. The trustee of the ILIT is directed to pay the proceeds to your heirs. The annual premiums on the insurance are paid with annual gifts to the ILIT, which are disclaimed by the policy beneficiaries.[8] Using an ILIT, you can leave a lot of money to your heirs without estate or income taxes. The only limitation on the use of this technique is the cost of the insurance and your ability to shelter the annual contributions using your annual gift tax exclusion.

An important use of ILITs is to provide liquid funds to your estate with which to pay the taxes due on assets that cannot be sold. Assume that you own a ranch in Montana worth $3,000,000. Your other assets are worth $1,250,000. You shelter the $1,250,000 using a Family Trust arrangement, but there will be $1,428,000 of federal estate taxes due on the value of the ranch. If you do not want your heirs to be forced to sell the ranch, you have to provide liquid assets on your death to pay the taxes. The most economical way to provide this liquidity is through the use of a second-to-die policy owned by an ILIT. The life insurance proceeds would be available to the heirs and they would not be forced to liquidate the ranch within nine months of the death to pay the taxes.

ANNUAL GIFT TAX EXCLUSION

A very popular technique for reducing estate tax liability and transferring wealth is the use of the $10,000 annual gift exclusion. The Taxpayer Relief Act of 1997 provides for indexing this $10,000 amount by the rate of inflation. Unfortunately, the indexed amount will be rounded down to the next lower $1,000, and thus, it will be several years until this increases to $11,000. This exclusion allows you to make gifts to as many people as you want as long as each gift does not exceed $10,000. Gifts can be made in cash or in other property. Using this technique, a married couple can gift up to $40,000 per year to a married child and that child's spouse. This is a very effective way to trim down an estate, and it can be altered from year to year according to investment results. If a regular pattern of gifting is

---

[8] The use of the so-called Crummey Powers—disclaiming the gifts—needs to be done exactly right. Your estate planning attorney should help the insurance advisor get this set up and advise the trustee on the appropriate procedures.

established, the tax law allows your surrogate to continue the gifting under a power of attorney, but only if the power of attorney contains specific language authorizing the continuation of the gifting.

FAMILY LIMITED PARTNERSHIP

A technique that is getting a lot of attention in estate planning circles is the use of the Family Limited Partnership or the Family Limited Liability Company (LLC). This technique is relatively new and court cases are defining the limits of its use. The basic idea is that, by placing your assets in a family limited partnership, you can retain control of the assets and conveniently gift fractional interests in those assets to other family members. In addition to the convenience and control, this technique allows the owners of the assets to get more bang for their annual $10,000 gifts. The theory is that, because the gift represents a minority interest in the ownership of the asset, it is worth less than "book value." The minority position lacks control and suffers from a lack of liquidity, so any valuation model supports the reduced value.

An example may help to make this complex device a little clearer. Assume that you own and operate a paint store. The store is valued at $1 million. You would like to begin transferring ownership to your three children, but you do not want to lose control of the business. (Presumably, you lost control of the kids a long time ago.) You create a Family LLC and transfer the ownership of the business to the LLC.[9] This is a non-taxable event, because it is simply a change of ownership form rather than a change of ownership. In the first year, you decide to transfer ownership interests to your three children. You give each of them a 2% interest in the LLC. It looks like a gift tax is going to be due because each interest appears to be worth $20,000 [$1,000,000 x .02 = $20,000] and that exceeds your annual $10,000 gift tax exclusion. In fact, this may not be a taxable event if you can convince the IRS that each gift is worth only $10,000 because the new owners do not control the asset, cannot sell their interests, and, in general, are subject to all the disabilities of minority owners of an illiquid asset. To make this even more interesting, you and your spouse could increase the gifts to a total

---

[9] Not all states allow one-person LLCs, so you may have to do this with your spouse.

of 4% of the LLC to each child by combining your gifting. If the children are married, you could increase the gifts to 8% of the LLC to each family unit. In two years, you could gift 48% of a $1 million business without paying taxes. Remember, the use of the Family LLC or Family Partnership is definitely not for amateurs. You need the help of an attorney who is well-versed and up-to-date on the latest court decisions and IRS rulings.

WHICH ASSETS TO GIFT

One of the controversial issues in estate planning is what kind of assets to gift. Some advisors recommend gifting appreciated assets because, they argue, your heirs may pay less taxes on the capital gains when the assets are liquidated. Under the present rules, the maximum tax on long-term capital gains is 20% and it only takes $41,200 of taxable income to put a married couple in the 28% tax bracket. A single filer needs only $24,650 of taxable income to be in a 28% bracket. There is another argument that says that if the asset is continuing to appreciate, you get that additional appreciation out of your estate.

That argument may hold some water, but the hole in the bucket is the management issue. Assume that, a few years ago, you invested $5,000 in a local technology company. The investment has been successful and is now worth $30,000. Your estate totals well over $1,250,000 and you can see this investment growing to $100,000 over the next few years. If you gift the shares to your three children right now, you get the $30,000 out of your estate, as well as the other $70,000 of appreciation that is expected over the next few years. It looks like a great strategy because it transfers $100,000 future value for this year's annual gift exclusions. There are two problems. First, the gift to the children is not really $30,000, it is only $25,000 because the asset carries with it your cost basis and a tax liability of $5,000. Second, how do the children know when to sell this? Typically, a rapidly appreciating asset needs management. If you lose the ability to manage this rapidly appreciating stock, it could turn into aggravation for both you and the recipient. Even if you are helping to manage the asset, the new owners may be reluctant to sell at the right time because, lacking your sophistication, they may see the taxes to be paid as an obstacle to selling. Depending on your age and other circumstances, I frequently recommend holding highly appreciated assets to get a stepped-up cost basis. (See Chapter 12 and the glossary.) Other alternatives are to use the highly appreciated asset to fund a Charitable Remainder Trust (CRT) or as an outright charitable gift.

CHARITABLE DONATIONS

If you donate an appreciated asset[10] to a bona fide charity, you generally get to deduct the fair market value of the donated asset from your taxable income.[11] Let's assume you bought some XYZ stock years ago for $100. Over the years, the stock has appreciated to $10,000. If you sell the stock, you will have to pay $1,980 in capital gains taxes. This makes the net value of the stock only $8,020—the sales price minus taxes. Instead of selling the stock, you decide to gift it to your favorite charity. You get a tax deduction of $10,000, the full market value of the stock. There are no income taxes to be paid—in fact, the $10,000 deduction saves you $3,600 in taxes if you are in a 36% tax bracket. The net cost of this gift is only $4,420 [$8,020 – $3,600] and the charity gets the full $10,000. If you have a charitable inclination, it is wise to make your donations with appreciated assets. Many charities have arrangements by which they can liquidate stocks and bonds at low cost or sometimes without cost. From an estate planning perspective, the gift may reduce your estate tax liability, but it also reduces the assets available for your heirs. Generally, charitable gifting needs to start with a desire to aid the charity, but sometimes it just makes pure economic sense.

Charitable Remainder Trust

Using a Charitable Remainder Trust (CRT) may create a situation where a charitable donation actually makes money for you. You and your spouse are both 67 years old. Let's assume that years ago, instead of investing only $100 in XYZ stock, you invested $1,000. Today, it is worth $100,000. If you sell the stock, your capital gains tax will be $19,800. If you give the stock to your heirs during your lifetime, they get your low cost basis, and will have to pay a large capital gain on the sale of the

---

[10] Special rules apply to personal property.

[11] See Chapter 12, Managing Taxes in The Prosperous Retirement, for more details.

stock. If you leave the stock in your estate, it will get a stepped-up cost basis, but will cost at least $37,000 in estate taxes. Either way, the stock actually is worth a lot less than $100,000.

Your financial advisor points out that XYZ stock pays no dividend, and asks if you would like to convert this asset to an income stream. Instead of giving the stock to your heirs or holding on to it, your financial advisor asks you to consider using the highly appreciated stock to fund a Charitable Remainder Trust. Your estate planning attorney is familiar with this technique and drafts the trust document. The document provides, that for as long as you and your spouse live, you can take 8% per year in income from the trust.[12] The document specifies that if, in a given year, the trust does not have 8% income, you can make up the shortfall in some future year when it has more than 8% income. When you and your spouse are both gone, the remainder in the trust will go to a specified charity. You execute the document, get a tax identification number for the trust, and open a brokerage account for the trust. Then you put the XYZ stock into the account. You sell the stock and reinvest the proceeds in whatever vehicle you wish and begin to draw income of $8,000 per year. At the time that you set up the trust, you get credit for a charitable donation of $22,694.[13] In your 36% tax bracket, this saves you $8,170 in taxes. In other words, the net cost of the CRT is only $72,030 [$100,000 − $19,800 − $8,170], but you are getting $8,000 per year of income. Your net investment was only $72,030 because, if you had sold the stock and paid taxes, you would have had only $80,200 to invest and you would not have had the tax savings of $8,170. Income of $8,000 on a net investment of $72,030 is a return of 11.1%. If you had sold the stock in your own account and paid the taxes, you would have had to invest the $80,200 at 10% to have gotten $8,000 per year of income. To get $8,000 in today's bond market, you would have to invest in some really terrible junk bonds with all the attendant risk.

There is still the issue that when you and your spouse are both gone, the value of the assets in your CRT will go to a bona fide charity of your

---

[12] The minimum annual income is 5%, but there are ways to avoid this—see Chapter 10.

[13] Assuming that the applicable IRC §7520 interest rate is 7.4%.

choosing. That is, however, not the end of the story. If you and your spouse live your statistical life expectancy of about 16 years, you will receive $128,000 of income from the CRT. The net present value of that stream of income discounted at 5.4%[14] is about $84,286. In other words, by giving away this stock, you have made a profit of about $15,000 if you live to your life expectancy. If either of you live longer than your life expectancy—and Chapter 4 explained why you probably will—the value will be even greater. In addition, when you are both dead, the remainder in the trust will go to the charity of your choice. This looks like an opportunity to do well while you are doing good.

Although the CRT is an irrevocable trust and the remainder must go to a qualified charity, your attorney can draft the trust in a way that allows you to change the designated charity if you wish. The cost of setting up the CRT can range from nothing to several thousand dollars. Many charities have arrangements with attorneys to draft the trust document without cost to you, the donor, if the charity is irrevocably named as the remainder beneficiary. Some assets are more complicated than others and some trusts are more complicated—both factors affect the cost. If you have highly appreciated assets in your estate, you should consider the benefits of a CRT. You get a terrific economic benefit, but—just like the outright charitable gift—it does deprive your heirs of the assets that you place in the trust.

WEALTH REPLACEMENT TRUST

If you feel guilty about depriving your heirs of the value of the XYZ stock, you can create another trust called a "Wealth Replacement Trust." The purpose of this irrevocable life insurance trust is to use an insurance policy to replace the value of the XYZ stock for your heirs. Using the income from the CRT, or other assets, you fund the ILIT with a $100,000 second-to-die policy and when you and your spouse are gone, and the charity has received the remainder of the CRT, your heirs will get $100,000 in life insurance benefits free of both income and estate taxes.

There are other, even more exotic, estate planning tools that can achieve beautiful results in the hands of skilled practitioners, but these tools are potentially dangerous in the hands of amateurs.

---

[14] The current interest rate on intermediate-term government bonds.

DURABLE POWER OF ATTORNEY

The same dynamic that has led to The Prosperous Retirement also has led to complications in the field of estate planning. The fact that Americans are living longer and longer greatly increases the probability that they will go through a period of ill health, incapacity, or even incompetence. It is an important part of the estate planning process to deal with these issues. It is probable that, at some point in your life, you will—at least for a short time—be unable to conduct your routine business. For instance, you could break a wrist in a skiing accident and for a few weeks be unable to write. Who will sign your checks? What happens if there is a business contract to sign?

The simple answer lies in a document called a durable power of attorney. A power of attorney is a document that delegates specific authority to another person (your "attorney-in-fact") to act on your behalf. A power of attorney normally is given for a specific purpose and for a limited time. For example, you might give your real estate agent the power to represent you at a real estate closing while you are out of town. A durable power of attorney generally has a broader mandate and a longer period, perhaps even an unlimited period. The word "durable" in this context means that the power of attorney remains in force even if you were to become incapacitated and could no longer execute a valid power of attorney. A durable power must provide that, even in the event of subsequent incapacity of the principal, the power remains in effect; this is the essence of its durability.

Special Durable Power of Attorney

An important issue that has arisen in recent years is whether your attorney-in-fact is empowered to make gifts on your behalf. The rule used to be that, if you had established a pattern of gift giving, your attorney-in-fact could continue that activity. In recent years, the IRS has taken the position that the durable power of attorney must contain specific authority for your attorney-in-fact to continue the gifting program that you have in effect. Without this specific authority in the durable power of attorney, the IRS has contested gifts made by attorneys-in-fact. A durable power of attorney with this specific authority is called by some a "special durable power of attorney."

Safeguarding the Power of Attorney

It is important to remember that a durable power of attorney is a very powerful document and can create a lot of mischief if misused. A technique that you might want to discuss with your attorney is placing the durable power of attorney in your attorney's safe. You then give the attorney instructions to release the power of attorney to your attorney-in-fact only under two circumstances. First would be if you give the attorney instructions to release it. Second would be if the attorney is informed by a doctor that you are no longer competent.

LIVING WILL

Another document that more and more Americans are including in their estate planning is the living will. The living will is a document that expresses your wishes concerning medical treatment in the event that you are terminally ill. All 50 states have recognized living wills and most have a prescribed statutory format. To be effective, the living will needs to be in the right format. Living wills were around for many years before all the states got around to recognizing them. If you have an old living will, you should show it to your estate planning attorney and ask if it meets your state's requirements. Even if your living will does meet your state's current requirements, you must recognize that it is effective only if you are certified as being "terminal." Being sick, incapacitated, in constant pain, or even in a coma is not enough to bring the living will into effect. One other condition to making the living will effective is that it must be in the hands of the attending physcian. I strongly recommend having a copy of your living will right in your medical files.

HEALTH CARE PROXY

There is a newer kind of document that gives more comprehensive guidance concerning your health care. This document is called by various names, including "health care proxy," "durable medical power of attorney," and "advanced health care directive." The law in this area is emerging as society grapples with the care of our burgeoning population of older people. Some states have established a statutory hierarchy of people who can make health care decisions for persons who are unable to act for themselves. Even if that statutory hierarchy exists in your state, there may be a problem if the people who are empowered to act for you do not know your views and preferences. It is not hard to imagine a scene around a hospital bed where various family members have differing recollections about what you have told them in the past.

Clearly, the best solution is to commit your thoughts on these matters to writing in the form of a medical memorandum. Certain attorneys, who are called "elder law" specialists, deal with documents like this. The document records your wishes about how you want to be treated in various circumstances, and gives authority to specific people to make decisions for you in the event that you are no longer able to do it for yourself. These decisions might concern life-support systems, forced feeding, organ donation, and other vital medical decisions. This document extends well beyond what a living will can do and, personally, I wouldn't leave home without one.

PERSONAL PROPERTY MEMORANDUM

Some people have personal property that may or may not be valuable, but which is important to them: a stamp collection, furniture, family heirlooms, a favorite piece of jewelry, or a painting. It is amazing how often items like these—not necessarily valuable things—are the focus of family disagreements.

A document called a personal property memorandum can direct the disposition of these important items. Such a memorandum obviously will be very helpful to the person designated to handle your estate. It details your accounts, your safe deposit boxes, and the location of documents that may be needed to settle your affairs. The memorandum also lists those special items that you want to go to specific people. Who gets the stamp collection, your grandfather's carved Meerschaum pipe, your great-grandmother's bureau, or the painting over the fireplace? Do you want to be buried with your wedding ring or does it go to a specific person? The memorandum also can give the details of how you want your funeral to be handled. This document is not strictly required, but if you were settling an estate for someone, wouldn't you prefer that they left a personal property memorandum?

CONSERVATORSHIP

One of the problems that can be avoided with a funded living trust arrangement is the need for a conservator. A conservator is a person appointed and supervised by a court to manage the affairs of a person who is no longer competent to manage his or her own affairs. The determination of competence is a public process done in the courts and a potential source of family disharmony. If the court determines that the person is not competent, a conservator is appointed to manage the person's affairs. A conservatorship is not common, but when it does happen, it can last for years and cost a lot of money. For all these reasons, it is worthwhile to avoid conservatorships. This can be accomplished by placing your assets in a funded living trust, and by executing a durable power of attorney and a durable medical power of attorney. With luck, these documents will prove to be unnecessary, but the risk—rare as it might be—is worth avoiding.

EXECUTOR

The last issue to be discussed is the choice of the person to administer your estate after your death. This person is variously called "administrator," "executor," or "personal representative," and is responsible for all the many steps involved in settling your affairs. This person arranges your funeral, distributes your assets according to your instructions, complies with the requirements of the state and federal governments, and manages your assets during the period of estate administration. This is a big job and whoever is burdened with this work is entitled to compensation. Usually, people look to a family member to be the executor of their estate. That may be fine if you have a family member who has the expertise, time, and energy to administer the estate. The person selected to act as executor should have fiduciary experience and expertise as a business person. Integrity is vital, but they also must have genuine compassion and concern for the welfare of your beneficiaries.

Most people expect that their attorney will guide the selected family member through the maze of decisions, regulations, and deadlines. If your choice for executor is one of your children, you need to consider the dynamics of your family to know if that is going to work without undue stress. If you hope to have your spouse act as your executor, remember that your spouse is getting old at the same rate that you are and estates can sometimes take years to settle. If the executor dies in the midst of settling an estate, it can be a major problem.

Some advisors suggest using the trust department of a bank as the executor of an estate. This is not a bad idea, but also not a cheap idea, and it has one major drawback. A trust officer, representing as he or she does the trust department of a bank, is likely to be rigid and legalistic. Trust officers often are as concerned about their fiduciary obligations as about the welfare of your beneficiaries. They probably would argue that strict compliance with your instructions and the rules is what they were hired to do and that is in the best interest of your beneficiaries. Unfortunately, the best set of instructions cannot foresee all the contingencies that might arise. In the event of an unexpected situation, you probably would like to see the executor resolve any doubts in favor of your beneficiaries. Therefore, if you elect to have a trust department carry this burden for you, you might want to consider an arrangement in which you name one of your family members as a co-trustee. The bank trust department is to do all the administration and the family member merely supervises the trust department. The family member's supervision is enforceable because the family member has the right to replace the trust department with another trust department if, for any reason, that seems desirable.

One of the other alternatives that some people consider is having one of their estate planning team act as their executor. Some members of your estate planning team may be reluctant to act as an executor because of a perceived conflict of interest. Never—I repeat, never—name a person or institution as your executor without consulting them and finding out if they are willing and able to serve.

CONCLUSION

This long and melancholy chapter would be hard enough to deal with if it were just once in your life. Unfortunately, the sad truth is that your estate planning needs to be reviewed every year. The only joy is knowing that you have dealt with your estate in the same thorough and responsible way that you have managed the rest of your life. I hope you get to review these issues many, many times before they come into play.

12.

TAX MANAGEMENT IN THE PROSPEROUS RETIREMENT

"Anyone may so arrange his affairs that his taxes shall be as low as possible. He is not bound to choose that pattern which best pays the Treasury. Everyone does it, rich and poor alike, and all do right; for nobody owes any public duty to pay more than the law demands."
—JUDGE LEARNED HAND

SYNOPSIS: Income taxes in retirement are no more complicated than they were before retirement, they just seem to be. The old problems that you have learned to deal with over the years tend to become less acute in retirement, while a whole new series of challenges appear. The basic rules continue to apply, but their relative importance may change. It still makes sense to do what you can to reduce your tax burden. It still makes sense to pay taxes later rather than sooner. It still makes sense to do year-end tax planning. It still makes sense to work with the best tax professional that you can find. The new challenges may lie in the field of medical deductions, charitable contributions, the management of taxable assets versus tax-deferred assets, and the production of the cash flow you need without producing excess taxes.

IT WOULD BE EASY TO ASSUME that anyone who has reached retirement has a basic understanding of how the income tax system works. As logical as that may seem, I would guess that a lot of retirees, just like a lot of working people, would not pass a test on basic tax facts. Years ago, my wife worked with a woman—an educated woman with professional responsibilities—who was certain that, when people turned 65, they no longer had to pay federal income taxes. She is now over 65 and I wonder if she still is at large? Even people who are well informed about taxes will find that, in retirement, some new issues may require research and a little thought. My thought about taxes is that I want to pay exactly what I owe, not one penny more and not one penny less. I also want to take Judge Hand's advice and arrange my affairs in the manner that reduces my obligation to the lowest legal amount.

Having said that, it is important to understand that a disagreement with the IRS can be very unpleasant and generally is something that people wisely shun. Therefore, most people try to avoid even the appearance of improprieties in their tax reporting. Your tax professional should be adept at knowing what patterns, what proportions, what kind of activities are likely to pique the IRS's interest. If you are going to hoist a lightning rod in your tax return, you want to know that you are doing it and be certain that you are well protected on everything in the return.

THE PROCESS OF DETERMINING YOUR TAX LIABILITY

The easiest way to understand the basic flow of taxes is to look at the Form 1040. You will find that the general flow of the form goes in the following order:

- Personal Information and Filing Status
- Gross Income
- Deductions
- Adjusted Gross Income (AGI) (gross income minus deductions)
- Itemized or Standard Deductions
- Exemptions
- Taxable Income (AGI minus deductions and exemptions)
- Tax Calculation (including other taxes, such as self-employment and alternative minimum tax)

•◦ Tax Credits
•◦ Tax Liability

FILING STATUS

The process of filing taxes begins with the selection of a filing status. This is not always as easy as it seems. Sometimes a joint filing for a married couple is not the most advantageous option. A typical example might be a situation where one spouse has huge medical expenses and the other earns most of the income. The medical expenses are deductible only to the extent that they exceed 7.5% of the adjusted gross income. If the couple files separately, there could be some tax savings. In some cases, unmarried people who are living together may wish to consider the tax implications of marriage. Sometimes there are opportunities to create additional taxable entities—trusts, businesses, and so on—rather than just filing a personal return. These are appropriate issues to review with your tax professional.

FIGURING YOUR GROSS INCOME

Gross income may include a lot more than just salary, dividends, interest, and capital gains. Pension income is taxable under the federal income tax, although some states exempt all or part of pensions from their state income tax calculation. Social Security benefits may be taxable depending on something called "provisional income," which will be discussed below. Gambling winnings in excess of losses are includible in income, as are any contest winnings. The value of "barter services" are taxable. Pages and pages of the code list items that are considered taxable income, some of which may not even occur to you. For instance, the accrual on a zero coupon bond (so-called Original Issue Discount—OID) is taxable as it accrues, even though you don't get any money until the bond matures. This means that you need to keep detailed records about the OID on which you pay taxes if the zero coupon bond is in a taxable account. If a partnership in which you had an interest goes bankrupt, the relief of indebtedness on your ownership interest is taxable even though you lost your investment. This is called "phantom income," and it is truly a bit of a mystery.

Some items that look like income but are not taxable include:

✔ Interest on municipal bonds
✔ Income that accrues and is not paid out in insurance contracts
✔ The living and traveling allowances of Peace Corps volunteers
✔ Veterans benefits
✔ Disability payments
✔ Benefits under a tax-qualified long-term care insurance policy, or a Medicare supplement, or health insurance policy
✔ Gifts and inheritances
✔ Educational benefits and scholarships, unless they are provided by an employer as a benefit

Entire books have been written on the subject of what is and what is not income for the purposes of the federal income tax, not to mention hundreds of court cases. Most of your income probably will fall into a regular pattern and you will soon know what is and what is not taxable. If a new source of income is added, make no assumptions about its tax status until you consult your tax professional. If there are business transactions, always inform your tax professional so he or she can evaluate the tax implications. The federal tax code is not logical, and reasoning by analogy can get you into an argument—or worse—with the Internal Revenue Service.

DEDUCTIONS

The question of deductions is even more complicated than the question of income.

✔ Some deductions are directly deductible from gross income.
✔ Some deductions are deductible from adjusted gross income.
✔ Some deductions are subject to a reduction based on your adjusted gross income.
✔ Some deductions must be amortized or taken over time.
✔ Some expenses just are not deductible.

Endless rules qualify or disqualify deductions, and the courts keep interpreting, changing, and modifying the rules. It probably would be possible to write a book just on the topic of the deductibility of business convention expenses.

Most people find that their deductions fall into predictable patterns and they learn about the rules that must be followed, the records that need to be kept, and the limitations that apply. As new situations arise, it is important to consult your tax professional. For example, say you buy 100 shares of XYZ Corporation. XYZ holds their annual shareholders' meeting in Fort Lauderdale, Florida, every year in January. You and your wife decide to go to Fort Lauderdale in January for a mid-winter get-a-way. While you are there, you decide to attend the shareholders' meeting. Is there a deduction available? It may surprise you to know that this is a legitimate business activity, so the cost of travel is deductible and perhaps a portion of your meals and lodging—depending on circumstances. Does this apply to both you and your spouse? Maybe yes and maybe no, depending on the title in which the shares actually are held. As legitimate as these deductions may be, if the IRS saw you taking 15 trips a year to exotic locations "to attend shareholder meetings" they might want to discuss this with you. Is it worth the possible hassle?

Limitations even exist on the gifts that you make to charitable organizations based on your income, the character of the property or services donated, and the nature of the charitable organization. More on this later. Gifts that you make to other individuals, no matter how charitable the purpose, are not deductible.

If you start a new business in retirement to generate some retirement earnings, the cost of setting up that business is deductible subject to a lot of restrictions.

Moving Expenses

The basic rule for deducting moving expenses is that they must be work-related and reasonable. If the expenses are deductible, they can be deducted directly from gross income. Many retirees move in the first few years of retirement. Few of them think in terms of making those moving expenses, which can be considerable, a tax deduction. Rules covering this topic vary depending on whether you are self-employed or just employed. The move must be more than 50 miles, and the expenses must be incurred within a year of the new employment. It could be very worthwhile to go over the requirements with your tax advisor and determine if you can meet them so that you can deduct these moving expenses.

The questions about deductions are almost endless, but the bottom line is that it probably is worthwhile to take an hour once a year to discuss your activities, expenses, and income with your financial advisor or tax professional to see if there are legitimate deductions that you are not claiming currently.

ADJUSTED GROSS INCOME

One of the tax questions that most people could not answer is "What is your adjusted gross income (AGI) plus or minus 10%?" Many people probably do not even know what adjusted gross income is. It is gross income minus certain deductions. It is a working number used in moving through the tax calculation from gross income (all income from all sources) to your calculated tax liability. The principal importance of AGI is that, at certain levels, the deductibility of some deductions is reduced and the taxability of Social Security benefits may be increased. For people with fairly high levels of income, it is worth watching. The principal deductions that come directly out of gross income to get AGI are:

✔ Pension plan and deductible IRA contributions
✔ Losses from sales and exchanges
✔ Alimony paid
✔ Expenses of producing royalty or rental income
✔ Trade or business expenses

It is worth noting that there are two ways to reduce AGI. One way is to have less income. This does not sound like a good idea, but if your current income is in excess of your current needs, it might make sense to investigate ways of reducing the income. For example, you might consider investing for capital gains rather than current income. You might consider using tax-deferred investment vehicles, such as annuities and life insurance. The use of municipal bonds to convert taxable income into tax-free income will reduce AGI, but municipal bond interest is added back to AGI to determine "provisional income" and the taxability of Social Security benefits. More about this below.

The second way to have less AGI is to increase deductions that are subtracted directly from gross income and are not deducted from AGI later in the process. Deductions like medical expenses, charitable contributions, and miscellaneous business expenses are deducted from AGI not from gross income. Accordingly, they do not reduce AGI. In some cases, AGI can be reduced with increased contributions to a retirement plan. This is another argument in favor of retirement earnings, if they allow you to make contributions to a retirement plan. The creation of a business vehicle to permit business expenses to be fully deducted from the business cash flow may increase the deductibility of those expenses and also make them deductible from gross income rather than from AGI. For example, let's say that you travel 5,000 miles per year for business purposes. The expense of business mileage is deductible as a business expense. If there is no business entity, the mileage expense is treated like a miscellaneous business expense and is subject to the 2% threshold, and the deduction comes off of AGI. If the expense is treated like a business expense through a business entity, it is fully deductible and the deduction comes off of gross income—a much better result. Other business expenses, such as the cost of business stationery, business phone lines, and so on, all can be treated in the same way, if there is a business purpose and a business entity.

ITEMIZED OR STANDARD DEDUCTIONS

This topic is a bit confusing, because we already have discussed deductions. However, those were the items that were deducted directly from gross income. A different set of items must be deducted—somewhat less advantageously—from adjusted gross income. A taxpayer has an election to take either the standard deduction or to itemize deductions. If the itemized deductions total more than the standard deduction, most people elect to itemize, but sometimes the hassle may not seem worth the effort. Remember what Judge Hand said.

Standard Deduction

The standard deduction on your 1998 return is $4,250 for a single filer and $7,100 for a couple filing jointly[1]. If a taxpayer is age 65 or older, he or she gets an additional deduction of $1,000 if single or $800 per person if married. If the taxpayer is legally blind, another deduction of $1,000 if single and $800 per person if married is available. Thus, if you and your spouse are over 65 and both blind, you could deduct $10,900 of AGI for purposes of the tax calculation. This is what passes for a good deal with the IRS.

Itemized Deductions

The big itemized deductions for retirees generally are medical expenses, taxes paid, interest paid, and charitable contributions. If the total of these deductions is about the same as the standard deduction, you may wish to think about grouping your deductions into alternate years and taking the standard deduction in between. This is particularly easy to do with charitable deductions. Say you give $1,000 a year to your public television station. Instead of giving them $1,000 this year and $1,000 next year, give them $2,000 this year and nothing next year. You also can elect to pay your state taxes in the year they accrue so they can be a deduction for that year on your federal taxes.

Medical Expenses

Like everything in the tax code, the definition of medical expenses is complicated. Generally, the definition includes the obvious: doctor bills, dentist bills, prescription glasses, medicine, and premiums paid for medical insurance, dental insurance, and tax-qualified long-term care insurance. Medical expenses also include travel expenses if the trip is "primarily for and essential to" medical care. Thus, a trip to the Mayo Clinic for purposes of a medical examination would be deductible. The limitations on these expenses, however, are an eye opener on the "logic" of the tax code. Meals on the trip are not deductible, nor is lodging in

---

[1] This figure and many of the other tax-related exemptions, allowances, restrictions, and deductible amounts are subject to change from year to year.

excess of $50 per night. If you are flying, the cost of travel is deductible, but if you are driving the deduction is limited to a statutory mileage allowance ($.10/mile in 1998) plus parking and tolls. Never mind the fact that it probably costs you more than $.36 per mile to operate your auto, including gas, maintenance, and depreciation; and that the deduction for charitable travel is $.14, business travel is $.325 and postal employees get $.4725. Now you know why the IRS has sharp pencils—to jab taxpayers.

Another obscure medical deduction is the cost of any special diet prescribed (in writing) by your doctor, over the cost of a normal diet.

After you have added up all of these expenses, deduct 7.5% of your AGI. The excess of medical expenses over 7.5% of AGI is deductible from AGI. Now you see one of the reasons why it is better to deduct against gross income rather than AGI. Knowing that you have to get over the 7.5% threshold to make your medical expenses deductible suggests that you should examine whether it might be possible to lump all your medical expenses into one year rather than spreading them over two or more years. Assume that you need a cataract operation and plan to have it done next spring. Suddenly, your spouse is hospitalized with a cancer scare. The doctors perform a series of expensive tests. Fortunately, the tests are all negative, but your medical expenses are well over the 7.5% of AGI threshold. From a tax point of view, it would make sense to move your cataract operation into this year, rather than waiting for next, because you know that the whole cost will be deductible this year.

Another planning opportunity is the situation in which one spouse has the preponderance of medical expenses and the other spouse earns most of the income. In this situation, the couple may be able to save taxes by filing separately. The medical expenses are deductible only to the extent that they exceed 7.5% of adjust gross income. Separating the income from the medical expenses by filing separate returns, the medical expenses would be subjected to a smaller reduction, but other changes will affect the separate returns. For example, if a married couple files separate returns and one spouse itemizes, the other spouse's standard deduction is reduced to zero, so they are both forced to itemize. To see how this strategy actually might work, the couple should have their tax professional prepare a comparison of the results of a joint return versus the separate returns. Your tax professional's software program makes comparisons like this quick and easy, and may save you a few hundred dollars in income taxes.

Taxes Paid

Property taxes are deductible, but levies for streets, sewers, sidewalks, and so on are not deductible. Taxes paid to foreign governments for income earned overseas generally is deductible from your AGI. Payments made to the state for estimated state taxes generally are deductible. Taxes assessed against the value of an automobile generally are deductible. The owner of an interest in a cooperative housing corporation can deduct his or her proportionate share of the real estate taxes paid on the cooperative's property.

Interest Paid

The basic rule on deductible interest used to be that a taxpayer generally could deduct interest paid or accrued on indebtedness. The indebtedness, however, had to be enforceable against the taxpayer. If, for example, parents paid interest on their child's car loan, they could not deduct that interest. In 1987, the rules were changed to exclude interest paid on personal indebtedness, with a few exceptions. Taxpayers still can deduct interest on a "qualified residence," subject to a $1 million limit on the mortgage. The "qualified residence" definition includes a principal residence and one other residence. As always, rules and restrictions exist, but the home mortgage deduction is a big one for most taxpayers. It should affect the thinking of retirees when they think about paying off their home mortgage. Be sure to read the section in Chapter 9 about paying off the mortgage.

Most taxpayers understand that the interest on consumer debt—car loans, credit card debt, and the like—is no longer deductible. As a result, most homeowners have arranged to replace those credit facilities with lines of credit based on their home equity. The interest on these home equity loans generally is deductible.

If a retiree owns more than two real estate properties, the extra properties probably should be organized into a business so that losses can be taken directly against gross income rather than against AGI. The business format also allows the taxpayer to use depreciation on the property to offset any income from the property. Normally, it is possible to show deductible losses in the first few years of ownership in spite of positive cash flow that exceeds the debt service. Another potential gambit for retirees who are building a new residence is to use margin borrowings on their investment portfolio in lieu of a construction loan. As long as the interest on the margin borrowings does not exceed the income from the portfolio, the interest is deductible in the year accrued. If the interest exceeds income, it can be carried forward and deducted in a subsequent year. This is not a tax savings, but it can save the retiree a lot of money in interest and origination fees.

Charitable Contributions

The deductibility of charitable contributions is limited to a percentage of the taxpayer's "contribution base." The percentage depends on two factors: the type of organization to which the contribution is made, and the type of property contributed. The contribution base is the AGI computed without using any net operating loss carryback. For most people, this means that the contribution base is their AGI. Deductions generally are limited to 50% of the contribution base, but lower limits may apply to gifts of property that are appreciated. More deep water. If you are thinking of making a large contribution to a charitable organization, be sure to check it out with your tax advisor before doing it. It might make sense to modify your plan.

There is some good news. If your contribution exceeds the limits, the excess can be carried forward for five years. The limits continue to apply, but being able to spread the deduction over five years should make it fully useful. All contributions need to be made to properly qualified organizations. If you are thinking of a big donation, be certain to verify that the organization is properly qualified. If you are embarrassed to ask, you can have your accountant or financial advisor ask for the verifying documentation.

Services contributed to charitable organizations—including blood donations—are not deductible. If you spend money for uniforms or equipment in conjunction with your service to a charitable organization, it is deductible, as are transportation and travel expenses incurred in your charitable service. If, for example, you travel 50 miles once a week to work as a volunteer in a hospital, you can deduct a standard mileage allowance ($.14 per mile), plus parking and tolls, for that travel.

Cash contributions of more than $250 must be substantiated by a written acknowledgment from the charity. If the donation shows up on a Form W-2 because it was a payroll deduction, no other documentation is required. In the case of larger donations, the charity may elect to report your contribution directly to the IRS. In this case, you technically do not require a written acknowledgment, but get it all the same.

Non-cash contributions are more complicated. Many retirees find themselves downsizing their household and having to find a new home for many serviceable items. If the total of non-cash contributions exceeds $500, the taxpayer must file Section A of Form 8283 with the details of the donation. If the non-cash donation exceeds $5,000, the taxpayer must get an appraisal of the contribution and fill out Section B of Form 8283, attaching it to the tax return. The appraisal generally is straightforward for most used property that is being appraised well below its acquisition cost. If the property has appreciated—it is worth more than you paid for it—there are other rules. Assume that, years ago, you bought a painting of the campus of the university you attended. The artist of that painting, for which you paid $100 45 years ago, became a renowned painter. The painting is now worth $10,000. If you donate this painting to the local hospital, which has no connection with the painting, you can deduct only $100. If, however, you donate the painting to the university, which has a function and purpose related to the painting, you can deduct the full $10,000 as long as you can document the fair market value of the painting. I offer this example, only one of many possible, to illustrate that if the tax deduction is an issue, always consult with your tax advisor before making a large contribution. There are many ins and outs and your charitable inclination could turn into an uncharitable aggravation.

Professional Fees

You probably noticed in Chapter 9 that I recommend using a number of professional advisors to help you manage your retirement. The Prosperous Retirement is a complicated undertaking and you don't want to spend any more of your time managing it than you must. Accordingly, there may be considerable fees for professional services incurred during the year. Fees paid in connection with the management of your investments generally are deductible as itemized deductions subject to the 2% floor for the total of such deductions. Fees paid for tax advice and the preparation of your taxes also are deductible, subject to the 2% floor.

Hobby Losses

No one would want to make a hobby out of losses, but when the IRS talks about "hobby losses," they are referring to losses that are related to business activities that seldom, if ever, show a profit. An activity is presumed to be a hobby if it does not produce profits in two of the five years ending with the current tax year. Horse breeding has special rules. I am reminded of the sign that I have seen on the wall of several small businesses: "This is a non-profit organization. It wasn't intended to be. It just turned out that way." I must note that any business that generates income should be able to show some kind of profit in two years out of five years. If you have trouble seeing how this might happen, you should talk with your tax advisor. Here is a hint. There is no law that says you have to be paid for the time you put in on your business. Even if your business activities fall into the hobby loss rules, the expenses for the business are deductible as itemized deductions to the extent that they do not exceed the income from the activity. If you start a business activity and it generates losses for a few years before it turns a profit, those losses are deductible as business losses, but eventually you need to become profitable.

EXEMPTIONS

Every taxpayer is allowed to exempt a certain amount of income from the federal income calculation. In 1998, the dollar amount for each exemption is $2,700.[2] This amount is adjusted each year to reflect

---

[2] In the spring of 1998, the IRS has not told us what these numbers will be. This figure is an estimate from CCH, Inc., in the 1998 Master Tax Guide.

inflation. On a joint return, two exemptions are allowed. Additional exemptions are allowed for "dependents." If a dependent exemption is claimed, the dependent must meet five tests (these are only brief summaries):

- ✔ Must have income of less than $2,650, or be under 24 years of age.
- ✔ Must receive more than half their total support from the taxpayer.
- ✔ Must be part of the taxpayer's family or a resident in the taxpayer's home.
- ✔ Must not file a joint return with his or her spouse.
- ✔ Must be a citizen or resident of the U.S., Canada, or Mexico for part of the year, or be an alien child adopted by and living with a U.S. citizen for the entire year.

If you are providing support for a relative, these rules may open some possibilities for tax savings. Let's assume that you and two siblings are providing support for your elderly mother. She receives $5,000 a year in Social Security benefits. In addition, each of the three of you give her $5,000 a year in support, so she is living on $20,000 a year of total income. Under the second rule, no one can claim her as a dependent because none of you are paying half of her support. She meets the income test, because her Social Security benefits are not taxable. She is certainly part of your family. Let's assume that your mother lived in the United States all last year. She meets all the rules except the second. If you and your siblings can agree that, each year, one of you will take the exemption, this meets the second requirement. The other two siblings must file an IRS declaration Form 2120, stating that they will not claim Mom as an exemption. The exemption can be passed around between the three siblings in succeeding years.

Phaseout of Exemption

Taxpayers with more than $124,500[3] of individual income or $186,800 of joint income lose a portion of their personal exemption. The exemption

---

[3] All the numbers in this paragraph are 1998 estimates from CCH, Inc.

is reduced by 2% ($50) for each $2,500 that the income exceeds the limit. Thus, when the taxpayer is $125,000 over the limit, he or she has lost the entire personal exemption. With $311,800 of taxable income, the taxpayer must pay about another $1,000 in taxes. This is what passes for a bad deal from the IRS's point of view.

TAX DEFERRAL

Many people think tax deferral is trivial. Pay now, pay later, what's the difference? Deferral may seem particularly trivial to these people in connection with retirement. They think that tax deferral will soon end as the funds are drawn out of the tax-deferred vehicle. Let's look at the numbers. Assume that, at age 59, you have accumulated $100,000 in savings which you believe probably will not be required to produce retirement income. You are considering two options, as illustrated in Figure 12-1. One account is fully taxable and the other is tax deferred. The fully taxable account is assumed to pay taxes each year on all its growth and dividends—a somewhat unreasonable assumption—but stick with me. The tax-deferred account accrues its growth and dividends without taxes until the investment is cashed in. When the tax-deferred asset is cashed in, taxes are paid on the increased value at the same rate that was paid on the taxable account. Both accounts have the same annual rate of return.

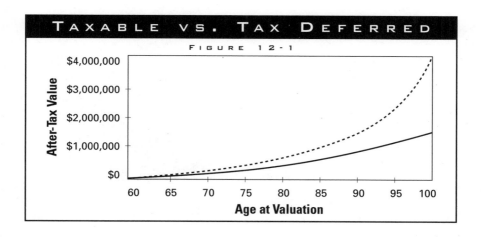

TAXABLE VS. TAX DEFERRED

FIGURE 12-1

Figure 12-2 shows the difference between the two accounts in terms of the percentage advantage of the tax-deferred account. In the first year, there is no difference. It takes a little over 10 years for the tax-deferred account to achieve a 10% advantage. By year 15, the advantage is over 20%, and by year 20, the advantage is pushing 40%. In the 33rd year, the advantage is a full 100%. The conclusion seems fairly clear. Tax deferred is almost always better than fully taxable.[4] In the first 10 years, tax deferral is not a significant advantage, but in longer periods, it offers a significant benefit.

Another way of understanding the benefit of tax deferral is to think about the net present cost of paying taxes. If you pay taxes currently as they accrue, the cost is 100% of the value of the taxes. If you can somehow defer the payment of the taxes, the net present value of the taxes paid in the future is less than 100%.

The idea of "net present value" may seem like a mystery, but it may become clearer when you answer the question, "Would you rather have $100 today or $100 10 years from now?" Obviously, you would rather have it today. The logic is that, if you can get it today and invest it, in 10 years it will be worth more than $100. How much more depends on the rate of return. Assume that 10-year Treasury bonds are yielding 5.5%. In

---

[4] This is not always true in practice because tax deferral normally has a cost. This is discussed in Chapter 7, Investment Alternatives.

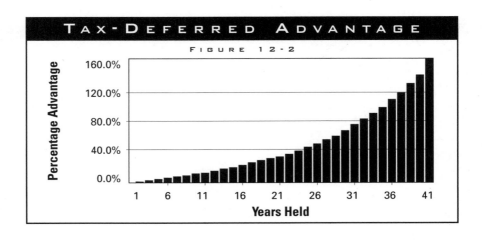

10 years, the $100 invested in those bonds will be worth $170.81. Conversely, if someone gave you just $58.54 today, and it were invested in these bonds, it would be worth $100 in 10 years.

We understand this concept almost intuitively, but somehow when someone says "tax deferral saves you money," it may seem more than a little questionable. It is simple. If something happens this year that causes you to owe the IRS $100, but you can somehow defer that payment— without penalty and interest—for 10 years, the net present value of that obligation is not $100, but only $58.54. The longer you can postpone the payment, the lower the net present value. Figure 12-3 shows how the value of deferral increases over time. It is amazing to think that if you can defer the payment of taxes for 38 years, you can literally pay a dime on the dollar, a 90% discount. Amazingly, this does not include the impact of inflation. If you throw in a 4.5% inflation, and you can defer the $100 tax liability for 23 years, you can pay it with the equivalent of $10. Who says that tax deferral in retirement is not important?

TAXABLE INCOME

Figuring your taxable income is relatively simple. It is just AGI minus your exemptions and itemized deductions or the standard deduction. We have spoken about exemptions and itemized deductions. If itemized deductions total less than the standard deduction, you are better off taking the standard deduction. A fairly esoteric point is that if your AGI is in excess

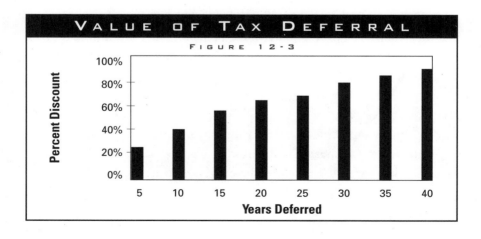

of the so-called "inflation-adjusted dollar amount," it triggers a reduction in the amount of your allowable deductions. In 1998, the inflation-adjusted dollar amount is $124,500.[5] If your AGI exceeds that amount, most of your deductions are reduced by 3% of the excess. Deductions for medical expenses, investment interest, or losses are not reduced. In other words, above $124,500 of joint income, most of your deductions are reduced. Another fairly esoteric point is that this amount may not actually turn out to be the income on which your tax liability is figured. There is another amount, called alternative minimum taxable income (AMTI), that may be the relevant amount if your alternative minimum tax liability is greater than your regular tax liability.

Alternative Minimum Tax (AMT)

The alternative minimum tax rules were devised to ensure that taxpayers could not avoid tax liabilities simply by the use of exemptions and deductions. In essence, the AMT reclaims some of the tax breaks available to high-income taxpayers in an attempt to maintain "tax equity." The rules for calculating AMT are complicated and arcane. Most taxpayers, even if they know what AMT is, do not know how it is calculated. The core of the revised calculation is a step which adds certain items, known as tax preference items (TPI), back into the taxable income to arrive at alternative minimum taxable income (AMTI). In addition to the TPIs, other adjustments are made to exemptions and deductions to further increase the AMTI. For individuals, the AMT is 20% of the AMTI. If the AMT liability is greater than the regular tax liability, then the AMT liability must be paid. The bottom line on this discussion is that, in the new tax situation that retirement represents for most retirees, it is possible that they may find themselves subject to AMT even if they were not previously. If retirees are used to preparing their own taxes and have done so without calculating their possible AMT liability on IRS Form 6251, they may have a problem. Even if you are using a tax preparation software that calculates the AMT, the software is helpless if you do not understand the definitions that control the revised calculation.

---

[5] Estimate by CCH, Inc.

One last additional caveat on AMT. The thresholds for the phase out of tax benefits on the regular income tax side are increased year after year to reflect inflation. The rules for AMT currently are not adjusted to reflect inflation. As a result, more and more Americans are being forced into paying AMT rather than the regular income tax. It is possible for a change like this to creep up unnoticed.

My advice is to have your taxes done by a highly qualified tax specialist. If you insist on doing your own taxes, pay a professional a fee to check your calculations and see if you appear to have done them correctly. You cannot ask the tax professional to sign the tax return or to defend it if he or she did not prepare your return, but professional insights may tell you if you have any obvious problems.

TAX CALCULATION

There are two basic methods for calculating your tax liability. If your taxable income is less than $100,000, you must use the Tax Table to determine the taxes due. If your taxable income is more than $100,000, you use the Tax Rate Schedule. (See Appendix 6 for the 1998 Tax Rate Schedules.)

TAX CREDITS

You can see from the flow of the tax liability calculation that, while deductions are subtracted from taxable income and only reduce your taxes by a fraction of their amount, credits reduce your tax liability on a dollar-for-dollar basis. If you are eligible for tax credits, they can be powerful tools for managing your tax liability. There are many sources of tax credits, some of which are not likely to apply to retirees: child care credit, earned income credit, or job credits. A tax credit does exist for people who are older than 65 or permanently and totally disabled. The amount is $5,000 for a single person and $7,500 for a couple filing jointly. The credit is reduced by the amount of your Social Security benefits that are excluded from gross income (see below) and then further reduced by one-half of your AGI in excess of $7,500 for single people and $10,000 for a married couple filing jointly. The bottom line is that anyone living The Prosperous Retirement is unlikely to qualify for this credit. Thank your lucky stars.

Foreign taxes paid during the year are credited against your tax liability. You should certainly keep track of these if you own foreign stocks or bonds or mutual funds that own foreign stocks or bonds and report them on your tax return.

A number of investments are available that potentially offer tax credits. Investments in alternative fuel sources, electric vehicles, low-income housing, and certain research activities may generate substantial tax credits. These programs are discussed in Chapter 7, Investment Alternatives, but I will reiterate one central point: "Never invest for tax benefits unless the economics of the project appear to be sound without regard to the tax benefits." Tax strategies are not just a game, they should, as a good friend[6] of mine is fond of pointing out, either add to your cash flow or your net worth.

In rare cases, a mutual fund may elect to retain realized capital gains and pay taxes on them. If the fund makes this election, each shareholder gets credit for a proportionate share of the taxes paid. Tax credits are powerful. For most prosperous retirees, tax credits can be counted as income rather than as a tax reduction strategy.

One last point is to remember to give yourself credit for all the taxes that were paid in estimated payments and which might have been paid with all or part of your refund from the previous year. Go ahead and laugh, it seems so obvious. I have overlooked this myself, but luckily my tax professional caught it!

TAX LIABILITY

After all the definitions and all the calculations, a tax liability emerges on the bottom of the second page of your IRS Form 1040. If you have been managing your retirement as recommended, the tax liability is, no doubt, about what you expected. You probably have made arrangements to have the necessary funds available to pay, your tax liability, but if not you might look at several sources that may not immediately come to mind. Are there funds available in the equity line of credit on your home? Is there a corporate retirement plan that allows you to take a loan? If you have stocks and bonds in a brokerage account, you can borrow up

[6] Vern Hayden, CFP, former Chairman of the Board of the National Endowment for Financial Education.

to 50% of their value under current rules. It also is legal to borrow up to 50% of the value of mutual funds in a brokerage account, but not every brokerage company will allow this. The cash value in life insurance contracts may be available on short notice. If the sum is not overwhelming, and you have a long-term relationship with your bank, they will probably be willing to give you a short-term loan until you can liquidate an asset to repay them. The best solution, of course, is to plan ahead and have your tax liability covered with liquid funds well before April 15, but you already knew that.

THE TAXPAYER RELIEF ACT OF 1997 (TRA '97)

As this book is going to the editors, President Clinton has signed the Taxpayer Relief Act of 1997 (TRA '97), showering taxpayers with more than 800 changes in the tax code. Among the major changes that affect The Prosperous Retirement are:

- Taxation of capital gains
- Individual Retirement Accounts
- Educational savings accounts
- Estate tax credits
- Using credit to pay taxes

CAPITAL GAINS

The old system recognized two classes of capital gains: long term and short term. Long-term capital gains or losses resulted from the sale of an asset held at least 12 months, and they were taxed at a maximum rate of 28%. Short-term gains or losses resulted from the sale of assets held less than 12 months, and they were taxed as ordinary income. In 1998 and beyond, there will be three holding periods: short (less than 12 months), long (more than 18 months), and intermediate (more than 12 months, but less than 18 months). The maximum tax rate on long-term gains is 20%, and if your income tax bracket is 15%, the tax rate on these long-term capital gains is only 10%. Intermediate-term gains are still taxed at a maximum rate of 28%, and short-term gains are taxes as ordinary income. Your mutual fund year-end statements now will have to report this new detail.

Appreciated personal property, artwork, collections, antiques, and so on, are not eligible for the new capital gains rate. They are still taxed at 28% if held long term.

INDIVIDUAL RETIREMENT ACCOUNTS

Most of the changes in the IRA rules will not have a huge effect on retirees, but several seem important. I will deal briefly with the changes that are less important to retirees before examining the new Education IRA and the Roth IRA.

Expanded eligibility for tax-deductible contributions is the first change. In the past, the spouse of a person participating in a company-sponsored retirement plan was not eligible to make a tax-deductible contribution. TRA '97 removes the spousal limitation, and over the next 10 years, will double the current income limitations on deductible contributions.

The Roth IRA

The Roth IRA is a new approach to IRAs that carries unique benefits for retirees. It allows individuals to contribute up to $2,000 per year (couples up to $4,000) as long as they have that much earned income. The contributions are not tax deductible, but the withdrawals are tax free (as long as the owner is 59-1/2 years of age and has held the IRA for at least 5 years).

The ability to contribute to the Roth IRA begins a phase-out at $150,000 of AGI. For individuals, the phaseout begins at $95,000 of AGI. Unlike traditional IRAs, a retiree can continue to contribute to a Roth IRA after they reach the age of 70-1/2, and there is no requirement to withdraw funds at any age. For retirees who are older than 59-1/2, and who have earned income that is not needed for the current budget, it makes good sense to save $2,000 a year in a Roth IRA rather than contributing it to a traditional IRA. There is an initial tax loss, because the Roth contribution is not tax deductible, but it builds flexibility into your retirement and avoids the need to start withdrawing the funds at age 70-1/2.

Many retirees are intrigued by their ability to convert their traditional IRAs into Roth IRAs, as long as their AGI in the transfer year is $100,000 or less. If you are planning to make a transfer to a Roth IRA, it makes sense to wait until the end of the year, to resolve any question that AGI may be more than $100,000. The amount of the funds converted does not increase your AGI for this calculation. If you convert from a traditional IRA to a Roth IRA, all the taxes on appreciation in the old IRA are payable in the year of the transfer. The IRS is offering a special deal if you convert in 1998—a one-time opportunity—you can spread the taxes over four years.

The big question is, obviously, does it make sense to convert to a Roth IRA? On the face of it, a conversion from a regular IRA to a Roth violates my principle of paying taxes later rather than sooner. The net result after any period of time will be the same for either account as long as tax brackets don't change. There are only two arguments that favor the Roth conversion. First is the fact that you are not forced to take distributions from a Roth IRA at 70-1/2 (or any other age), as you must from a regular IRA. There are ways to minimize the distributions from the regular IRA at age 70-1/2, but distributions are not completely avoidable. This is a benefit for the Roth IRA if you don't need the distributions, but the benefit is not enormous unless you really live a very long time. The other argument in favor of the Roth conversion arises if you expect to have lower taxes in retirement than you did before retiring. The only way that is likely to happen for prosperous retirees is if tax rates are reduced by some new legislation. This is pure speculation, but a flat tax is not impossible. Your tax and financial advisors probably have computer programs for analyzing your situation, but pay careful attention to the assumptions. One neat twist on the Roth IRA is to make a grandchild the beneficiary and use it as a gift that will grow tax free. Imagine the benefit of having this grow tax free for more than 100 years![7]

The Education IRA

The new Education IRA is very attractive for retirees who want to contribute to the educational funding for their grandchildren and great-grandchildren. The new law allows a $500-per-year contribution for each designated beneficiary of a specially designated Education IRA. The contribution is not tax deductible, but earnings accumulate tax free. Additionally, no taxes are due on withdrawal to pay qualified educational expenses. If the designated beneficiary does not use the funds, the account

---

[7] If your calculator is not handy, a single $2,000 contribution compounded at 8% for 100 years is almost $4.5 million—tax free!

can be rolled to another beneficiary. The $500-per-year limitation may make this seem trivial—it is not. The advantage of tax deferral over the 18 years the funds are building increases the after-tax yield by more than 50%. Remember, both you and your spouse can each make a $500 contribution, and so can the youngster's mom and dad, other grandparents, aunts and uncles, and so on.

OTHER TRA '97 CHANGES

Another change from TRA '97 includes the Lifetime Learning credits. If your AGI is less than $80,000 for a couple (phases out between $80,000 and $100,000), you may be eligible for an annual tax credit of up to $1,500 per year for educational expenses. There is a legitimate question as to whether these credits truly extend to retired persons, because they are supposed to reimburse expenses in the pursuit of job skills.

An intriguing new opportunity, beginning in 1998, is to pay your tax bill with a credit card. If you have a frequent flier card or other credit card with supplemental benefits, and if you can pay the bill promptly, it probably makes sense to use this new facility.

The main change in TRA '97 on the estate tax front was the increase in the unified gift and estate tax exemption, from $600,000 in 1997 to $625,000 per person in 1998. There are gradual increases scheduled over the next 10 years, ultimately raising the exemption to $1 million. I know I shouldn't look a gift horse in the mouth, but that is a rate of increase of only 5.2% per year and your investments are likely to increase more rapidly (see Appendix 5).

These comments on TRA '97 barely scratch the surface, and, as usual, this big tax change contains a number of issues that are going to need clarification and adjudication. Stay tuned to your tax professional's wavelength.

TAXATION OF SOCIAL SECURITY

Up to 85% of the benefits you receive under Social Security may be subject to income taxes. To figure how much of your Social Security benefits are taxable, you go through a three-step calculation. Begin with your AGI and add to it any municipal bond interest that you received during the year. This combination is called "modified adjusted gross income." Then add one-half of your Social Security benefits to the modified adjusted gross income to arrive at "provisional income." Then subtract something called the "base amount." The base amount for married taxpayers filing jointly is currently $32,000. Married taxpayers filing separately who lived with their spouse at any time during the year have a $0 base amount. Everyone else gets a base amount of $25,000. (How is that for a "marriage" penalty and a "separation" penalty?) Then increase your gross income by the lesser of one-half of your Social Security benefits or one-half of the excess of provisional income minus the base amount. An example may make this clearer.

Fred and Fern Nextdoor have adjusted gross income of $25,000 for 1997. Fred receives Social Security benefits of $7,000 per year. The Nextdoors have a mutual fund that distributed $6,500 this year in tax-exempt municipal bond interest. The following computation will determine how much of Fred's Social Security benefits will be included in their gross income.

1. Adjusted gross income	$25,000
2. Plus: All tax-exempt interest	$ 6,500
3. Modified adjusted gross income	$31,500
4. Plus: One-half of Social Security benefits	$ 3,500
5. Provisional income	$35,000
6. Less: Base amount	$32,000
7. Excess above base amount	$ 3,000
8. One-half of excess	$ 1,500
9. One-half of Social Security benefits	$ 3,500
10. Amount includible in gross income	$ 1,500
(Lesser of 8 or 9)	

The Nextdoors have to add $1,500 of their Social Security benefits to their taxable income.

Since 1994—if you are a married taxpayer filing jointly and you have provisional income in excess of $44,000—additional amounts of your

Social Security benefits up to 85% of the total are includible in gross income. Married taxpayers filing separately and not living apart for the entire year get a $0 provisional income allowance, all other taxpayers get $34,000 of exempted provisional income.

Taxpayers whose income exceeds the higher threshold "adjusted base" amounts must include the lesser of:

- 85% of their Social Security benefits
————————————OR————————————
- 85% of the excess of provisional income over the threshold amount, plus the sum of the smaller of the following:

The amount that would be includible if the second threshold did not apply
————————————OR————————————
$4,500 ($6,000 for married joint filers)

The addition works like this: let's assume that the Goodfences are your other neighbors. Their situation is identical to the Nextdoors' except their provisional income is increased from $34,000 to $54,000.

1. Provisional income	$54,000
2. Adjusted base amount	$44,000
3. Excess of 1 over 2	$10,000
4. 85% of the excess (3)	$ 8,500
Amount Otherwise Includible	
5. One-half of Social Security benefits	$ 3,500
6. Base amount for joint filers	$ 6,000
7. Lesser of 5 or 6	$ 3,500
8. Sum of 4 plus 7	$12,000
9. 85% of Social Security benefits	$ 5,950
10. Amount includible in gross income	$ 5,950
(Lesser of 8 or 9)	

The Goodfences have to add $5,950, 85% of their Social Security benefits, to their taxable income.

TAX-FREE INTEREST

One of the basic recommendations for reducing your tax liability is to switch from investments that yield taxable interest to investments that yield tax-free interest. This strategy usually takes the form of a switch from taxable bonds to municipal bonds. As we discussed in Chapter 7, the tax-exempt bonds usually are priced so that their after-tax yield is competitive with the after-tax yield on taxable bonds. Normally, the comparison is made at a 28% tax bracket and the person making the comparison will throw in, ". . . and larger savings for people in higher brackets." You can see that this kind of a comparison is not entirely correct. The interest from the tax-exempt bonds still may drag some of your Social Security benefits into gross income. Let's take an example.

Fred and Fern Nextdoor are still in the same situation as they were previously, but they wonder how they would fare if they switched from municipal bonds to taxable bonds. Let's assume that they have $110,000 invested in their municipal bond mutual fund that yields 5.9% and pays them $6,500 a year in tax-exempt interest. They switch those funds to a high-quality, taxable bond mutual fund yielding 8.2%. The taxable fund would pay them $9,020 a year in taxable interest. You will note that the 5.9% tax-exempt interest is 28% less than the 8.2% taxable interest. This is a typical market adjustment. The Nextdoors are in a 15% tax bracket. The additional interest would cost them another $378 in income taxes and would drag another $1,260 of Social Security benefits into gross income. This would cost another $189. The total extra taxes would be $567, but they have an extra $2,520 in interest to pay the extra taxes. In their case, municipal bonds are not a wonderful solution. Each case is a separate calculation. In general, taxpayers with adjusted gross income in excess of $50,000 are better off with municipal bonds than taxable bonds.

SALE OF RESIDENCE

The Taxpayer Relief Act of 1997 introduced a real bonanza for many retirees. A married couple can sell their principal residence and exclude up to $500,000 of capital gains from their taxable income. A single person gets an exclusion of $250,000. There are no age restrictions and the exclusion can be repeated. There is no limit on the number of times this exemption can be used, as long as the property has been the principal residence for at least two of the five years prior to the sale. Just to make this more interesting, yachts, houseboats, and vacation residences all may qualify if they meet the principal residence rule. This opens the opportunity for retirees to sell their home and take up to $500,000 in tax-free gain. They could move into their second home, live there for two years, to qualify that as their principal residence, and take another $500,000 in capital gains without taxes. The old technique of rolling capital gains forward into a home that costs more than the old one, a technique that wasn't useful to very many retirees, is no longer allowed.

TAX DEFERRAL STRATEGIES

Now that you are convinced that tax deferral is important, even in retirement, you do not want to rush out and move all your investments to tax-deferred accounts. However, you may want to make some use of this strategy, so we will examine it in more detail. There are fundamentally only three ways to defer taxes on investments.

1. Retirement accounts
2. Insurance contracts (life insurance and annuities) that are given tax-deferred status under current law
3. Own stock until you die

There are advantages and disadvantages to each of these strategies.

RETIREMENT ACCOUNTS

Among these three strategies, investments in retirement accounts may carry the unique benefit of tax savings as well as tax deferral, and with the new Roth IRA, total exemption from taxes. Different retirement accounts have various eligibility requirements and various contribution limits. This is a complex area that we will not cover in this book. The point, in this section, is that contributions to most retirement accounts have three principal benefits:

✔ Contributions are deducted from your taxable income.
✔ Contributions can grow tax deferred.
✔ The tax benefits are an added incentive to save.

The structure of benefits in the new Roth IRA is totally different.

✔ Contributions are made with after-tax dollars.
✔ Contributions grow tax free.
✔ Withdrawals are not subject to taxation.

Of the three tax-deferral strategies, retirement accounts are the most powerful. The contributions are increased by the fact that they are tax deductible. To illustrate, let's say you got a $2,000 bonus from your business and decided to save it. If you took the cash, paid the taxes, and invested the remainder, the investment amount might be $1,200. If you could contribute the entire $2,000 to a retirement account and avoid the taxes, the investment amount would be $2,000. Another reason that retirement accounts are powerful tools is that the cost of making investments in this form is less than if you have to pay for an insurance contract to get the tax deferral. It really makes sense to keep contributing to retirement accounts as long as you can. It is not possible to continue to add to traditional IRAs after you reach the age of 70-1/2, but the new Roth IRA allows contributions, albeit non-deductible, at any age and the Roth IRA does not require distributions at any age.

INSURANCE CONTRACTS

Under current tax laws, the build-up of cash value in insurance contracts is not taxable. This could conceivably be changed at some time in the future. On the other hand, the insurance lobby has a powerful voice in Washington partly because they speak for so many millions of policy holders. In recent years, Congress has made some in-roads on this rule. In each case, existing policies were "grandfathered," in other words, the benefits in existing policies were preserved. New policies might not be able to offer all the benefits of the older contracts, but the benefits of the old policies continue to be respected. We might hope that the same will be true of any future changes, but there are no guarantees. In addition, to the tax-deferred build-up of value, the death benefit of life insurance contracts is paid without income tax liability. Apparently, Congress thinks that if you are willing to die to get the benefit, you ought to be able to give this to your heirs without taxes. The proceeds from insurance policies that you own are included in your estate, so estate taxes may be due on the proceeds. We have spoken in several places (see Chapter 10) about the benefits of using an irrevocable life insurance trust (ILIT) and I will not repeat it here. In addition to the tax benefits of normal life insurance policies, other kinds of life insurance combine the benefits of insurance and investment.

Variable Life Insurance

In a normal cash value life insurance contract, the insurance company invests the cash value in their investment pool. You earn whatever rate of return they are earning minus their expenses. By contrast, variable life insurance contracts allow you to direct the investment of the cash value of the contract. The variable policy has several investment options, like a small family of mutual funds. You can pick whichever investment option you want and move the investment from fund to fund within the policy without tax consequences. These policies normally are funded with as much cash and as little insurance as the IRS rules will allow and still treat the contract as insurance. You then direct the investment of the funds in a way that is intended to get you a higher rate of return than you would expect from the guaranteed account in a normal cash value insurance contract. A policy such as this can be a very productive investment vehicle if it is obtained at a relatively young age. By the time most people are retired, it is generally too late. The burden of the life insurance premiums on the investment pool at older ages is a heavy load to carry. If you are older than 55 years of age, look very carefully at the benefits before deciding that you want to purchase a variable life insurance contract. It may not be too late, however, to start using a variable annuity, which does not have the insurance costs but does provide tax deferral.

Tax-Free Exchange

If you have an old cash value life insurance policy that you have had for years, the cash value may have grown to be close to the death benefit. It may make sense to do something with this policy. One of the options is to exchange—without tax consequences—the cash value in the policy for another insurance policy or an annuity.

Fixed Annuities

Fixed annuities allow you to invest money with the insurance company at a fixed rate of interest that is tax deferred until it is withdrawn from the contract. There are many different kinds of fixed annuities and it is important to understand the terms and conditions of any annuity you buy. If you decide to move your investment from one annuity to another, it is possible to make the exchange to another annuity without tax consequences. It is not possible to move funds from an annuity to a life insurance policy without paying taxes. There may be penalties from the insurance company if you agreed to have the investment remain with the company for a period of time. Some contracts have a feature by which the insurance company pays you "bonus interest." If you move the funds before the contract expires, they may charge you a penalty and reclaim the "bonus" that they have already credited to your account. If you plan to make a move, let the company know what you are planning to do and make certain that there will be no unexpected penalties or costs.

Variable Annuities

The variable annuity is like a small mutual fund family wrapped with an insurance contract. The insurance wrap gives you tax-deferred growth, but it also increases the cost of the investment. This is discussed in detail in Chapter 10, but the bottom line here is that if you can allow funds to stay in the variable annuity for a long period of time, it can increase the after-tax, effective yield of the investment by as much as 20%. In other words, if the after-tax yield on a mutual fund is 8% after taxes, the after-tax yield on the same investment organized as a variable annuity might be as high as 9.6%. Variable annuities are complicated, expensive, and restrictive. Do not buy one without a thorough evaluation of the costs and benefits, but that does not mean not to buy one.

OWN STOCKS AND HOLD THEM

You may not have heard of this as a tax management strategy, but it is among the best. The idea is that if you never sell a stock, there are no capital gains taxes to pay and your heirs get a stepped-up cost basis (see glossary) on your death. Whether you own the stock in your name or in the name of your revocable living trust, the assets receive a stepped-up basis on your death. That means your heirs will get the assets with a current cost basis and no one will ever pay the income taxes on the gains that have accrued between your purchase and your death.[8] The trick here is that you need to buy stocks that are capable of being held for all those years. Generally, this means very strong, blue-chip stocks with long records of increasing dividends. One of the classics in this category used to be AT&T, but after the break-up of the company, the remaining stocks were of varying quality and the company was really in a new business. I cite this example just to point out that the prospects for the company have to be very solid into the foreseeable future. There are a number of companies that fall into this category and your financial advisor should be able to identify them for you. The low dividend yields of most blue-chip companies is currently a drawback to this strategy, but that only argues for a smaller commitment to this idea, not for abandoning it.

Timing Asset Sales

Even if you are not able to hold individual stocks until your death, the ability to time the sale of the stock may yield some tax benefits. When you hold mutual funds, the fund manager decides when to buy and sell. The tax laws require that the fund's realized gains be distributed to the shareholders in the year they are realized. When you hold individual stocks, the sale of the stocks can be timed for your convenience or for minimum impact on your taxes. If you have a stock with a loss, you can liquidate that in a year when income is high. If you have a stock with a gain, you can liquidate that in a year when income is lower. If you need the cash now, you can borrow against the stock without tax consequences. There are many other advantages to mutual funds, but tax management is a plus for individual stocks.

---

[8] Your estate tax liability will include the full market value of securities owned at the time of your death.

Netting Capital Gains and Losses

When stocks are sold, the capital gains and losses are segregated by short term, intermediate term, and long term. Gains and losses within groups are netted out, and then netted category against category. If the net result is a gain, there is no limit on how much gain is added to your taxable income. If the net result is a loss, the annual loss is limited to $3,000. Losses in excess of $3,000 can be carried forward, but it makes more sense to realize some gains to net out against the losses. This is the flip side of delaying the payment of taxes. The rule here is to use tax reductions as soon as possible.

RETIREMENT WITHDRAWALS

You have been advised in this book and from many other sources that you should contribute as much as possible to your retirement plan and allow those tax-deferred savings to grow as long as possible. In general, that is the right advice, but there are some exceptions. I hope you are lucky enough to be affected by one of the exceptions, which have to do with the fact that the IRS has what I call the "Goldilocks Theory" of pension plan withdrawals. They don't want you to start too soon. They don't want you to wait too long. They don't want you to take too little, and it used to be that they didn't want you to take too much. They want your pension withdrawals to be "just right." If you start withdrawing funds from your pension plan before you are 59-1/2 years of age, you may be subject to a 10% premature withdrawal penalty. (See the following section on early withdrawals.) Prior to 1997, if you withdrew more than $150,000 per year, you were subject to a penalty. If you died with "too much" in the plan, the "excess" was subject to a penalty. (See the section on overfunded plan.) The penalties on excess withdrawals and excess accumulations were repealed by TRA '97.

Early Distributions

A distribution from a retirement account before the participant is 59-1/2 years old is considered an early withdrawal and is subject to a special 10% excise tax. Early withdrawals are not a great idea, but sometimes they are unavoidable and there are ways to avoid the penalty. Years ago, I had a client who bought a large number of shares of a small company for his IRA account. The shares soared in price, making him a very wealthy person and helping him to retire in his early 50s. However, the IRA held the bulk of his wealth, and he had no alternative but to start drawing funds from the IRA even though he was subject to the 10% early withdrawal penalty.

One of the exemptions from the penalty is if the participant sets up a series of substantially equal periodic payments over the life expectancy of the participant or the joint lives of the participant and his or her beneficiary. The client set up such a series of periodic payments and was able to draw the required funds without penalty even though he was not yet age 59-1/2.

Another exemption allows you to cover tax-deductible medical expenses by withdrawals without penalty. If you have to make a withdrawal to pay tax-deductible medical expenses, you can at least reduce the taxability of the withdrawal by the amount of the medical expenses.

Late Distributions

The owner of a traditional IRA is required to begin distributions from the account before April 1 of the year in which he or she reaches the age of 70-1/2. If there is more than one traditional IRA, the required distributions from all the plans can be taken from one or more of the plans in any manner that the owner wishes as long as the total withdrawal is made. If the withdrawal is not made, the plan is subject to a 50% penalty on the amount that should have been withdrawn. A rich complexity of rules provide a mind-boggling variety of withdrawal options. This complexity offers a worthwhile planning opportunity if there are substantial funds in the plan. There are specialists who counsel people with large IRA accounts on the best methods for withdrawing the funds.

Excess Distributions

There used to be a 15% excise tax levied on aggregate distributions from qualified plans, tax-sheltered annuities, and IRAs to the extent that the distributions exceeded an indexed dollar amount. This penalty was repealed by the Taxpayer Relief Act of 1997.

Overfunded Retirement Plans

The Taxpayer Relief Act of 1997 also repealed the penalty on so-called "overfunded" qualified plan accounts. This opens an opportunity for retirees to continue to enjoy the tax-deferred accumulation of value in their retirement accounts. The pitfall, if there is one, in this strategy is that the assets in the retirement plan account will not receive a stepped-up cost basis on the death of the owner. The heirs will have to pay taxes on the value of the plan at ordinary income rates.

RETIREMENT EARNINGS AS A TAX STRATEGY

The retirement earnings strategy has been touted in various places in this book as a great idea. It generates additional retirement income and keeps you involved and interested in the world around you. In addition to those benefits, it also provides a reason for continuing a business in retirement and the benefits that brings.

One of the typical delights of retirement is the opportunity to travel, the chance to visit family and friends, and to see places you have always wanted to see. To the extent that there is a legitimate business purpose, your retirement earnings activities can make the cost of that travel partially deductible or allow you to pay for the travel with before-tax dollars. That could easily save you a third of the cost of the travel. Let's assume that you are an avid doll collector. You decide to start a publishing company to produce a newsletter about dolls and publish books about dolls. You call this new venture The Doll Press. The business requires you to travel around the country attending the many doll shows, interviewing people for the newsletter, looking for authors, and promoting your publications. Is this travel a deductible expense? You bet it is. (See the section above on Hobby Losses.) If your spouse is an employee of The Doll Press, the spouse's presence on these business trips may serve an important business purpose and the spouse's expenses also may be deductible. If dolls are your passion, it may not be too much of a burden to spend three or four months of the year traveling around the country visiting doll shows and talking with people about your business.

Another tax benefit associated with retirement earnings is that they may allow you to move some of your deductible expenses onto the business and deduct them from gross income rather than AGI. If medical insurance is one of your main medical expenses, you may be able to pay that out of the business as a benefit rather than paying it as a personal expense subject to the 7.5% threshold. If you are the owner-employee of your retirement earnings company, the medical insurance premiums will be deductible. If, however, you are regarded as "self-employed," only 40%[9] of the cost of your medical insurance is deductible to the company, the rest is deductible to the extent that it exceeds the 7.5% threshold.

YEAR-END TAX PLANNING

The essence of tax planning is the year-end meeting with your accountant. This is when you make year-end adjustments, get briefed on changes in the tax laws that affect you, and lay your plans for the year ahead. If there are stock positions that should be sold to realize tax losses, this is the time to do it. (See the paragraph on wash sales below.) If there was unexpected income during the year from your retirement earnings, it may be possible to adjust your year-end withholding rather than pay a penalty for a late estimated payment. If your retirement earnings are coming from something like a consulting practice where the income may be hard to predict from quarter to quarter, you need to be alert to the fact that estimated taxes must be paid in the quarter that the earnings are received. Rather than be penalized for late payments, it may be advantageous to ask a client to postpone payment until the beginning of the next quarter.

WASH SALES

One of the potential pitfalls in year-end tax planning is the danger of "wash sales." Wash sales refer to the sale of an asset in which a loss is incurred if substantially identical assets then are purchased within the following 30 days. An example or two may help make this clear. Let's assume that you own 500 shares of XYZ corporation. XYZ has taken a big tumble and you decide to sell the 500 shares to realize the tax loss to offset a gain you had on another stock. You sell the XYZ on November 1. If you buy back XYZ shares before December 1 (30 days), the loss on the sale will not be allowed. Another variation might be that, on November 1, you decide that you want to sell the XYZ stock to realize the loss, but

---

[9] In 1997, up from 30% in 1996.

you think the stock could go up in the near term and don't want to be out of the stock when it does. Accordingly, you buy a second lot of 500 shares on November 1, increasing your position to 1,000 shares. If you sell the 500 original shares before December 1 (30 days), the loss on the sale will not be allowed. There are many more variations on this theme involving options, short sales, and future delivery contracts. The IRS has pretty well covered this base.

RECORD KEEPING

One of the tricks to following Judge Hand's advice is to keep good records. Keep records of all your investments. Keep the confirmation notices for every securities purchase in one file folder. Keep a file for income taxes and, during the year, accumulate everything in that one folder that may be useful in preparing your taxes.

Keep detailed records of all contributions to your tax-deferred accounts. Keep your Individual Retirement Accounts separate according to the source of the funds. Do not mix tax-deductible IRAs with IRAs funded with after-tax contributions. Do not mix any other assets with your new Roth IRA. If you have a "conduit IRA," which contains funds rolled over from a corporate plan, do not mix this with other IRAs.

If you own zero coupon bonds in taxable accounts, keep records of the amounts added each year for the Original Issue Discount (OID). These amounts add to your cost basis and reduce the taxes to be paid when the bonds finally mature or are sold.

If you have a dividend reinvestment account on stock that you own, keep those records as long as you own the stock. The difficulty of accounting for the cost of these shares acquired through dividend reinvest has kept many an investor in a stock long after they would have liked to have sold it. Keeping these records is the key to being able to sell the shares when you want.

Keep good records of all mutual fund dividends and add them to the cost basis of the mutual fund. This will keep you from paying too much in taxes when shares are sold or exchanged. Some of the better families of mutual funds will now provide you this cost basis information when you sell shares.

In the past, it was necessary to keep records on real estate for as long as you were rolling forward the capital gains. Many retirees have records on real estate transactions going back decades to document these capital gains rollovers. The Taxpayer Relief Act of 1997 eliminated the old rules and substituted a system that gives anyone the opportunity to take up to $500,000 on the sale of their principal residence. The bad news is that the cost basis of your residence is still reduced by all the capital gains that you have been rolling forward from the sale of previous residences. Do not throw away all those papers until after you have sold your last residence.

MEDICAL SAVINGS ACCOUNTS

There are currently 750,000 individuals who are being permitted to maintain medical savings accounts (MSAs). These accounts allow the employer to make tax deductible contributions to the plan, that can be used to make tax free payments for qualified medical expenses. These plans are not relevant to retirees, but after December 31, 1998, eligible seniors will be allowed to establish MSAs called Medicare Plus Choice MSAs. This pilot program will be limited on a first-come, first-served basis to the first 390,000 seniors. More information will be coming out about the details of this program. It may be worthwhile to keep an eye on this opportunity.

CHAPTER 12

ACTION PLAN:

- ❏ Examine your gross income. Is there more income than is currently required?

- ❏ Can some income-generating assets be put into tax-deferred form?

- ❏ Is there income that should be converted to tax-free form?

- ❏ Should you convert some or all of your IRA assets to a Roth IRA?

- ❏ Study your deductions. Are there possible deductions that you are not currently using?

- ❏ Would a business entity improve the deductibility of your expenses and your overall tax posture?

- ❏ Have you considered grouping medical or business expenses into alternate years to increase their deductibility?

- ❏ Are you taking any required distributions from retirement accounts?

- ❏ Are you using all your charitable contributions and services to charitable organizations to reduce your taxes?

- ❏ Have you considered the use of tax credits?

- ❏ Include tax dates on your retirement management calendar: tax planning, tax filing, estimated taxes.

- ❏ Keep good tax records, including the cost basis of your residence.

- ❏ Are you getting the advice and service that you expect from your tax professional?

13.

RETIRED IN THE 21ST CENTURY

"We should all be concerned about the future because we will have to spend the rest of our lives there."
—CHARLES FRANCIS KETTERING, 1949

SYNOPSIS: The future is a mystery. No one can know what it will bring, but you need to have a model to provide some basis for your plans and actions. Knowledge, diversification, and persistence have proven useful in the past and are likely to be helpful in the future. There are some shadows on the economic landscape that may bear watching. A positive attitude will help deal with whatever surprises, challenges, and opportunities are in front of you. This chapter offers some counsel on how to approach the future, how to deal with some challenges that may be coming, and how to take advantage of the opportunities that may present themselves.

THE FUTURE IS A MYSTERY. No one knows what the future will bring, neither the kinds of events that will happen, nor the sequence in which they will happen. In spite of these fundamental problems, useful thoughts about the future abound. The future probably will be some combination of events that have happened before and the unprecedented. Of the occurrences that have happened before, some will be clearly recognizable and some will be barely recognizable. The future probably also will include a very few things that have never happened before. The shadow of some of these unprecedented events is already on the landscape, while others will be total bolts out of the blue. The future is more fundamentally mysterious than most of us realize.

Having said all that, some force in human nature seems to demand that we act as though we understand history and current events, and, therefore, have some clue about the future. In the next few paragraphs, I am responding to that basic force that makes me want to act as though I understand and can, therefore, predict the future. Here I go.

KEEP INFORMED

There are certain tactics that have served people well in good times and in bad. It is always a good idea to be aware of what is going on around you. You should follow the markets, the economy, the political news, and the international news. Nothing that you get from that survey of information is likely to have operational importance, but it will help create a sound background for your decision making. **Keeping informed is the first principle.** In retirement, it is important that you make an effort to bring in the information that you need because you may be cut off from some of the sources that used to bring information to you automatically. Be certain to spend the time and develop the sources to stay well informed.

DIVERSIFY

The second principle is diversification. One obvious consequence of our inability to predict the future is that we should not act as though we can predict the future. If I could predict the future, I would concentrate all my assets in a way that would profit from the predicted event. Since I cannot predict events, not even trivial ones like which stock will go up and which will go down, I have to hedge my bets by not putting all my eggs in one basket. I have been investing for more than 40 years, and the only thing I have learned is that diversification is wise. In Chapter 8, we discussed the most advanced form of investment diversification that the theoreticians have come up with—asset allocation. Diversification also applies to our activities. You should keep a diversified range of personal contacts, activities, and interests. You do not want to be isolated. You want to stay active, involved, and feeling connected. Do not put yourself in the position where the loss of any one element in your life will totally disconnect you.

STAY FLEXIBLE

The third principle is flexibility. The recognition of the need for flexibility also flows out of our inability to predict the future. Imagine that you are standing on the deck of a sailing ship. The sea is choppy and tosses the ship this way and that. How do you position yourself to resist those random motions? You would stand squarely on both feet and grab on to something to steady yourself. You would relax and be prepared to move with the motion of the ship. You would not try to outsmart the sea by lunging this way and that. You would not stand on one foot. You would not stand rigidly erect, and if it really got bad you might get down on all fours. So it is with your retirement. You should position yourself—financially, emotionally, and psychologically—to expect change. Anticipate events that are surprises and evaluate them for risk and opportunity. When we were young, we tended to feel powerful and in charge. As we get older, that self-confidence may become less strong; we may feel threatened by change. Change continues to be the same mixture of risk and opportunity that it always was, you just need to keep focused on the positive aspects.

WATCH THE SIGNS

There are a number of factors that the experts keep talking about as if they were potential sources of problems.

- Interest rates
- Inflation
- The economy

- Employment
- Population
- Political stability
- Trade balance
- Federal deficit
- Entitlement programs
- Technology
- Foreign affairs

Somewhere in this laundry list of issues are the roots of future developments. If you keep scanning the clouds on the horizon, you may get a little advance warning that something is coming. If you pay no attention, every event will be a surprise and a shock. As we get older, the last thing that we need is shocks and surprises, and so it makes good sense to pay attention to developments in these key areas. It seems to me that some of these things are fundamentally unpredictable: politics, the economy and technology. Other factors are a bit more predictable and may help us to guess wisely about the future.

Demographics

It seems to me that the most predictable of all of these issues is demographics. We already know how many people were born in 1955, so we know with some precision how many people will be 45 years of age in the year 2000. Harry Dent has written a book, called *The Great Boom Ahead*,[1] in which he argues that the economy is largely driven by consumer spending, that people hit their peak spending years when they are in their mid-40s, and therefore the "baby boom" will cause the economy to do well until the second decade of the 21st Century. Many smart people are persuaded that Dent is on to something and that economic prospects for the next couple of decades look bright. I am convinced that there is validity in Dent's arguments, but I would quibble over some of the details Dent's book leads me to believe that age 45 is no longer the period of peak consumption in most people's lives. I think that the peak comes a little later, and the decline in consumption will not be as radical as it was

---

[1] Dent, Harry S., Jr.. *The Great Boom Ahead*, (NY: Hyperion, 1993).

in past generations. I also believe that there is a rising wave of consumerism building world wide as massive population segments in Asia come into the middle class. I believe that this wave of international consumerism will tend to prolong the economic expansion in the United States. Having said all that, I would not argue for one moment that economic activity is no longer cyclical. It seems clear from everything we see that economic cycles are still alive and well and that, in the words of the Wall Street aphorism, "trees do not grow to the sky." The unprecedented prosperity of the last 50 years is not a permanent condition. There will be excesses, there will be corrections and there are likely to be crashes—even in the lifetime of today's retirees. No one knows when, why, or how bad, but the odds are strong that these fluctuations will occur.

Debt

It seems to me that one of the characteristics of the late 20th Century is an excessive sense of capacity. I think Americans of our generation are under the impression that we can, collectively, do whatever we make up our minds to do. Evidence abounds that this is not correct, but there are also many examples of our failure to recognize our limitations. Many experts tell us that the federal deficit, the rising obligations of entitlement programs, high levels of personal debt, riskier investment postures, and the burgeoning foreign trade imbalance are not matters for immediate concern. I think that they are right in terms of where we are in 1998, but I am concerned about the trends. I plan to watch the trends carefully and worry about when these problems, which we seem to have little resolve to fix, will turn into full-fledged crises. Seeing the crisis approaching may provide some protection, or it may not. What it will provide is the opportunity to adjust expectations and to respond promptly to the new reality, whatever it may be.

Interest Rates

Current dogma has it that rising interest rates are a death knell for the stock market. The thinking runs that when inflation goes up, interest rates will follow, and the market will fall. Every sign of rising employment, increased housing starts, rising fuel prices, or anything else that could give a boost to inflation is a reason for a sinking spell in the stock market. The reasons seem clear enough. We are currently in a period where growth of earnings is a driving factor in stock valuations. Future earnings are translated into stock prices by using a discount rate that is related to current interest rates. Thus, when interest rates rise, the present value of future earnings falls, and the valuations of stocks fall with it. Furthermore, there is the notion that rising interest rates will add to the cost of doing business, and that profits and earnings will fall. Another reason for stock prices to fall. This syllogism is not always correct. There are phases in the market cycle when inflation and interest rates are compatible with rising stock prices. I offer this as one example of the need for flexibility. Yesterday's rules may be powerless in tomorrow's light. We need to be guided by our experience and the wisdom that age has given us, but we must not be dogmatic. Things change, and our views need to take those changes into consideration.

Technology

Many observers believe that the current wave of affluence affecting the world economy is based on technology. The argument is multidimensional, but it certainly starts with the idea that technology has allowed workers all over the world to be more productive. Further, technology manufacture has allowed the export of jobs and wealth to areas that previously had little basis for creating wealth.[2] We can see that there have been earlier waves of technology, in past centuries, which boosted the world economy in similar ways. When will the current cycle of technology slow down and falter? Will it slow down and falter? It seems to me that this wave of technological innovation is fundamentally different than earlier waves and may be much more long-lived than earlier waves. This wave of technological innovation may motivate the world economy for more than a century. If that idea turns out to be correct, the fear that technology will lose its power to lift the world economy may prove to be baseless in the 21st Century. If technological change continues at its current rapid pace, it could greatly affect our longevity and pose many chal-

---

[2] In 1996, I observed the Scottish authorities extending fiber optic cables to the Outer Hebrides so that the local population on these poor, isolated islands could be employed as data entry specialists.

lenges—practically, emotionally, and ethically. One of the burdens of old age is the feeling of being left behind. It is not easy to stay abreast of technology and yet, to a great extent, technology defines our time. If we fall behind in our understanding and mastery of technology, we are in danger of isolating ourselves and making ourselves feel like relics of an older age, out of touch with modern reality.

ATTITUDE

The older I get, the more I like the motto, "Your attitude determines your altitude." You are not likely to be successful, prosperous, or happy unless you expect to be. I am certainly no Pollyanna, but I have learned that if you are not looking for opportunities, you will not see them. If you are looking for problems, you are likely to find them. I urge you to move into the 21st Century looking for the opportunities, wary of the dangers, and determined to prosper, whatever may come. Of course, there will be challenges. It would not be fun if there were no challenges, but we must stay resolved to take a positive view, and be determined to stay connected and relevant. The world really can be a better place because we are here and determined to make it a better place for ourselves and everyone around us.

BON VOYAGE

Here we are again, on the deck of our sailing ship. We expect the winds to keep coming, we know the sea will be restless, but we are determined to keep our sails trimmed and our course constant. We intend to enjoy our prosperous retirement whatever the weather and to let our example inspire those who will someday face the challenges that we face today.

LIST OF APPENDICES

1. MEASURING YOUR MOOD

THIS TEST, CALLED THE Geriatric Depression Scale*, is one of several tests used by mental health specialists to identify depression in older adults. The 15 questions each require a Yes or No answer. Mark your answer, then score your answers using the Scoring Guide below the questions. If your answers suggest that you are depressed, you should discuss your concerns with your primary-care physician or a mental health specialist. Depression can be a very serious disease, even life-threatening. It deserves your attention.

---

* Source: Sheikh, Javaid I., MD, Jerome A. Yesavage, MD. "Geriatric Depression Scale (GDS): Recent Evidence and Development of a Shorter Version." *Clinical Gerontologist*, June 1986. pp 165-173.

GERIATRIC DEPRESSION SCALE

(Short Form)

Choose the best answer to describe how you have felt over the past week.

1. Are you basically satisfied with your life? ❏ Yes ❏ No
2. Have you dropped many of your activities and interests? ❏ Yes ❏ No
3. Do you feel that your life is empty? ❏ Yes ❏ No
4. Do you often get bored? ❏ Yes ❏ No
5. Are you in good spirits most of the time? ❏ Yes ❏ No
6. Are you afraid that something bad is going to happen to you? ❏ Yes ❏ No
7. Do you feel happy most of the time? ❏ Yes ❏ No
8. Do you often feel helpless? ❏ Yes ❏ No
9. Do you prefer to stay at home rather than go out and do new things? ❏ Yes ❏ No
10. Do you feel that you have more problems with memory than most? ❏ Yes ❏ No
11. Do you think that it is wonderful to be alive now? ❏ Yes ❏ No
12. Do you feel pretty worthless the way you are now? ❏ Yes ❏ No
13. Do you feel full of energy? ❏ Yes ❏ No
14. Do you feel that your situation is hopeless? ❏ Yes ❏ No
15. Do you think that most people are better off than you are? ❏ Yes ❏ No

SCORING: Match your answers to the answers given below. Score one point for each matching answer. A score of 0 to 5 is normal. A score above 5 suggests depression.

1. No	4. Yes	7. No	10. Yes	13. No
2. Yes	5. No	8. Yes	11. No	14. Yes
3. Yes	6. Yes	9. Yes	12. Yes	15. Yes

2. BOND RATING SYSTEMS

There are several bond rating services that command the respect of the investment community. Among these, Standard & Poor's and Moody's are the oldest and most well-known.

MOODY'S

Aaa - Investment grade - The best bonds. Interest payments are protected by a large or exceptionally stable margin and the principal is secure. The issuing entity is considered so stable that any changes by the issuer are thought unlikely to impair its strong position for the foreseeable future.

Aa - Investment grade - High-quality bonds by all standards. Margin for protection is less than Aaa and their potential for fluctuation may be greater.

A - Investment grade - Upper medium-grade bonds with many favorable investment attributes. Security for payment of principal and interest is adequate, but certain factors, such as consistent profitability, suggest a susceptibility to impairment at some time in the future.

Baa - Investment grade - Medium grade obligations, neither highly protected nor poorly secured. Principal and interest payments appear secure but cannot be projected for a substantial period of time. The bonds also lack outstanding investment characteristics and have the flavor of speculation about them. Bonds rated Baa or higher are considered "prudent-man" investments under rules of law.

Ba - Speculative - Have speculative elements and their future cannot be considered well assured. Protection of interest and principal may be moderate, and therefore not well safeguarded during bad times. Uncertainty characterizes bonds in this class and they are not considered "prudent-man" investments.

B - Speculative - Generally lack the characteristics of a desirable investment. The assurance of interest and principal payments or the maintenance of other terms of the bond's contract over any sustained period of time is small.

Caa - Speculative - Have poor standing. May be in default, or have elements of danger in terms of paying interest or principal.

Ca - Speculative - Highly speculative. Such issues are often in default or have other marked shortcomings.

C - In Default - Lowest rated class of bonds. Considered poor prospects for any real investment standing.

STANDARD AND POOR'S

AAA - Investment grade - The best bonds. Interest payments are protected by a large or exceptionally stable margin and the principal is secure. The issuing entity is considered so stable that any changes by the issuer are thought unlikely to impair its strong position for the foreseeable future.

AA - Investment grade - High-quality bonds by all standards. Margin for protection is less than AAA and their potential for fluctuation may be greater.

A - Investment grade - Upper medium-grade bonds with many favorable investment attributes. Security for payment of principal and interest is adequate, but certain factors, such as consistent profitability, suggest a susceptibility to impairment at some time in the future.

BBB - Investment grade - Medium-grade obligations, neither highly protected nor poorly secured. Principal and interest payments appear secure but cannot be projected for a substantial period of time. The bonds also lack outstanding investment characteristics and have the flavor of speculation about them. Bonds rated BBB or higher are considered "prudent-man" investments under rules of law.

BB - Speculative - Have speculative elements and their future cannot be considered well assured. Protection of interest and principal may be moderate, and therefore not well safeguarded during bad times. Uncertainty characterizes bonds in this class and they are not considered "prudent-man" investments.

B - Speculative - Generally lack the characteristics of a desirable investment. The assurance of interest and principal payments or the maintenance of other terms of the bond's contract over any sustained period of time is small.

CCC - Speculative - Have poor standing. May be in default, or have elements of danger in terms of paying interest or principal.

CC - Speculative - Highly speculative. Such issues are often in default or have other marked shortcomings.

C - In Default - Lowest-rated class of bonds. Considered poor prospects for any real investment standing.

CI - Income bonds which are currently not paying interest.

D - Bonds in default in payment of interest and repayment of principal is in arrears.

Other bond rating services are Fitch and Duff & Phelps.

3. FINANCIAL ADVISOR SOURCES

The best source of a competent advisor is a referral from a satisfied client, an accountant, or attorney with whom you are working. Be sure to ask how well they know the financial advisor and the nature of their relationship. If this doesn't work, you can look in your local Yellow Pages. Look for the credentials in the ads. If that doesn't work, or you want more information about the credentials, you can contact the sponsoring organizations.

Concerning Certified Financial Planners (CFP)

The Institute of Certified Financial Planners
3801 E. Florida Avenue, Suite 708
Denver, CO 80210-2544
1-800-282-7526

Concerning Chartered Financial Consultants (ChFC)

The American College
270 Bryn Mawr Avenue
Bryn Mawr, PA 19010
1-610-526-1000

Concerning Fee-Only Planners

National Association of Personal Financial Advisors
1130 Lake Cook Road, Suite 150
Buffalo Grove, IL 60089
1-888-333-6659

Concerning CPA, Personal Financial Specialists (PFS)

American Institute of CPAs
1-800-862-4272
This organization does not make referrals, but will refer you to the local CPA society, which generally does have a referral service.

Concerning Chartered Retirement Planning Counselors

College for Financial Planning
4695 S. Monaco Street
Denver, CO 80237-3408
1-303-220-1200

Concerning Certified Investment Management Analysts (CIMA)

Investment Management Consultants Association
9101 Kenyon Avenue, Suite 3000
Denver, CO 80237
1-303-770-3377

If you have problems with a financial advisor, you may wish to speak with the organization that sponsors their credential or the following regulatory agencies:

Every state has a Securities Department or Commission. You can find them in the Yellow Pages for your state's capitol.

The National Association of Securities Dealers
1-301-590-6500

The Securities and Exchange Commission
Office of Consumer Affairs and Information
450 5th Street, NW
Washington, DC 20549
1-202-272-7440

4. INSURANCE COMPANY RATING SYSTEMS

A. M. BEST COMPANY

Rating	Explanation
A++, A+	Superior; very strong ability to meet obligations
A, A–	Excellent; strong ability to meet obligations
B++, B+	Very Good; strong ability to meet obligations
B, B–	Good; adequate ability to meet obligations
C++, C+	Fair; reasonable ability to meet obligations
C, C–	Marginal; currently has the ability to meet obligations
D	Below minimum standards
E	Under state supervision
F	In liquidation

STANDARD & POOR'S

Rating	Explanation
AAA	Superior; highest safety
AA	Excellent financial security
A	Good financial security
BBB	Adequate financial security
BB	Adequate financial security; ability to meet obligation may not be adequate for long-term policies
B	Currently able to meet obligations, but highly vulnerable to adverse conditions
CCC	Questionable ability to meet obligations
CC, C	May not be meeting obligations; vulnerable to liquidation
D	Under order of liquidation

DUFF AND PHELPS

Rating	Explanation
AAA	Highest claims-paying ability; negligible risk
AA+, AA	Very high claims-paying ability; moderate risk
A+, A, A–	High claim-paying ability; variable risk over time
BBB+, BBB, BBB–	Below average claims-paying ability; considerable variability in risk over time
BB+, BB, BB–	Uncertain claims-paying ability
CCC	Substantial claims-paying ability risk; likely to be placed under state supervision
D	Under an order of liquidation
E	Under state supervision
F	In liquidation

MOODY'S INVESTOR SERVICES

Rating	Explanation
Aaa	Exceptional security
Aa	Excellent security
A	Good Security
Baa	Adequate security
Ba	Questionable security: moderate ability to meet obligations
B	Poor Security
Caa	Very poor security; elements of danger regarding payment of obligations
Ca	Extremely poor security; may be in default.
C	Lowest security

5. INCREASE IN UNIFIED CREDIT

THE TAXPAYER RELIEF ACT OF 1997 was signed into law on August 5, 1997. Among its provisions is a gradual increase in the unified gift and estate tax credit. This credit exempts a limited value of lifetime gifts and/or testamentary bequests from taxation. In 1997, the credit was $192,800, which allows each taxpayer a lifetime exemption of $600,000 in gifts and bequests. In addition to the estate and gift taxes shown in Figure 11-1, the government imposes a 5% surcharge on cumulative taxable transfers in excess of $10,000,000 up to $21,040,000. In essence, this recaptures the taxes on the exempted amount. The upper limit of this imposition also will be gradually increased to recapture the increased exemption.

Year	Credit	Effective Exemption	Upper Limit on 5% Surcharge
1997	$192,800	$600,000	$21,040,000
1998	$202,050	$625,000	$21,225,000
1999	$211,300	$650,000	$21,410,000
2000-01	$220,550	$675,000	$21,595,000
2002-03	$229,800	$700,000	$21,780,000
2004	$287,300	$850,000	$22,930,000
2005	$326,300	$950,000	$23,710,000
2006	$345,800	$1,000,000	$24,100,000

The astute reader will quickly grasp that $600,000 has to compound at only 5.25% for 10 years to equal $1,000,000. If the $600,000 compounds at 10% for 10 years it grows to $1,556,245.

6. 1998 FEDERAL INCOME TAX RATES

SINGLE INDIVIDUALS

TAXABLE INCOME Over - But not Over	Pay +	% on Excess	of Amount Over
$ 0 - $25,350	$ 0	15%	$ 0
25,350 - 61,400	3,802.50	28%	25,350
61,400 - 128,100	13,896.50	31%	61,400
128,100 - 278,450	34,573.50	36%	128,100
278,450 and up	88,699.50	39.6%	278,450

MARRIED FILING JOINTLY

TAXABLE INCOME Over - But not Over	Pay +	% on Excess	of Amount Over
$ 0 - $42,350	$ 0	15%	$ 0
42,350 - 102,300	6,352.50	28%	42,350
102,300 - 155,950	23,138.50	31%	102,300
155,950 - 278,450	39,770.00	36%	155,950
278,450 and up	83,870.00	39.6%	278,450

HEADS OF HOUSEHOLD

TAXABLE INCOME Over - But not Over	Pay +	% on Excess	of Amount Over
$ 0 - $33,950	$ 0	15%	$ 0
33,950 - 87,700	5,092.50	28%	33,950
87,700 - 142,000	20,142.50	31%	87,700
142,000 - 278,450	36,975.50	36%	142,000
278,450 and up	86,097.50	39.6%	278,450

ESTATES AND TRUSTS

TAXABLE INCOME Over - But not Over	Pay +	% on Excess	of Amount Over
$ 0 - $1,700	$ 0	15%	$ 0
1,700 - 4,000	255.00	28%	1,700
4,000 - 6,100	899.00	31%	4,000
6,100 - 8,350	1,550.00	36%	6,100
8,350 and up	2,360.00	39.6%	8,350

A

Active Retirement - The first phase of The Prosperous Retirement, during which retirees lead an active life-style including travel, social activities, and sports. We generally assume this phase will last until the mid-70s. (*See also Chapter 2, Passive Retirement, and Final Phase Retirement*)

Active to Passive Offset Factor (APO Factor) - A reduction in the amount of retirement income required as a retiree becomes older and slows the pace of retirement activities. In retirement modeling, we express this as a percentage reduction of the active retirement budget. (*See also Chapter 6*)

Adjusted Cost Basis - The amount that can be deducted from the sales proceeds of an asset in determining the taxable capital gain or loss.

Adjusted Gross Income (AGI) - An intermediate step in calculating taxable income for income tax purposes. It represents gross income minus deductions. (*See also Gross Income*)

After-Tax Rate of Return - The return on an investment after the payment of taxes. (*See also Real Return and Internal Rate of Return*)

Alternative Minimum Tax (AMT) - An alternative method of calculating income tax liability which is intended to ensure that high-income taxpayers pay at least a minimum amount of taxes. The calculation is extremely complicated.

Annual Renewable Term Insurance - The form of life insurance with the lowest current premium. The policy can be renewed for one year at a time, but the premium goes up each year.

Annuitant - A person who receives a series of fixed payments, usually for the lifetime of the person, but possibly for a stipulated period of time. (*See also Period Certain*)

Annuity - (1) A series of fixed payments, generally for the lifetime of the annuitant, but possibly for a stipulated period of time. (*See also Deferred Annuity, Joint Annuitant, Period Certain, and Variable Annuity*) (2) An insurance contract that can be annuitized.

Annuitize - To convert an asset into a series of fixed payments, either for the lifetime of the annuitant or for a stipulated period of time. Frequently used in connection with insurance contracts, but it also may refer to other assets. (*See also Reverse Mortgage*)

APO Factor - *See Active to Passive Offset Factor*

Asset - Anything owned by a person or company that has value. (*See also Liability and Net Worth*)

Asset Allocation - A method, based on Modern Portfolio Theory (MPT), of diversifying an investment portfolio to optimize the risk/reward relationship. (*See also Modern Portfolio Theory*)

B

Back-End Load Mutual Fund - A mutual fund that pays a commission to the financial advisor who services the account, but which is not deducted from the initial investment. The advisor collects the commission at the time of investment and the account is charged a so-called "12b-1 fee" each year until the investment company is reimbursed for the commission. This type of account is subject to contingent deferred sales charges that will be charged in the first few years after the investment is made if the account is liquidated.

Basis - *See Adjusted Cost Basis*

Bear Market - A term used to describe the stock market when the value of the market is dropping. (*See also Bull Market and Trading Range*)

Beneficiary - A person or organization who is designated to receive benefits. (1) A person who receives government benefits, such as Social Security,

Medicare, or Medicaid. (2) A person or organization designated in an insurance contract to receive the contractual benefits. (3) A person or organization named in a will or trust to receive benefits. (4) A person or other entity designated in a retirement plan to receive benefits in the event that the owner of the retirement account dies.

Beta (β) - A measure of the volatility of a specific asset versus the market. Technically, it is the covariance of an asset versus the broad market. Beta generally is used as a measure of the risk in the asset, although there are questions about its usefulness. (*See also Covariance*)

Blue-Chip Stock - The common stock of a corporation that is considered to be well-established and, therefore, a relatively secure investment. It generally is characterized by a long history of rising dividends, a well-established market position, sound finances, and a good reputation. (*See also Common Stock and Dividend*)

Bond - An obligation issued by a company or a government that carries two guarantees: a guarantee to return the investor's principal at a stipulated time, and a guarantee to pay a certain rate of interest as long as the principal is outstanding. The guarantees are only as good as the issuer's credit rating . (*See also Principal, Interest, and Credit Rating*)

Bond Fund - A mutual fund or closed-end investment company that invests in bonds.

Book Value - The balance sheet value (assets minus liabilities) of a corporation. Usually expressed in book value per share (BVPS), which is the book value divided by the outstanding shares.

Broker-Dealer - A firm that is registered as a dealer in securities (stocks and bonds). In the role of "broker," the firm is acting for its customers in buying or selling securities. In the role of "dealer," the firm is buying or selling securities for its own account. (*See also New York Stock Exchange and National Association of Securities Dealers*)

Bull Market - A term used to describe the stock market when the value of the market is rising. (*See also Bear Market and Trading Range*)

By-Pass Trust - *See Credit Shelter Trust*

C

Call On A Bond - The right reserved by the issuers of some bonds to pay off the principal before the maturity date of the bond to end their obligation to pay interest. Sometimes the call is at par and sometimes a premium is paid to the investor. (*See also Maturity and Par*)

Capital - Wealth, assets. (*See also Retirement Capital Base*)

Capital Gains/Losses - The difference in value between the acquisition cost of an asset and the sales proceeds. Currently, taxable at a special tax rate. (*See also Cost Basis*)

Captive Agents - Financial planners, insurance agents, or brokers who work for a specific company and are obligated, to a greater or lesser degree, to sell the financial products of their employer.

Cash Flow - The funds available to support retirement from pensions, annuities, earnings, dividends, interest, and the liquidation of assets. (*See also Income*)

Cash Value - The value of an insurance contract if surrendered, also called cash surrender value. It is the value of the contract minus any surrender penalties imposed by the insurance company.

Cash Value Insurance - Any insurance contract in which a portion of the premium accumulates within the contract to create cash value. (*See also Term Insurance*)

Certificate of Deposit (CD) - An investment contract available from banks and other financial institutions that carries a fixed rate of interest for a specified period. Generally, CDs are guaranteed by the Federal Deposit Insurance Corporation up to $100,000.

Certified Divorce Planner (CDP) - A financial planner who has been trained and accredited by Quantum Financial, a leading proponent of financial planning as part of the divorce process.

Certified Financial Planner (CFP) - A financial planner who has been accredited and licensed by the Certified Financial Planner Board of Standards, Inc. (CFP Board). (*See also Appendix 3*)

Charitable Remainder Trust (CRT) - A trust created to provide a stream of income for the lifetime of the beneficiary or beneficiaries and to leave the assets remaining in the trust at the death of the beneficiary to a charity.

Chartered Financial Analyst (CFA) - A person who has completed the courses and examinations given by the Financial Analysts Federation and who is a specialist in analyzing companies for investment purposes.

Chartered Financial Consultant (ChFC) - A financial planner who has completed the courses and examinations sponsored by the American College of Bryn Mawr, Pennsylvania. (*See Appendix 3*)

Chartered Life Underwriter (CLU) - A life insurance agent who has completed the courses and examinations required by the American College of Bryn Mawr, Pennsylvania.

Chartered Property Casualty Underwriter (CPCU) - A property/casualty insurance agent (automobile and home insurance) who has completed the courses and examinations required by the American College of Bryn Mawr, Pennsylvania.

Chartered Retirement Planning Counselor (CRPC) - A financial professional who has completed a special program of instruction concerning personal retirement planning and a test sponsored by the College for Financial Planning.

Churning - Excessive buying and selling of securities in a customer account by a registered representative to generate commissions. A prohibited practice.

Closed-End Investment Company - An investment company that has issued a fixed number of shares. These shares are traded like stock on a stock exchange.

COLA - *See Cost-of-Living Adjustment*

Collateralized Mortgage Obligation (CMO) - A security that derives its value from some form of interest in and underlying pool of mortgages. There are many varieties of CMOs, ranging from conservative to aggressive investments. (*See also Derivatives*)

Commission-Only Financial Planner - A financial planner who is compensated only by commissions earned on products sold. Generally, these planners are not registered investment advisors. This is different than a "fee-based" financial planner. (*See also Registered Investment Advisor and Fee-Based Financial Planner*)

Common Stock - A security that represents fractional ownership of a corporation. The assets of a corporation belong to the owners of the common stock after all other debts are paid.

Compound Interest - A form of interest in which the interest is added to the principal rather than being paid out on a current basis. The interest accrued then earns interest in subsequent years. (*See also Simple Interest*)

Consumer Price Index (CPI) - The Consumer Price Index is the price of a "basket" of goods and services. The Bureau of Labor Statistics of the Department of Commerce tracks this on a monthly basis and reports the changes in the prices as the basic measure of inflation/deflation.

Convexity - A measure of the sensitivity of a bond's price to changes in interest rates. Positive convexity describes the tendency of the price of most traditional bonds to respond more to falling interest rates than rising interest rates. Negative convexity is the reverse. (*See also Duration*)

Correlation Coefficient - A measure of the sensitivity of returns on one asset to the returns on another. It answers the question, "If Asset A goes up, is Asset B likely to go up, down, or stay the same?" (*See also Covariance*)

Cost Basis - The cost of an asset for the purpose of calculating the capital gain or loss on the sale of the asset. This includes the total purchase price, plus commissions, minus returns of capital. In mutual fund accounts, it also includes reinvested dividends. (*See also Stepped-Up Cost Basis*)

Cost-of-Living Adjustment (COLA) -
An adjustment made periodically to
Social Security, an annuity, a pension,
or wage based on the increase in the
Consumer Price Index (CPI).

Covariance - A measure of the degree
to which the prices of different assets
move in conjunction or independently.
(*See also Correlation Coefficient, Beta,
and Standard Deviation*)

Credit Rating - A measure of the financial strength of a business. There are
several organizations that analyze the
financial strength and assign ratings to
indicate the probability that the organization will be able to pay its debts.
(*See also Appendices 2 and 4*)

Credit Shelter Trust - An arrangement
used in estate planning to ensure that
a decedent's estate gets the fullest possible use of the decedent's Unified
Transfer Tax. (*See also Decedent and
Unified Transfer Tax*)

Currency Risk - The danger that an
investment denominated in a foreign
currency will lose value because the
currency will lose value versus the
U.S. dollar. (*See also Risk*)

Current Yield - A percentage derived by
dividing the dividend or interest payment on a security by the current
price of the security.

D

Debt-Based Assets - Assets that reflect
the indirect ownership of bonds or
other income assets. The principal
examples of debt-based assets are bond
mutual funds, closed-ended investment companies investing in bonds,
unit investment trusts owning bonds
and assets like collateralized mortgage
obligations, and GNMAs that are
based on mortgages.

Deferred Annuity - An insurance contract in which the payment of benefits
is deferred into the future. This allows
the accumulation of value without
paying current taxation. (*See also
Variable Annuity*)

Deflation - A general decrease in the
prices of goods and services. Typically
measured by changes in the Consumer
Price Index. (*See also Inflation*)

Depression - (1) An economic condition characterized by a rapid decline
in the value of commodities and a collapse of financial institutions. (2) A
mental state characterized by inactivity and feelings of hopelessness and
powerlessness.

Derivatives - Technically, any investment that derives its value from some
other security. For example, a put or
call derives its value from the price of
the underlying stock. Many derivatives
are created by dividing the potential
benefits of the basic securities. For
example, a treasury bond can be divided into a security representing the
redemption value of the bond and
another security representing the value
of the stream of interest payments.
Many derivatives are extremely esoteric
and are best avoided by anyone who is
not a full-time financial professional.

Discount - The negative difference
between current price and face value
or net asset value. A discount bond
sells for less than face value because
its coupon is below current market, or
the credit rating has been lowered.
Shares of a closed-end investment
company are said to sell at a discount
if the share price is below the net asset
value of the shares. (*See also Face
Value, Premium, and Net Asset Value*)

Dispository Intentions - An individual's
plan for leaving wealth to heirs or
charity after his or her death.

Diversification - A risk management
technique which dictates that investments should be divided among a
number of different investment categories to reduce the overall risk in the
investment portfolio. (*See also Asset
Allocation*)

Dividend - A share of the operating
profits or retained earnings of a corporation paid to the owners of the stock
of the corporation. (*See also Common
Stock and Preferred Stock*)

Durable Power of Attorney - A legal
document in which a competent adult
appoints another person to act on his
or her behalf if he or she becomes
incapacitated or unable to act. The
document retains its authority even
after the incapacity of the grantor.

Duration - A measure of the sensitivity of a bond to changes in interest. For a bond that pays current interest, duration equals maturity, but for other bonds, there can be significant differences between the two.

E

EAFE Index (Europe/Australasia/Far East Index) - The most widely followed of the Morgan Stanley Capital International Indices. It covers the stock markets of 18 countries, not including the United States.

Earnings - Profit. Earnings frequently are stated as Earnings Per Share (EPS), which are the profits of a corporation divided by the number of shares outstanding.

Eighty Percent Channel - The idea that the U.S. economy is likely to keep going as it has for 70 years without falling into hyper-inflation on one side or deep depression on the other. (*See also Chapter 5 and Hyper-Inflation*)

Equity Investments - Investments that represent an ownership interest in a business enterprise. Generally, these fall into three categories: direct ownership, stocks, or composite ownership in the form of partnerships. It generally is believed that equity investments are inflation hedges. (*See also Growth Investments*)

Estate - The property of a deceased person.

Estate Planning - The process by which steps are taken to deal with the transfer of property, taxes, medical treatment, and other matters associated with the end of life. (*See also Chapter 11*)

Exemption - An amount that a taxpayer is allowed to subtract from adjusted gross income for the taxpayer and any dependents.

F

Face Value - The value of a bond stated on the face of the bond. The current value may be more or less than the face value. (*See also Discount and Premium*)

Federal Deposit Insurance Corporation (FDIC) - A quasi-governmental agency that collects a fee from participating institutions to create a pool of capital with which to guarantee eligible deposits.

Fee-Based Financial Planner - A financial planner whose compensation is based on fees, but not necessarily restricted to fees.

Fee-Offset Financial Planner - A financial planner who is compensated by a fee for their financial planning work and who reduces that fee to reflect any compensation from commissions received from transactions made by the client. (*See also Fee-Plus-Commission Financial Planner*)

Fee-Only Financial Planner - A financial planner whose compensation is exclusively from fees received from clients.

Fee-Plus-Commission Financial Planner - A financial planner who is compensated both by fees and commissions. There are many varieties of this arrangement, but a common one is for the planner to collect a small fee for financial planning work and commissions for any transactions made by the client.

Fiduciary - (1) A person who holds property in trust for other persons. (2) A person who exercises management authority over funds belonging to other persons. (*See also Prudent Man Rule*)

Filing Status - The categorization of a taxpayer based on IRS definitions. A taxpayer may be taxed as a single person, married filing jointly, married filing separately, or head-of-a-household.

Final Phase Retirement - The third and final phase of The Prosperous Retirement, in which retirees experience declining physical and mental health. Typically, the period begins in the mid-80s and ends with death. The main expenses in this period are associated with medical and nursing care. (*See also Active Retirement and Passive Retirement*)

Financial Risk - The danger that an investment may not function properly as a business. (*See also Risk*)

Form 1040 - The basic Internal Revenue Service form on which income taxes are filed. There are various kinds of 1040s and many related forms.

Form ADV, Part II - A part of the form that Registered Investment Advisors must file annually with the SEC. This part of the form is required to be offered to the clients of the RIA each year.

401(k) Plan - A type of defined-contribution retirement plan set up by an employer under Section 401(k) of the Internal Revenue Code. A plan like this allows employees to contribute a limited amount of pre-tax earnings to their retirement savings account. Some 401(k) plans also include contributions from the employer. Contributions are not taxable and the account grows tax-deferred. Sometimes called a "cash or deferred account (CODA)."

403(b) Plan - A type of defined-contribution retirement plan that can be set up by non-profit organizations and government agencies under Section 403(b) of the Internal Revenue Code. A plan like this allows employees to contribute a limited amount of pre-tax earnings to their retirement savings account. Some 403(b) plans also include contributions from the employer. Contributions are not taxable and the account grows tax-deferred. Often called a "deferred annuity."

Front-End Load Mutual Fund - A loaded mutual fund in which the sales charges paid to the financial advisor are deducted directly from the amount invested. (*See also Mutual Fund and Back-End Load Mutual Fund*)

G

GNMA (Government National Mortgage Association) (Ginnie Mae) - A government corporation that forms and distributes securities based on pools of mortgages. GNMAs are backed by the full faith and credit of the U.S. government and generally are the highest yielding government security.

Gross Income - Income from all sources before any deductions are made for taxes or other adjustments.

Growth Investments - Investments that are intended to grow in value, as distinct from investments that are intended to produce income. Growth investments can involve a variety of assets and various ownership forms. The most common growth investments are stocks, mutual funds investing in stocks, business or real estate interests owned directly or indirectly through partnerships, limited liability companies, or closely held corporations. (*See also Income Investments and Equity Investments*)

Growth Mutual Fund - (1) A mutual fund that invests primarily for appreciation of capital rather than income. (2) A mutual fund that selects stocks on the basis of how rapidly the earnings of the company are growing. (*See also Value Mutual Fund*)

Growth Stock - A stock with rapidly rising earnings that is expected to increase rapidly in price. While there is no universally accepted definition, growth stocks generally have price-to-earnings ratios that are twice the average for the market. (*See also P/E Ratio*)

H

Health Care Proxy - An important estate planning document (also called a Durable Health Care Power of Attorney) that designates another person to make health care decisions in the event the signer of the proxy is not capable of making their own decisions.

High-Yield Bonds - *See Junk Bonds*

Hyper-Inflation - A period of extremely rapidly rising inflation generally leading to a currency collapse.

I

Income - Funds available to support retirement from earnings, pensions, annuities, interest, and dividends. (*See also Cash Flow*)

Income Investments - Investments intended to produce income rather than growth. Income investments can involve a variety of assets and various ownership forms. The most common income investments are bonds, bank deposits, mortgages, preferred stock, insurance contracts, income producing real estate, and leasing. These assets may be owned directly or indirectly through partnerships, limited liability companies, real estate investment trusts, mutual funds, or closely held corporations. (*See also Growth Investments and Debt-Based Assets*)

Inflation - A general rise in the price of goods and services typically measured by changes in the Consumer Price Index (CPI). (*See also Chapter 5 and Consumer Price Index*)

Interest Rate Risk - The danger that an investment will lose value because of interest rate fluctuations. This affects all investments whose value is based on their yield, not just bonds, but some real estate and stocks, as well. The value of these investments falls as interest rates rise, and vice versa. (*See also Risk*)

Interest - Money paid for the use of money. A sort of rent paid for the use of money. Expressed as a percent of the principal per period of time, e.g., 6% per year.

Investment Company - An investment vehicle that allows investors to place their investment funds under professional management. There are two basic types: closed-end and open-end or mutual funds. (*See also Closed-End Investment Company and Mutual Fund*)

Internal Rate of Return (IRR) - A complex method of calculating investment returns that compares net present value of cash flows to net present value of costs. It may include tax consequences and transaction costs. It does not consider inflation. (*See also Real Return*)

Investment Policy - A written document guiding the investment of funds. There is no standard form, but generally it should include: objectives, time horizon, risk tolerance, expected returns, investments allowed or prohibited, tax considerations, and possibly a model asset allocation.

J

Joint Annuitant - A person designated to receive annuity payments along with or in the event of the death of the primary annuitant.

Joint Tenancy - A form of ownership, usually Joint Tenancy with Right of Survivorship (JTWROS), which transmits ownership of property to the survivor in the event that one of the owners dies. One of the will substitutes.

Junk Bonds - Low-grade bonds. Generally, bonds rated below BBB are considered to be below investment quality and are called "junk bonds" or "high-yield bonds."

K, L

Large Cap Stock - The shares of a company with a market capitalization of more than $5 billion. (*See also Market Capitalization*)

Level Load Mutual Fund - A mutual fund that pays a periodic, on-going commission to the financial advisor servicing the account.

Level Term Insurance - A form of term life insurance in which the benefit and premium are fixed for a specified period of time.

Liability - The obligation of a person or company to pay some debt. (*See also Asset and Net Worth*)

Life Expectancy - (1) A number of years, based on statistical tables, that the average person is expected to live. (2) A number of years, based on statistical tables and other factors like health, family history, and personal habits, that an individual is expected to live.

Liquid Assets - Assets that can be easily converted into cash.

Living Trust - An "inter vivos" trust that is established while the maker of the trust is alive, as distinct from a testamentary trust. Living trusts can be revocable or irrevocable. The term is widely used to denote a form of estate planning in which a person's property is transferred to a revocable, living trust to avoid probate. (*See also Chapter 11 and Testamentary Trust*)

Living Will - A legal form that gives instructions for medical treatment in the event that the maker is determined to have a terminal illness. Most states have legally enforceable forms of living wills while others rely on generic forms.

Load Fund - A mutual fund that is sold by a financial advisor at net asset value plus some sales charge. There are various forms of sales charges: front-end loads, back-end loads, and level loads.

Longevity - Length of life. An expectation concerning the length of a person's life, as in, "Does your family have good longevity?" (*See also Life Expectancy*)

Long-Term Care Insurance - An insurance policy that provides financial benefits in the event that the insured requires nursing home or home health care under the terms of the policy.

M

Marital By-Pass Trust - *See Credit Shelter Trust*

Marital Deduction - The current federal estate tax regulation allows decedents to leave an unlimited amount of wealth to their surviving spouse without the payment of estate taxes.

Market Capitalization - A measure of the size of a publicly traded company. It is calculated by multiplying the number of shares of the company outstanding times the market price of the shares. (*See also Large, Small, and Medium Cap Stocks*)

Market Risk - The danger that an asset will lose value because of a general market decline. Some assets tend to fluctuate more or less than the general market. The measure of market risk in a specific investment generally is thought to be Beta (β). (*See also Beta*)

Market Value - The value of a company in the stock market as calculated by adding up the total value of all securities (stocks and bonds) issued by the company.

Maturity - The date on which the principal of a bond is due to be repaid to the investor. Also the length of time until a bond matures. (*See also Duration, Principal, and Bond*)

Medicare - A government program that provides basic medical insurance

coverage for everyone over the age of 65 who is eligible for Social Security benefits.

Medicare Supplemental Policy - A type of commercial insurance that covers all or some of the medical payments not paid by Medicare.

Medigap Policy - *See Medicare Supplemental Policy*

Medium Cap Stock - The shares of a company with a market capitalization between $1 billion and $5 billion. (*See also Market Capitalization*)

Modern Portfolio Theory (MPT) - The currently predominant method of managing investment portfolios. Based on the work of Harry Markowitz, this theory focuses on the portfolio as the basic unit of investment management, rather than individual securities.

Mutual Fund - Also called an "open-end investment company." An investment vehicle that allows investors to pool their investment funds together and place them under professional management. The investments are controlled by the prospectus and are continuously offered at net asset value (NAV). There are two basic types: load funds and no-load funds. (*See also Prospectus, Load Fund, and No-Load Fund*)

N

NASDAQ - The National Association of Securities Dealers Automated Quotation system is a computer network of NASD members for trading stocks and bonds. Unlike the exchanges it is not a physical meeting place. This is the "over-the-counter (OTC) market."

National Association of Securities Dealers (NASD) - A self-regulatory organization mandated by Congress to establish standards and provide oversight for the operations of broker/dealers who are not members of the major stock exchanges.

Net Asset Value - The value of a pool of investments divided by the outstanding shares. Calculated daily for mutual funds and closed-end investment companies by totaling the value of all assets owned and dividing by the number of shares outstanding.

Net Worth - The net value of all assets minus all liabilities. (*See also Retirement Capital Base*)

New York Stock Exchange (NYSE) - The largest and oldest (founded in 1792) U.S. centralized stock exchange. It operates under the guidance of its board of directors and the supervision of the SEC. It is a physical meeting place where the buying and selling of stocks and bonds is conducted by the members of the exchange. The listing requirements for a stock to be listed on the NYSE are the most stringent of any of the U.S. exchanges.

No-Load Fund - A mutual fund that charges no sales charge. Generally, investors buy these funds without the assistance of a financial advisor or compensate the advisor by the payment of fees not directly related to the purchase.

O

Original Issue Discount (OID) - A factor used by the IRS to determine the amount of taxable accrual associated with the ownership of a zero coupon bond. (*See also Zero Coupon Bond*)

Offset - *see Active to Passive Offset Factor*

P

Par - (1) The face value of a bond. (*See also Principal*) (2) The stated value of a share of stock. Not all stocks have a par value.

Passive Retirement - The second phase of The Prosperous Retirement in which the retiree's life-style slows down. Retirees travel less or not at all, they are less active socially and athletically, and their need for income declines. We typically expect this to last about 10 years, from the mid-70s to the mid-80s. (*See also Active Retirement* and *Final Phase Retirement*)

Pension - A regular payment received for prior service.

P/E Ratio - The ratio of the price of a share of a corporation's stock divided by the earnings per share reported by the corporation. It is a fundamental measure of the market's evaluation of the corporation's future prospects.

Period Certain - A pay-out option on an annuity which specifies that if the annuitant dies, the annuitant's heirs will continue to receive payments until payments have been made for a specified period of time.

Personal Financial Specialist (PFS) - A financial planner who, in addition to being a Certified Public Accountant (CPA), has undergone special training and been accredited by the American Institute of Certified Public Accountants (AICPA) as a personal financial specialist. (*See also Retirement Advisor* and *Appendix 3*)

Portfolio - A group of investment securities, more than one.

Portfolio Management - The art, science, and business of managing investment portfolios.

Preferred Stock - An ownership interest that has a preferential position for receiving any distributions from the corporation. There are various forms.

Premium - (1) The amount paid for insurance coverage. (2) The amount paid for an asset in excess of its face value. (*See also Face Value and Discount*)

Principal - The face amount of a bond due on the maturity date of the bond.

Probate - A judicial process used to establish the validity of a will and to supervise the execution of its terms. Also used in a broader sense to mean the entire process of dealing with the estate of a deceased person. (*See also Will*)

Prospectus - A document required to be provided to an investor prior to investing in certain types of investments. The document describes the investment, the people associated with the investment, and the risks involved. The prospectus should be read, but it may not answer all the investor's questions.

Prudent Expert Rule - An elaboration of the Prudent Man Rule that pertains to fiduciaries exercising authority over pension funds. It raises the level of knowledge and skill required from the prudent man level to the level of a prudent expert.

Prudent Man Rule - A classic legal principle which states that a fiduciary must act "with the care, skill, prudence, and diligence under the circumstances then prevailing that a prudent man acting in a like capacity and familiar with such matters would use in the conduct of an enterprise of a like character and with like aims." (*See also Prudent Expert Rule*)

Purchasing Power Risk - The danger that the value of an investment will not keep pace with inflation. If the asset increases 10% during a period when inflation rises 15%, there is a 5% loss in purchasing power. (*See also Risk*)

R

Rate of Return - *See Internal Rate of Return and Total Return*

Real Estate Investment Trust (REIT) - A company organized under regulations passed by Congress in 1960 that allow the company to avoid taxation on their earnings if they comply with the provisions. In general, they must distribute at least 90% of their earnings, have an outside board, and not engage in short-term trading. Shares of REITs are traded on the exchanges or in the NASDAQ system.

Real Return - Investment return adjusted for inflation over the period of the investment.

Registered Investment Advisor (RIA) - A person or company registered with the Securities and Exchange Commission as an investment advisor. Financial advisors cannot legally charge fees for providing financial advice unless they are registered and provide clients with their Form ADV, Part II. This is not a professional qualification. (*See also Form ADV, Part II*)

Retirement Advisor - A person who offers advice concerning retirement. See Chapter 9 for a discussion of various types of professional advisors.

Retirement Capital Base - The total of all assets available to generate the cash flow required to support The Prosperous Retirement.

Reverse Mortgage - A contract between a property owner and a mortgage company that provides regular payments to the property owner until the owner's death. On the owner's death, the property transfers to the mortgage company. There are many different forms.

Risk - The common sense meaning of "risk" is the danger of losing an asset. Investment risk generally is divided into several risks: financial risk, market risk, purchasing-power risk, interest-rate risk, currency risk. Other risks—death, sickness, accidents, disability, flood, fire, etc.—are the subject of risk management. (*See also Chapter 10 and Risk Management*)

Risk Management - The science of reducing the financial risks in a person's life. Many of the risk management techniques involve the use of insurance, but others may involve life-style decisions, e.g., to stop hang gliding, or to wear a helmet when bicycling.

Risk Tolerance - The ability of an investor to undertake investment risk. It is composed of two parts: objective risk tolerance and subjective risk tolerance. Most investors have a greater objective risk tolerance than subjective risk tolerance. (*See also Chapters 9 and 10*)

S

Securities Investors Protection Corporation (SIPC) - A quasi-governmental agency that pools fees from participating broker/dealers to create a pool of capital with which to guarantee qualified accounts against loss through fraud or bankruptcy of the broker/dealer.

Simple Interest - A form of interest payment that is made to the investor on a current basis and is not added to the principal. (*See also Interest*)

Small Cap Stock - The shares of a company with a market capitalization of less than $1 billion. (*See also Market Capitalization*)

Social Security - The Social Security Act of 1935 went into effect on January 1, 1937. The program is administered by the U.S. Department of Health and Human Services. The original act provided modest retirement benefits for wage and salary earners. Over the years, the program has been expanded and modified to provide a very broad range of benefits to the elderly, retirees, handicapped persons, and a broad range of other beneficiaries.

Standard Deviation - A measure of variability of asset returns. It measures the degree to which returns vary from the arithmetic mean. Modern Portfolio Theory assumes that standard deviation is a measure of the risk involved in a given investment.

Stepped-Up Cost Basis - The new cost basis given to assets owned by a decedent as the time of death. The stepped-up cost basis is used by the heirs in figuring the capital gains due on the sale of the asset. The stepped-up cost basis is the value of the asset on a date elected by the executor for all assets in the estate. The executor may elect to evaluate all assets as of the date of death or a date six months after the death. (*See also Cost Basis*)

T

Tax Credits - An amount that may be subtracted directly from a taxpayer's tax liability. The credit may result from overpayment of taxes, from involvement in certain economic activities, or as a result of certain kinds of investments. In planning retirement cash flow, tax credits can be counted as income.

Tax-Deferred Investment - An investment that is not required to pay current taxation on income or capital gains. The deferral normally results either from the type of account in which the investment is held, or from the form of the investment, e.g., an insurance contract.

Term Insurance - A form of life insurance with low current premiums and no cash value. (*See also Annual Renewable Term and Level Term Insurance*)

Testamentary Trust - A trust set up by the will of a deceased person. (*See also Living Trust*)

Total Return - The economic benefit of asset ownership over a period of time

expressed as a percentage. For stocks, this is dividends, plus or minus the change in value of the stock over a period of time, divided by the value of the stock. For bonds, this is interest, plus or minus the change in value of the bond over a period of time, divided by the value of the bond. (*See also Internal Rate of Return* and *Real Return*)

Trading Range - (1) A term used to describe the stock market when the value of the market has been relatively stable for a prolonged period. (2) Describes the movement in the price of a security when it is relatively stable. (*See also Bull Market* and *Bear Market*)

U

Undervalued Stock - A stock that sells for less than its proportionate share of the value of the company. The analyst calculates the "book value" of the company and divides that by the number of shares outstanding. If that value is greater than the current market value of the shares, the stock is said to be "undervalued." (*See also Value Stock*)

Unified Transfer Tax - Since 1976, the federal taxation system has imposed a unified system of taxes on transfers made during a lifetime, at death, or in a generation-skipping mode. Transfers made in excess of the limits are subject to a unified lifetime credit, and then a high level of taxation.

Unit Investment Trust (UIT) - A form of investment ownership that offers fractional ownership (units) in a fixed portfolio of investments. A UIT may contain specific stocks or bonds that are professionally selected, but not managed. Units are traded like stocks on the exchanges or on the NASDAQ.

V

Value Mutual Fund - A mutual fund which selects stocks on the basis of their perception that the market valuation of the stock is less than the "true" value of the company. Value managers seek "undervalued" stocks.

Value Stock - There is no universally accepted definition of a value stock, but it generally is understood to be the shares of a company which has a market value less than the perceived value of the company. A classic measure, but certainly not the only one, is the ratio of book value to market value of the company.

Variable Annuity - An insurance contract that allows the accumulation of investment value without current taxation, and which allows the investor to select from a variety of investment alternatives within the contract. The insurance protection under the contract is minimal. (*See also Annuity and Fixed Annuity*)

Variable Insurance - A life insurance contract that allows the insured to direct the investment of the cash value of the contract. The range of investment options is typically like a small family of mutual funds. The ability of the investment account to grow tax deferred, and to be accessed on a tax-free basis, makes contracts like this useful for a variety of purposes.

Volatility - The extent to which the value of an asset fluctuates over time. (*See also Beta*)

W

Will - A legal document in which a person directs the disposition of his or her wealth and property after death.

Will Substitute - A form of property ownership that automatically transfers ownership of property to another person in the event of the death of the owner. A will substitute operates outside the control of the will and the probate process. (*See also Probate*)

X, Y

Yield to Maturity - The "true yield" on bonds, which considers the price paid for the bond, the maturity value, and the interest to be received during the entire period of ownership. (*See also Current Yield, Premium, and Discount*)

Z

Zero Coupon Bond - A bond that does not pay current interest. These bonds are sold at deep discounts from their maturity value. The difference between the purchase price and the maturity value is the only return. The annual accrual is subject to taxation. (*See also Original Issue Discount*)